Clarendon
and the Rhetoric of
Historical Form

Clarendon
and the Rhetoric of
Historical Form

Martine Watson Brownley

University of Pennsylvania Press   *Philadelphia* · *1985*

Quotations from Clarendon's *The History of the Rebellion and Civil Wars in England*, ed. W. Dunn Macray, 6 vols. (1888; reprint ed., Oxford: Oxford University Press, 1969) are reproduced with permission of the publisher.

Quotations from Joan E. Hartman, "Clarendon: History, Biography, Style" (Ph.D. diss., Radcliffe College, 1960) are reproduced with permission of Joan E. Hartman.

Small portions of this book are taken from earlier essays by the author and are printed with permission of the publishers. These essays include "Some Sources of Problems in Clarendon's Prose Style in the *History of the Rebellion*," *Prose Studies* 4 (1981); "Why Clarendon Served the Stuarts," *Biography: An Interdisciplinary Quarterly* 4, no. 2 (Spring 1981), published by the Biographical Research Center; "The Women in Clarendon's Life and Works," *The Eighteenth Century: Theory and Interpretation* 22, no. 2 (1981); "Johnson's *Lives* and Some Earlier Traditions of the Character Sketch in England," in *Johnson and His Age*, ed. James Engell, *Harvard English Studies* 12 (Cambridge, Mass.: Harvard University Press, 1984).

Library of Congress Cataloging in Publication Data

Brownley, Martine Watson.
    Clarendon and the rhetoric of historical form.

    Bibliography: p.
    Includes index.
    1. Clarendon, Edward Hyde, Earl of, 1609–1674.
History of the rebellion and civil wars in England
begun in the year 1641.   2. Clarendon, Edward Hyde,
Earl of, 1609–1674.   3. Great Britain—History—Puritan
Revolution, 1642–1660—Historiography.   4. Historians—
Great Britain—Biography.   I. Title.
DA400.C63B76   1985   941.06'092'4   85-1197
ISBN 0-8122-7988-3 (alk. paper)

Printed in the United States of America

To Geraldine M. Meroney

Contents

Contents

Acknowledgments

Various institutions and organizations have given me support over the course of this study, and it is a pleasure to acknowledge my debts to them. The Melanie R. Rosborough Fellowship from the American Association of University Women in 1978 supported initial research and writing in a particularly crucial phase of the project. Grants from the Emory University Research Committee in the summer of 1978 and the spring of 1981 allowed supplementary research and a good deal of writing. Preliminary studies for parts of the last two chapters were completed in 1980 during a summer fellowship at the William Andrews Clark Memorial Library, University of California, Los Angeles; the entire staff at the Clark was extremely helpful.

I am also grateful for access given to the following libraries: the Ashmolean Library and the Bodleian Library, Oxford University; the British Library; the Ida Jane Dacus Library, Winthrop College; the Folger Shakespeare Library; Goldsmiths' Library, the University of London; the Houghton Library, Harvard University; the Huntington Library; the Library of Congress; the Pierpont Morgan Library; the Newberry Library; and the Woodruff Library, Emory University.

Finally, individuals have been extremely generous. The following people have helped me in many different ways at various times while I was working on this book, and the lack of specificity in an alphabetical list in no way reflects the extent of the gratitude which I feel to each one of them for the assistance he or she gave: W. J. Bate; F. I. Brownley; Martine Watson Brownley; Karen Ruth Brownley; Georgia B. Christopher; William B. Dillingham; Helen Fontsere; J. Paul Hunter; John N. King; Paul J. Korshin; Trudy Kretchman; Patrick McCloskey; Lore Metzger; Jo Mugnolo; Janet Greenwood; Eric Nitschke; Marie Nitschke; Margaret W. Pepperdene; Jeffrey Portnoy; Raymond A. Reece; Kathleen Robinson; Peter Seary; John E. Sitter; Floyd C. Watkins; and Cynthia M. Wilkinson. My greatest debt throughout this study, however, has been to the teacher and scholar to whom it is dedicated.

Introduction

The very nature of historical study and writing usually dictates that an individual work of history will endure as a living part of a culture for only a limited period of time. Factual evidence, the bedrock of history, is a shifting foundation. With new information accumulating that supplements and alters earlier interpretations, a history that becomes a classic must show more than simply a mastery of the evidence available at the time it first appeared. Even without additional evidence, different perspectives in each generation's present require reinterpretations of its past. In a historical classic, something must compensate for the diminished accuracy and the changing perspectives made inevitable by time. Those histories that have survived to be read as well as quarried, to be enjoyed for their own sake as well as to provide evidence for later historians, have done so because they have qualities that allow them to function at least partly as literary texts. Such works are rare because the necessary relationship between literary art and historical evidence is elusive and difficult to create.

Among English histories written in the seventeenth century, only *The History of the Rebellion and Civil Wars in England* by Edward Hyde, the first Earl of Clarendon, has managed to achieve this kind of stature, to survive as both a historical narrative in its own right and a historical source for others. As an interpretation of the events of a turbulent era, it immediately assumed a central place in English historiography after it appeared early in the eighteenth century. For the rest of the century, much English historical writing developed directly out of reactions to Clarendon, as historians from White Kennet to David Hume attacked, defended, annexed, or reworked the *History of the Rebellion*. It influenced the general reading public as well, who in buying edition after edition over the century made it a best seller for the press at Oxford. By the mid-nineteenth century, Leopold von Ranke declared:

The effect which an historical work can have is perhaps nowhere seen more strongly than in the History of the Rebellion. The view of the event in England itself and in the educated world generally has been . . . determined by the book. . . . Clarendon belongs to those who have essentially fixed the circle of ideas for the English nation.[1]

A hundred years later, David Underdown's verdict remained surprisingly similar: "Clarendon so dominates the period that the most self-consciously critical reader can hardly escape being overwhelmed by his majestic synthesis."[2]

The success of the *History of the Rebellion* was due to its form as well as its content. From the beginning, even those who disagreed with Clarendon's version of events paid tribute to the literary quality of his work. John Oldmixon, who vehemently attacked Clarendon in the early eighteenth century, attributed the high reputation of the *History* to its style, while Samuel Rawson Gardiner, the great nineteenth-century historian who was also a severe critic of Clarendon, termed the work "one of the masterpieces of English prose."[3] Twentieth-century historians and literary critics have continued the tradition of lavishing encomia on his writing: "all that nobility"; "those long, rich, serpentine, polychromatic sentences"; "its clear, forward-moving narrative strength"; "the ample, easy flow of a great river"; "that wonderful style of his."[4] Christopher Hill sums up the reactions of almost three centuries of Clarendon's readers when he writes: "Above all it is his style that we remember."[5]

Clarendon produced a great historical narrative because he was able to create the language and the perspective to write about his own time and his own life in ways that permanently illumined his age for future readers. He managed to function as a literary historiographer against enormous odds. The problems that he faced illuminate not only his own particular situation, but also important changes during the period in the traditional relationship between history and literature. What F. S. Fussner has described as a "revolution" was occurring in English historiography from 1580 to 1640,[6] as the antiquarian movement permanently altered traditional methods and approaches in history. Clio was one of the first casualties of this revolution, as literary art, which had been an accepted element of historical writing since classical times, came under increasing attack for distorting the presentation of historical evidence. The civil wars at midcentury, which provided an enormous impetus for writing history, further crippled it as literature. Finally, English prose itself, in transition throughout much of the century, was proving to be increasingly inadequate for effective narrative history. To these general difficulties, Clarendon added other handicaps that were specifically personal. He was an avowed partisan, determined to render an account of his times while simultaneously justifying his own central role in the tumultuous events in which he had participated. The final version of his *History* was written while he was exiled in disgrace, far from many of the materials he needed. Chapter I of this study delineates the contemporary and personal contexts of Clarendon's *History* to explain the conditions under which it evolved in terms of the general criteria for any historical writing that endures as literature. The remaining chapters focus on what Clarendon's literary achievement was in the *History* and what in his own character and experiences enabled him to produce literary historiography in so unpropitious an age.

Over the centuries the substantial literary merit of Clarendon's *History* has become a critical and historical commonplace. Commentators from Jonathan Swift to T. S. Eliot and from John Le Clerc to Sir Charles Firth considered Clarendon important both as a literary figure and as a historian, according him a position in seventeenth-century literature roughly analogous to Gibbon's in the eighteenth century and Macaulay's in the nineteenth. That his modern reputation seems somewhat less secure has more to do with changes in critical outlook and definition, which by the mid-twentieth century had narrowed the field of literature mainly to belles-lettres, than with Clarendon's own stature. He is still faithfully included in anthologies of seventeenth-century literature, and his name is inevitably invoked in studies of the prose of the period. But since with a few exceptions the twentieth century has proffered Clarendon lip service rather than analysis, precisely where his literary claims can be staked has become increasingly obscure.[7]

Evaluations of Clarendon's work as literature have so far remained too limited and too general, eclipsing the scope of his actual achievement. Mainly interested in Clarendon's reliability as a source, historians have tended to commend his style in vague descriptive terms before retiring to their particular areas of professional interest in the *History*. In addition, until recently most historians have not tended to be interested in the larger questions about the role of literary elements in historical writing that judgments of any individual style involve. Literary scholars, while echoing the historians' comments about the prose, have usually focused on Clarendon's character sketches, the magnificent gallery of contemporaries with whom he peopled his account. Critics are still in the early stages of evolving methods for dealing with nonfictional prose—and particularly with longer works—as art. Although structuralists and other recent critics have made substantial contributions in opening the general area, their emphasis on synchronic rather than diachronic concerns has meant that history, which is of course in essence a study of temporal process, has received relatively little attention. For all of these reasons and also because seventeenth-century studies have traditionally been oriented toward genre, literary attention has been focused on the most obvious of Clarendon's successes in the *History*. But his almost perfect fusion of literary art and historical evidence in the characters is a cumulative rather than an isolated achievement. Because it can be most accurately evaluated from the perspective of his other accomplishments, Chapter 2 focuses on Clarendon's literary art in the *History* exclusive of the character sketches.

Clarendon's work directly reflects his personal perspective on events. The origins and development of this unique vision in his character and experiences are traced in Chapter 3. Despite the abundance of material by and about him, Clarendon the man has remained an elusive figure. Biographies so far have effectively rendered his political career, but not his personality and private life.[8] However, the relentless subordination of personal concerns to public ones that characterized his life, and that largely accounts for his historical inaccessibility as a human being, contributed a great deal to his success in the *History of the Rebellion*. Moreover, Clarendon combined in uneasy synthesis various attitudes and values of both the Renaissance and the Augustan Age, and many of his public and private conflicts strikingly mirrored those of his era. As a result, in politics and in literary historiography he was able to play a pivotal role in helping England through the many transitions that occurred during the mid-seventeenth century. Not surprisingly, in view of his own circumstances and those of historical study and writing at the time, Clarendon's achievement was a mixed one. The *History* became in certain ways an experiment in form and expression, as Clarendon sought the proper style, narrative structure, and thematic approach to subsume the public and the private, the particular and the universal, into effective historical discourse. His own evolving relationship with literature, which is the subject of Chapter 4, accounts to a great extent for the kinds of literary abilities he developed and the ways he chose to employ literary art in the *History*. Clarendon's experiences provide specific examples of the kinds of biographical and cultural influences that lead historians to consider literary concerns among their priorities as they shape their works.

This study concludes with a chapter on the character sketches in order to summarize the ways in which Clarendon succeeded in uniting literature and history. The *History of the Rebellion* has its flaws and imperfections, as any long work does. Great Gibbon sometimes nods, and Macaulay has his gray as well as purple patches. But if Clarendon's *History* does not show the complete integration of literary art and historical method that would come in England only in the next century with Robertson, Hume, and Gibbon, it nevertheless stands as the most significant step in English literary historiography before the Age of Johnson. The work is particularly useful in comparatively illuminating larger issues because of the thick matrix of contemporary historical accounts that surrounds it. Using many of the same basic approaches and materials as other historians, Clarendon transformed them to produce the only work of history written during the period that was also literature. He did so because he alone managed to bring the creative imagination of an artist to bear on the manner and matter of historical writing. Before and during the composition of the *History*, he evolved from his own experiences, knowledge, research, and values what I have termed an "imaginative referent," a personal conception of the meaning of the events he was depicting that provided the kind of thematic structure characteristic of works of literature. It is this kind of unique informing concept that has shaped the style and structure of the works of all of the great literary historiographers, and that makes their writings works of art rather than simply collections of evidence arranged in chronological narratives.

Clarendon's achievement can only be fairly evaluated within its own context, a turbulent period that imposed crucial limitations on what could be accomplished in historical writing. In any age, his would have been a solid achievement; in mid-seventeenth-century England, it is a genuinely astonishing one. During this early stage in the development of literary historiography, questions about the general role of style in historical writing—the nature of a prose suitable to it, the use and misuse of rhetoric, the proportions of various narrative elements, the deployment of alternative thematic structures—emerge with particular clarity and intensity. What Clarendon was able to accomplish working with and against the literary and historical trends of his age offers one perspective on the volatile partnership of art and evidence that produces great literary historiography.

1

Clarendon's Historical Writing in Context

The truth is, there hath been never a good History writ since *Camden's Annals*, of our affairs that ever yet came to my knowledge; nor perhaps have the times been such as to bear one.

Degory Wheare, *The Method and Order of Reading Both Civil and Ecclesiastical Histories*, 1623

The Argument of our English historie hath bene so soiled heretofore by some unworthie writers, that men of qualitie may esteeme themselves discredited by dealing in it.

Sir John Hayward, *The Lives of the III Normans, Kings of England*, 1613

Among the critics in history it is not contested whether truth ought to be preserved, but by what mode of diction it is best adorned.

Samuel Johnson, *Rambler 152*

Let us guard against stripping our science of its share of poetry. Let us also beware of the inclination, which I have detected in some, to be ashamed of this poetic quality.

Marc Bloch, *The Historian's Craft*

PROBLEMS OF LITERARY HISTORIOGRAPHY IN SEVENTEENTH-CENTURY ENGLAND

The middle years of the seventeenth century in England offered certain advantages to a historian attempting to create a work having literary value. At this time writers had an audience eager for history in any form, whether in the history play, which for over a decade had been the most popular kind of drama when the century opened,[1] or in poems such as Samuel Daniel's *The Civil Wars Between the Two Houses of York and Lancaster* and Michael Drayton's *The Barons' Wars* and *Poly-Olbion*. Some poets not only focused their verse on history, but actually became historians. Thus Daniel and John Milton wrote histories of England, and John Dryden later in the century would hold the position of Historiographer Royal. The readers of the period devoured more editions of Sir Walter Raleigh's *History of the World* than of William Shakespeare's collected plays.[2] For the learned, antiquarians were producing massive collections of national records; neighborhood antiquaries lovingly compiled local histories. Those who were intimidated or bored by such erudition occupied themselves with the chronicles of John Speed and Sir Richard Baker. Along with Raleigh's history, Puritans looked to the moralistic writings of John Foxe and John Bale, who used historical subjects to reveal God's purposes and instruct man in his proper behavior. Even popular street ballads employed historical themes.[3] Throughout the century, the interest in history remained constant, although the form it took did not. If the heroic plays of the Restoration reflected a move away from the actual past, the poetry of the period turned from more subjective verse and private concerns to concentrate on politics and the state. Nevertheless, despite the proliferation of historical writings at every intellectual level and the many connections of history with drama and poetry, what the wide reading public seldom received during this period were historical narratives with any real literary merit.

Since classical times, critical discussions of historical writing had centered on content rather than literary style, in part because there had been wide agreement on the kind of language that history required. Cicero had remarked that rhetoricians were not particularly concerned with historical writing because "its rules lie open to the view."[4] Quintilian and Lucian agreed that because history shared some affinities with poetry, it demanded a limited amount of ornament. Lucian emphasized, however, that as a whole "the diction is to be content with *terra firma*," avoiding

both overly poetical and overly prosaic expression.[5] The classical preference for maintaining a middle course between the elegant and the plain
styles continued well into the sixteenth century, when Polydore Vergil
called for "a brefe perspicuite . . . wyth moderate and peaceable orna-
mentes."[6] It was generally recognized that appropriate historical language
involved more than simply a mean between extremes; the desired level
of expression should combine both poetic and colloquial elements. As
Roger Ascham explained, effective style "must be always plain and open,
yet sometimes higher and lower, as matters do rise and fall."[7]

By the middle of the seventeenth century, however, various circumstances had seriously undermined the consensus concerning style in history. Insofar as historical practice tended toward the middle style that
earlier commentators described, it did so mainly by reactions when a prevailing style came to be considered either too high or too low. Partially in
reaction to what was seen in some of the early Continental humanists as
excessive concern for expression, an enthusiasm for good Latin rather
than for historical substance, writers in the late sixteenth and early seventeenth centuries had begun to redress the balance.[8] They warned that
rhetorical ornamentation could threaten history's primary duty of im-
parting truth and instruction. Edmund Bolton was typical in remarking
that "without Truth, Art and Style come into the Nature of Crimes by
Imposture."[9] The emphasis on truth as the historian's first concern had, of
course, been conventional since Cicero; what was new was the emphasis
on matter at the direct expense of manner. Jean Bodin went so far as to
proclaim that "I have made up my mind that it is practically an impos-
sibility for the man who writes to give pleasure, to impart the truth of the
matter also."[10]

The increasing separation between literary art and history, and the
resulting distrust of stylistic elegance by historians, was fueled by the
antiquarians, who pioneered the great advances in historical methods that
were made during the period. For the first time since most English history was written by monks, scholars once more began to take over this
sort of writing from politicians and statesmen, inaugurating the movement that over the course of three centuries would make history the prov-
ince of academics rather than of men of affairs. After 1580[11] the English
antiquarians' critical scrutiny of early records combined with their stricter
standards for evaluating evidence to place an overwhelming emphasis
on the importance of documentary sources in writing history. William
Camden's description of himself amid "great Piles and Heaps of Papers
and Writings of all sorts" provides a glimpse of the prodigious work in-

volved in the examination of collected manuscripts: "In searching and turning over whereof . . . I laboured till I sweat again, covered all over with Dust, to gather fit Matter together." [12] But despite such efforts, in their concentration on more technical problems, the antiquarians were at best uninterested in and at worst hostile to literary art in historical writing. They glutted their histories with lengthy quotations from sources, more concerned with making the texts available than with constructing coherent narratives. Although Camden uneasily questioned whether the extensive documentation in his text was perhaps an offense against "the Laws of an History," [13] few others seemed aware of the literary damage they were doing. Their focus on documentary evidence was encouraged by Baconian empiricism and the resulting naive concept of "fact," as well as by the century's growing interest in the sciences and its concomitant distrust of imagination, rhetoric, and poetry.

The later humanists' and early antiquarians' increasing sophistication about precisely what historical evidence was and how it could be properly deployed was central to the problem of literary style in the writing of history. In beginning to establish history on a more rigorously inductive basis, they neglected it as an art. Historians failed to distinguish between excessively poetic or rhetorical expression and effective prose. If the imaginary speeches, elaborate battle scenes, and other rhetorical distortions which had marked the histories of the ancients and the early Renaissance humanists began to disappear, so, too often, did the literary style which had formerly been prized. Various commentators throughout the seventeenth century continued to pay lip service to the idea that form as well as content was vital to good historical writing. Thomas Hobbes, for example, emphasized that "in *truth* consisteth the *soul*, and in *elocution* the *body* of history. The latter without the former, is but a picture of history; and the former without the latter, unapt to instruct." [14] In the early eighteenth century, John Hughes also wrote that "tho' the Matter of History is the first thing to recommend it, the Form, which depends wholly on the Writer, is almost of equal Consequence." [15] But in practice most historians forgot Cicero's warning that those who "did not embellish their facts" would end up "chroniclers and nothing more." [16]

The emphasis on substance to the neglect of style set the standard for every seventeenth-century historian after Raleigh, whose rich and rolling periods made him as much an anachronism in historical writing as in his other ventures. Camden, defending his "courser and curter" historical style as peculiar to annals, presented the characteristic excuses. He wrote that he had "somewhat polished the Phrase of it, howbeit without any

4

curious trimming or bravery of pleasing words. For it is enough (I think) for me, if, like a Picture ill drawn with weak and faint Colours, I place it in a good and advantageous Light."[17] The attitudes toward style of the literary men who wrote history during the period are particularly disappointing. In a general discussion of historical writers in one of his letters, Milton proclaimed grandly that "the decorations of style I do not greatly heed; for I require an historian, and not a rhetorician."[18] Daniel scarcely mentioned style in the preface to his prose history, except in a brief reference to his desire "to deliver things done, in as even and quiet an Order, as such an heape will permit."[19] Similar remarks were ubiquitous among seventeenth-century antiquarians and historians. The practices of these men indicate that their comments were not merely the conventional rhetorical disavowals of rhetoric to disarm audiences; in context, it is clear that what they were offering were justifications for actual stylistic neglect, ineptness, or failure. When Thomas Carlyle read Milton's history, he compared it to "a stone-dike of ugly whinstones" and concluded that "perhaps the moderns *have* improved in their mode of writing history."[20] Daniel deliberately moved to literal and colorless expression when he wrote history.[21] Seeking more direct expression of historical truth, seventeenth-century historians too often ended up not with a plain style, but with no style at all. Thus, later in the century, John Aubrey could defend his almost formless garrulity by stressing the content and accuracy of his work: "Historia quoque scripta, bona est [In whatever way history is written, it is good]; and though this be writt, as I rode, [at] gallop; yet the novelty of it, and the faithfulness of the delivery, may make some amends for the uncorrectness of the stile."[22]

Even if antiquarians and contemporary historians had not been so eager to separate literary art from what they considered to be truthful history, the state of English prose style in the seventeenth century would have created serious difficulties for them.[23] Seventeenth-century stylistics is basically the history of the breakdown of inherited styles and the search for more adequate forms of expression for new kinds of insights. As the century progressed, writers in every field found themselves forced to abandon Ciceronian and Senecan styles, which were more static in their certainties because of restricted movements within the forms, to find simpler structures, a prose that was plainer because of a different kind of art. Rhetorical conventions crumbled as writers sought to reflect reality by using informally structured sentences, striving to mirror directly the ways in which the individual mind formed ideas. Although no particular syntax was traditionally associated with historical writing—Quintilian described the only requirement as "a certain continuity of motion and connexion of style" and Lucian mentioned "smooth, level, and consistent progress"[24]—the prose of the age could not meet the syntactical needs of historians. The large patterns of Ciceronian style were inadequate for reflecting the emerging sense of process and progress that research into the past was making central to historical perception. The dichotomies produced by Senecan oppositions were also too limiting for history. Even Sir Francis Bacon in his *History of the Reign of King Henry VII* had abandoned his characteristic terse style to work in looser periods. Nor was the escape into vividly egocentric syntax that was possible for a Browne or a Burton an option for historians, whose subject matter precluded such eccentric subjectivity in their prose. The demands of narrative in particular were only beginning to be understood at the time; a prose suitable for it would not emerge in England until almost the turn of the century.

The retreat from any semblance of literary style in historical writing was accelerated by changes which the English civil wars brought about in the content and perspective of histories. The conflicts reversed historiographical patterns that had evolved earlier in the century by plunging historical writing into the present. Beginning in the Tudor period, patriotic and utilitarian motives had combined to focus historians' interest on their own national history, particularly the more recent parts of it. As John Hayward later explained, "because it is dangerous to frame rules of Policie out of Countreys differing from us, both in nature, and custome of life, and forme of government; no Histories are so profitable as our owne."[25] However, at the end of the sixteenth century, governmental sensitivity to the potential political volatility of these writings had begun to turn historians away from contemporary history and the more recent past. In 1599 all histories were required to be licensed by the Privy Council; by 1637 this task was considered important enough to be proposed as the responsibility of one of the two principal secretaries of state.[26] The century opened with Hayward's incarceration in the Tower because of possibly treasonable allusions in his *First Part of the Life and Reign of King Henry IV*. Raleigh's *History of the World* and Sir Robert Cotton's *Life and Reign of Henry III* were threatened with suppression for similar reasons.[27] Governmental intimidation and censorship were ultimately powerless to purge politics from history—indeed, many of the antiquarians were motivated to write by political concerns[28]—but such interference did encourage prudent historians to concentrate on more remote eras. In such a threatening climate, even those with official encouragement to write on recent events proceeded gingerly. Camden, who had been persuaded by

6

Lord Burghley himself to write the history of Queen Elizabeth's reign, wrote in Latin to avoid popular attacks. No translation of his *Annals* was allowed during his lifetime.[29]

The civil wars abruptly ended this historiographical retreat into the more distant past. With their subject a weapon, historians entered the political arena. Using the testimony of history, Parliamentarians defended themselves from charges of rebellion by claiming past precedents for their political actions. Similarly, Royalists appealed to history to show the traditions supporting their cause. In some cases, ephemeral polemical elements made history degenerate into political propaganda. Other writers, despairing of practical expedients in the crises, explained events so completely in otherworldly terms that they produced sermon or jeremiad rather than history. Caught between the overly immediate and the eternal, historical writing floundered. More important, in the peculiar merging of public and private concerns that was characteristic of the English civil wars, history became reduced not only to personal polemical views, but also to individual experiences. Those who had been shattered by the events they had witnessed—or in some cases had created—tried to come to grips with their own pasts by writing about them. The resulting distortions in the content and language of the histories produced during the period were painfully clear as early as the next generation. Thus in the early eighteenth century, John Oldmixon, himself a virulent polemicist, noted when evaluating his sources that he had "cautiously made Use of" the *Memoirs* of Edmund Ludlow, who "too often mixes Gall with his Ink."[30]

Contemporary historians who sought to give an accurate and objective account of the events of the wars consciously avoided the taints of the extravagant rhetoric that marked partisan propaganda and the subjective language of personal memoir. But they insisted that the magnitude and dignity of their matter made the manner of its presentation irrelevant. Joshua Sprigge, whose account of Sir Thomas Fairfax's campaigns in *Anglia Rediviva* was one of the first histories of the civil wars, is typical in maintaining that the glory of his account is "*not to need* the *Trappings* of Words." He defended his lackluster narrative as a virtue: "I should count myself unhappy, to detain the Reader in the *Artifice* of the *Style*, from the *Greatnesse* of the *Matter*; Lofty language, is but to Mount *Pigmee* actions, and to please a *lower* Sense."[31] Rhetorical excesses during the conflicts increased the general fear of any art in historical writing. Thomas May, another of the earliest contemporary historians of the period, noted in his preface that the civil war had produced "as much bitternesse of Pens, both publike and private,—as was ever knowne." He complained that even historians "who seeme to abhorre direct falsehood" would use "rhetorical disguises" and other verbal tactics "to seduce a Reader, and carry the judgement of Posterity after that Byas which themselves have made." [32] As secretary to the Parliament, May was writing his *History of the Long Parliament* in 1647 at the behest of his employers; his own awkward position as a historian undoubtedly heightened his awareness of such dangers. The dull and prosaic compilation he produced perhaps assuaged some of the uneasiness revealed in his preface. In addition to the public and partisan considerations of historians like May, overriding private concerns in many of the narratives of the period made style seem a negligible concern. Sir Thomas Fairfax explained that his *Short Memorial of the Northern Actions* was written "not in that methodical and polished manner as might have been done; being but intended only for my own satisfaction, and the help of memory." [33] It was surely Fairfax's lame and halting prose as much as his content that led Horace Walpole a century later to observe that "one can easily believe his having been the tool of Cromwell, when one sees, by his own memoirs, how little idea he had of what he had been about." [34]

In attempting to deal with contemporary affairs during and after the wars, writers found that the complexity of events combined with the immediacy of their personal perspectives to place an almost unbearable burden on existing syntaxes. For example, Milton's review of English affairs since 1641 in *The Ready and Easy Way* proceeds with few problems until his prose becomes hopelessly entangled in relating the negotiations between Charles I and Parliament in 1647 and 1648. The elaborate rhetorical periods of Sir William Waller's *Vindication* similarly collapse among details of what he himself admitted was a "tedious relation" of feuds between Parliament and the Army. [35] But if the periodic style proved insufficient to order the chaos of the 1640s and 1650s, the loose style was no better. John Price, one of Monck's chaplains, wrote an account of his patron's role in the Restoration in artless but straightforward prose. Even he loses syntactical control when he tries to discuss the messages sent to and from Coldstream as Monck's men "fought in Paper," [36] or when he details Monck's interminable meetings with political leaders in London.

Seventeenth-century historians were no more fortunate with narrative structure than they were with prose style. The problems these writers faced can most precisely be explained in terms of some of the descriptive categories of recent narrative theory, altered in certain ways to reflect the particular demands of writing history. Most critics working with narrative agree on a basic distinction between the actual sequence of events on which a narrative is based and the depiction of these events within the narrative itself.[37] For historical writing, all of the raw material from which the historian works—other written accounts, state papers and various official records, eyewitnesses' information, personal experiences—can be described as the "chronicle," to reflect not only the progression of events in time around which the work is composed, but also its documentary component. The historical narrative that is constructed from the chronicle has in turn two primary components: the past events it portrays, including characters and settings as well as actions, and implicit or explicit commentary on these events and circumstances, in the form of explanations, analyses, interpretations, or judgments. In history, the part of the narrative that is concerned with depicting events can be termed the "story."[38] Although currently the term "discourse" is often applied simply to the expressive component of the narrative—the formal manipulations of the words themselves within a text—it can also be extended more specifically to evaluative or persuasive elements in an account.[39] In this sense, the interpretive or analytical commentary in historical writing can be called "discourse." At one level, historical explanation resides in the story itself, in the way the historian selects his evidence and separates the causal from the casual by constructing a sequence of events from the chronicle. In addition, in discourse he creates further levels of historical explanation. Through interpretation and analysis, he shows the significance of each past event in itself and establishes additional linkages of various kinds between individual actions. The part of the discourse that renders the singular significance of each event can be described as "contextual discourse," while the discourse that establishes relationships between events and thus supplies continuity in the text can be called "connective discourse." In practice, contextual and connective discourse often overlap in historical narrative, since the significance of most events obviously derives in part from their relationship to other events. Nevertheless, a distinction between the two kinds of discourse is useful for showing literary developments in seventeenth-century historiography.

In its earliest phases, the evolution of history from raw chronicle to literary historiography was a struggle to find suitable ways of structuring available evidence in order to produce a story. Since imposing form on fact necessarily imposes meaning, problems in narrative construction during the period were related to a lack of understanding of the comparative significance and relevance of documentary evidence and also to an inadequate grasp of historical causation. Both weakened history as readable narrative. Although Tudor historians had learned a great deal about limiting their materials, John Donne could still satirize the gossip of a court bore by claiming that "more then [*sic*] ten Hollensheads, or Halls, or Stowes, / Of triviall houshold trash he knowes."[40] Some of the same kind of overinclusiveness still lingered in seventeenth-century histories. Thomas Sprat pointed out that even Bacon's theory outran his practice: "His rules were admirable: yet his *History* not so faithful, as might have been wish'd in many places, he seems rather to take all that comes, then [*sic*] to choose; and to heap, rather, then [*sic*] to register."[41] The antiquarians' tendency to amass rather than order evidence led too often to literary regression into the chroniclers' habit of writing history as an unconnected series of events. Many of their works lacked any narrative or analytical connections, emerging simply as successive conflations of documents. From John Stowe early in the century to Robert Brady at the end, the antiquarians prided themselves on presenting their materials with minimal authorial interpolations.[42] Thus, in narrative terms, these historians remained at an elementary level between chronicle and story, with no discourse and only a modicum of story.

In those seventeenth-century histories where the story was more developed, a major obstruction to effective narrative history was the tyranny of time, the overdependence on chronology for structure. Thomas Blundeville in *The true order and Methode of wryting and reading Hystories* (1574) was reflecting centuries of rhetoricians' commonplaces when he wrote that a "hystorye ought to declare the thynges in suche order, as they were done."[43] But with their increasing historical sophistication, seventeenth-century historians were beginning to recognize the manifold difficulties inherent in this ostensibly straightforward approach, dimly perceiving that insofar as it was viable at all, it could reflect little beyond the chaos of the raw chronicle. Although writers desperately needed more flexible methods of organization in order to incorporate the learning of the antiquarians into readable narrative and to include more extended analyses in their works, they remained blocked by the annal. Its arbitrarily confined chronological format limited the development of literary narrative; in addition, as Camden and others noted, the annal was traditionally associated with a less literary style.[44] Nevertheless, historians failed to devise a workable alternative. Tacitus, Livy, and other classical writers, whose character sketches and political analyses proved powerful literary influences on historians of the century, were of course of no assistance here. The main approach other than annalistic was biographical, by

lives or reigns, but in the hands of seventeenth-century historians this organization also inevitably subsided into chronology. In addition to annals
and lives, Bacon and other descriptive theorists had noted that history
could be written by focusing on a single action or event of magnitude,
such as a military campaign. Although Bacon praised such "Narrations
or Relations" for "verity and sincerity" and Bolton found them best for
"presenting to the Mind the whole State of every particular great Business,"[45] few English historians of the time explored this narrative option.

The midcentury movement toward chronicling contemporary events
also had serious implications for literary structure. The immediacy of
perspective that made contemporary accounts irreplaceable to later historians usually damaged narrative coherence, for to impose any literary
order on what had happened in the 1640s and 1650s was beyond the capacity of most writers of the time. Even the caustically reductive Denzil
Holles, contemplating the strange twists and turns of events during the
period, was reduced at the end of his *Memoirs* to a Brownean "*O Alti-
tudo!*"[46] As every man became his own historian, placing the self at the
center of a historical work required an aesthetic detachment that few
could sustain under the circumstances. The test was how much they
could come to terms with beyond themselves, to what extent they could
incorporate personal elements while subsuming them within the larger
context of events. The artistic costs tended to be high because most writers limited their scope overmuch, failing to find anything beyond private
concerns to provide either contextual or connective discourse in their records. Sir John Ashburnham was typical in asserting that the "buisinesse"
of his narrative was "onlie to deliver so much as my duty was particularly
concern'd in."[47] The military focus of Fairfax's two brief memorials combined with his own inadequate comprehension of political events to make
his writings useful mainly for details of battles.

Some personal perspectives sacrificed history entirely to other modes.
A generation unable to produce traditional history turned to memoir, the
most characteristic historical derivative of the seventeenth century. At
best some of the memoirs of the time became good autobiographies,
enriching an emerging genre with enlarged scope. At worst history de-
scended to personal apologia. Men like Ashburnham and Sir John Berkeley were so anxious to avoid culpability for Charles I's disaster at the Isle
of Wight that their accounts ended up obscuring events rather than exon-
erating the writers. Similarly, Holles structured his blistering *Memoirs* to
blame all of England's difficulties on the Independent Party and in the

process produced satirical polemic rather than autobiography or history. Such blurred generic distinctions threatened the very identity of historical narrative as a distinct literary form.

Finally, in addition to more flexible chronological bases and larger scopes for story, literary historiography required the development of both contextual and connective discourse. The major existing structural models in the first half of the seventeenth century tended to focus on one kind of discourse to the exclusion of the other, emphasizing either single events or the course of affairs as a whole. Providential and propagandist histories, using past events to illuminate general principles of belief, included mainly connective discourse. These writers sacrificed examination of the complexities of individual actions to teleological or ideological continuity. For example, Tom May, when writing his history for Parliament, haphazardly assembled dates, treated events in vague summaries, and slighted particulars of the war: "[Sir William Brereton] marched thence along through those Counties, and took some places of great import, as the affaires of both Parties stood at that time."[48] On the other hand, histories focusing on moral or political instruction, which were concerned with general precepts for behavior, contained mainly contextual discourse. Thus they offered more comprehensive treatments of individual events but lacked sufficient narrative continuity. Sir Robert Cotton's brief history of Henry III (1627), which was reprinted several times during the early 1640s because of parallels with Charles I, loses the reader in a maze of motives and fails to make clear exactly what was happening at any given point during the reign. Whatever their structural model, all early seventeenth-century historians experienced difficulties in effectively integrating discourse and story. Analyses of politics or personal digressions, often the most interesting parts of histories such as Raleigh's or Bacon's, were awkwardly handled in ways that disrupted the narrative. Hobbes complained that since Thucydides such sections had been "discourse inserted, and not of the contexture of the narration."[49] The structure of historical works was crippled by historians' failures to fuse story and discourse into literary wholes.

Thus by the middle of the seventeenth century, history, which from classical times had been considered a branch of literature, was gaining stature as an independent field of intellectual endeavor, but only at substantial stylistic and narrative costs. But the careless prose and poor arrangement that marred the histories of the time were in a larger context surface indicators of deeper literary problems. If a good prose style and narrative skill, combined of course with the necessary ability to evaluate and synthesize evidence, were the only talents required for literary historiography, the histories written by such distinguished eighteenth-century authors as Defoe, Goldsmith, and Smollett—all of whom wrote well and conscientiously collected materials—would have endured. Similarly, the Italian public historiographers of the early Renaissance, who were appointed mainly because of their literary talents to turn the research of others into works of artistic value, tended to produce bland and superficial histories.[50] A history whose only merits are an effective narrative and prose style will simply be supplanted by the next well-written history that appears.

The technical difficulties with style and narrative in seventeenth-century histories reflect the absence of a deeper engagement of the creative imagination that gives form to rationally evaluated and ordered research. Although careful weighing of evidence, discernment of causal relationships, analyses of events and characters, and clarity of explanation may produce an accurate narrative account of past events, they cannot create a work of art. The genesis of any literary work, whether a novel, a poem, or a history, is a unique personal image or vision in the mind of the author. However, most historians of the seventeenth century, attracted to the new rational methods of science and despising both the empty rhetoric of the later humanists and the exaggerated language of the civil war partisans, not only abandoned literary style but completely ignored or forgot that the most necessary ingredient of literary historiography is not reason but imagination. It is the creative image in the mind of the historian that gives literary form to the evidence as it is assembled and evaluated, that dictates the deployment of both story and discourse, and that determines the appropriate style of the narrative account. As Hayden White observes, "In the poetic act which precedes the formal analysis of the field, the historian both creates his object of analysis and predetermines the modality of the conceptual strategies he will use to explain it."[51] An intermediate stage of this "poetic act" is the formation of what can be called an imaginative referent, the prestructural component of the eventual narrative history. Since history is not fiction, this unique prefigurement of the historian not only derives from the evidence studied, but, in turn, also gives its own form to the raw materials of the history. Thus the imaginative referent is more dynamic than White's "poetic act," for it expands and alters as the historical field is examined and analyzed, developing by successive stages into a full image of the particular society or events under study. As it is both imposed on and evolved through the historian's material in the process of research and writing, the imaginative referent makes the historical text a work of art rather than simply a collection of evidence organized into narrative form.

On the relationship between the imaginative referent and the historical record as it survives—the satisfactory congruence of the imaginative and the documentary and the ability of the historian to imbue the evidence with his vision—rests the value of any work that aims to be more than material for future histories. In addition, the imaginative referent, though not generally in itself a strictly literary paradigm, plays a crucial role in determining the literary value of a history. The success of the historical text as a work of art depends on how well the historian's imaginative referent lends itself to literary embodiment, and of course on the skill with which he himself can employ literary means to render it. An imaginative referent can give thematic structure and aesthetic coherence to the evidence and create that sense of reality, of actuality, that produces for the reader the sense that what he is encountering is the historical truth. For example, whether or not one accepts F. M. Cornford's original argument completely, subsequent commentators have shown that Thucydides saw the events of the Peloponnesian War as a working out of tragic patterns of self-destruction in Athens and the other Greek city-states. His unrevised Book 8 suggests how carefully he molded earlier sections to express his imaginative referent, his personal vision of the disintegrating society of the late fifth century.[52] Similarly, Livy's conception of the formative value of individual moral character in the Roman past and future and Tacitus' vision of Roman republican virtue destroyed by imperial evils are themes derived from the imaginative referents of these historians. Edward Gibbon subsumes Tacitus' view into his own presentation of the Roman empire as external grandeur masking internal deterioration, closing the system by poising the declining empire between the values of early Rome and the revitalization of these values in new forms during the Renaissance and the Enlightenment. The imaginative referents of the literary historiographers are so intrinsically bound up with their factual evidence as to be inseparable from it, and thus give it that profound meaning which ultimately converts a chronicle into a history that is also literature.

Seventeenth-century English historians in general either lacked imaginative referents entirely or evolved ones that were not suitable for literary embodiment. On the one hand, historical writing to have literary value had to move beyond the combination of fact and time that controlled the outlook and therefore limited the structure of the chronicler. But the extant structural thematic alternatives were not useful. Providential and propagandist models, relying on external referents that were neither unique to the individual historians nor strictly imaginative, distorted evidence to serve their causes and thereby crippled history. Moreover, their formulaic nature seldom encouraged serious literary efforts. In both cases ideological ends eclipsed literary means. Early seventeenth-century historians managed to skirt the problem for a while by focusing on individual lives and reigns, usually applying principles of Italian Renaissance political historiography to English affairs. Biographical history, with an imaginative referent limited, as in the memoir, to a view of a single character that dictates his relationship to his time, is potentially the simplest nonformulaic history. But if the list of titles is impressive—Sir Thomas More's *Richard III*, Hayward's *Henry IV* and *Edward VI*, William Habington's *Edward IV*, Cotton's *Henry III*, Bacon's *Henry VII*, Sir Edward Cary's *Edward II*, Sir George Buck's *Richard III*, and Lord Herbert of Cherbury's *Henry VIII*—the level of literary achievement is not. Only Bacon and More managed to produce histories in this form that had any literary value, but More's was never taken up by other writers as a model. Bacon's factual inexactitude, ironically in contrast to his methodological stance, made his *Henry VII* even more worthless as history than More's work.[53] Moreover, a biographically based imaginative referent creates serious difficulties in any attempts to structure units of history larger than an individual reign.

It is the presence or absence of the writer's imaginative referent that above all determines to what extent a historical narrative will yield the kinds of effects that literary works produce. At one level the imaginative referent creates aesthetic patterns in the work, providing artistic coherence and pleasure for the reader. At another level its role is intellectual as well as aesthetic. Although not in itself an explanation, the imaginative referent carries explanatory force because it is interpretive at a level higher than the merely causal. H. Stuart Hughes, following Georges Sorel, points out that "most people do not understand their history in terms of careful chronology or reasoned explanation; they *see* it rather, as images of the apocalyptic battles which have changed the world."[54] To a large extent, the great literary historiographers have shaped the kinds of vivid depictions that live in the public memory with a force which Hughes and George Steiner have described as almost mythological.[55] But in addition to individual historical events—great battles, seminal documents, crucial moments of debate in council—certain larger historical patterns also live on in the popular understanding of the past. (Various adaptations of the haunting and powerful specter of Rome provide obvious examples.) The literary historiographer's imaginative referent shapes within his work these larger noetic patterns that create responsive images in the reader's own mind.

Carl Becker wrote of the ways in which "Mr. Everyman" produces "a mythical adaptation" of what actually happened in the past to help him function in the present.[56] In addition to creating most of the noetic patterns that allow "Mr. Everyman" to domesticate and use history, imaginative referents also fuse the individual life with the record of the past at another level. Until modern narrative studies began to emphasize the similarities between history and literature, the conventional wisdom from Aristotle on held that history, tied to the actual, expressed the particular, while literature, freed into the realm of the imagination, focused on the universal. But of course literature universalizes experience only through the particular, and thus history, which recreates particular experience, can do so in ways that reflect those aspects of the universal in the particular usually associated with literature.

Because the past the historian recreates in his work is irrevocably gone, he, like the literary artist but with more strictly referential constraints, constructs a world that is at some level imaginary. When he chooses to construct it not only by reproducing as accurately as possible what is known of the past, but also by using this information wherever he can to show the universal in the particular, he writes literature as well as history. The past can be accurately depicted in ways that invoke larger questions of human value and significance; the Latin root of the English word "moral" is after all *mos, moris*, which simply means "custom" or "habitual practice." The historian's imaginative referent determines whether or not he will deal with such concerns. Because of his referential obligations, the historian usually has fewer opportunities than the fictional artist to show the universal in the particular. Nevertheless, at the points where he can do so, the truth of fact and the truth of fiction, which Virginia Woolf found antagonistic,[57] merge, and the truth of the past, in as accurate a form as it can be known, becomes for a moment the reader's personal truth. From such a perspective, the reader's understanding of history becomes an understanding of himself and of his own capacities. The lasting appeal of the great literary historiographers has been the ability, shared with other literary artists, to tell their true stories of the past in ways that enlarge the emotional, intellectual, and finally the moral worlds of the common reader. It is for this reason that subsequent more accurate accounts cannot supplant their works. Though new evidence may be discovered, the views of life and of human beings in the classic histories retain a timeless validity: Thucydides' Athens, Machiavelli's Florence, Gibbon's Rome.

Even as they illumine the timeless within time, the great literary historiographers have their own limitations. Almost without exception, they have been synthesizers of the already known, and their contributions to history as a field are occasionally denigrated by other historians. Thus a distinguished contemporary historian comments that although Americans who have won Pulitzer Prizes for history "have been highly respected by the profession" for their style, narrative abilities, and accurate scholarship, "they have not usually been regarded as path-breaking innovators in the field of history. Very few of them, for example, have received that final accolade of the profession, nomination as president of the American Historical Association."[58] Whatever the merits of the academic assessment of a "final accolade" (one recalls, for instance, the University of Glasgow faculty in 1752 preferring James Clow over David Hume to fill their vacant chair for a professorship of logic),[59] it is true that the literary historiographers have stood as innovators not in their discoveries of factual evidence, but in their ability to transmute their historical apprehension of evidence into broadly applicable literary terms. Theirs is another kind of historical creativity and originality.

Precisely why historical innovation and literary depiction of discoveries have tended to be separate achievements remains unclear. The two tasks may require minds too markedly dissimilar and imaginative capacities that vary too widely to be united in one historian.[60] Alternatively, it may simply be a question of a predominant interest or ability that leaves little energy for the other task. Whatever the reason, the literary historiographers' primary appeal has tended to be more to the general reading public than to those who are actively involved in historical research. Insofar as history has remained a living part of any culture, it has done so because certain writers have been able to express their insights through literary means to reach a general audience. When this kind of writing atrophies, history reverts to chronography or antiquarianism and becomes a concern only to professional historians. If such a narrowing of history is one of the problems modern historians face, it has also been a recurring concern in the past. By the middle of the seventeenth century, it had emerged in a particularly acute form.

THE WRITING OF CLARENDON'S *HISTORY*

During this period, when history was fragmenting into arid antiquarian compilation, memoir, local chronicle, propaganda, satire, autobiography, apologia, and jeremiad, Edward Hyde, the first Earl of Clarendon, wrote *The History of the Rebellion and Civil Wars in England.* Hyde's personal situation and the circumstances under which he wrote were hardly more auspicious than the state of history itself for producing a historical work of literary significance. He was a committed partisan, writing the history of events in which he had played a major role. Moreover, the final *History of the Rebellion* was actually an amalgam of two works, one written as a history and the other originally an autobiography. They were composed during two different exiles separated by a hiatus of almost twenty years.[61] In both periods Hyde was forced to work without access to many of the materials he needed. His optimism in believing that he could produce literary historiography under such conditions was equalled only by his persistence in the task. And in spite of all the odds against him, he succeeded. Although the final *History* shows some of the weaknesses of the historical works of Hyde's contemporaries, as well as certain shortcomings imposed by the conditions under which it was written, Hyde managed to create a structured historical synthesis of annal, memoir, polemic, and apologia that was the greatest—indeed, probably the only—work of literary historiography produced in England during the seventeenth century.

Hyde began writing his history in the Scilly Islands on March 18, 1646. With the collapse of the Royalist armies in the west of England, he and other members of the Prince of Wales' council had fled there from Cornwall with the Prince for safety. However, the islands provided only temporary asylum, for supplies were short and Parliamentary warships patrolled the surrounding waters. Within a month, the group had moved to the island of Jersey, which was better fortified. When the Prince left for Paris three months later at Queen Henrietta Maria's command, Hyde stayed behind because he bitterly opposed Charles' coming under the French and maternal influences that he considered pernicious. After the Prince and his other attendants departed, Hyde settled in to do what he could to help the King's cause. Far from the centers of Royalist activity, hampered by poor communications, he could offer little immediate assistance. The Royalists' prospects were bleak; it was by then clear that they would lose the initial round of fighting. But it was unclear that ahead of them lay a royal scaffold and fourteen years of suffering, deprivation, and, in some cases, exile. At the time, the situation did not seem hopeless, and Hyde was in any case a sanguine man. Thus he wrote to his close friend, Secretary Edward Nicholas: "As soon as I found myself alone, I thought the best way to provide myself for new business against the time I should be called to it . . . was to look over the faults of the old."[62] He had long considered writing a history of the war;[63] marooned by choice on Jersey, he now had the time to do so.

Hyde set to work with enthusiasm, for he possessed an unbounded confidence in the direct utility of historical writing. He wrote in his commentaries on the Psalms that "we want little more than very good Memories to make us very good Men."[64] Although in general he was not one to underestimate man's capacity for corruption—his years in political life had afforded him ample exposure to it,—he retained to the end a touching faith that human knowledge of past mistakes would be sufficient to prevent similar errors in the present and future. While writing his history, he remarked in his commonplace book: "If all Historyes were written by as wise men as Machivell, and the true groundes & originalls of all diseases to the State observed, and ther remedyes, surely ther neede little more wisdome for governors, than a dispassyoned and sober perusill of those Storyes."[65]

Because Hyde saw the practical efficacy of history across a broad spectrum, the work as he conceived it was an ambitious undertaking. He was determined to do all he could to see that the truth, which he held to be the "soul" of history,[66] would be preserved as a lasting record for the future. To do so he intended to draw on every major approach in seventeenth-century historiography. As a deeply religious man who had become a Royalist in part because the Parliamentarians had turned against the Anglican church, Hyde had an abiding sense of the Providential in human affairs that was reflected in his history: "The immediate finger and wrath of God must be acknowledged in these perplexities and distractions" (*HR*, 1:2). He also shared traditional classical and Renaissance views of history's secular instructional value. To produce the kind of history that could guide rulers of the state, he planned to incorporate extensive political analyses into his text. As he explained in his answer to Hobbes' *Leviathan*:

Few accidents fall out in States and Empires, which have not in former times happened in such conjunctures, and then if the same hath bin faithfully represented to posterity, with all the circumstances and successes, which is the natural end of all good Histories to transmit, nothing can more properly be reflected on, or bring clearer light to the present difficulties in debate, then [*sic*] the memory of what was upon those occasions don fortunatly, or unhappily left undon.[67]

In addition to being a seasoned politician, Hyde was an extremely moral man. He had no intention of abandoning the older tradition that history should offer moral and ethical instruction. He considered the "celebrating the memory of eminent and extraordinary persons, and transmitting their great virtues for the imitation of posterity" to be "one of the principal ends and duties of history" (*HR*, 3:178). His work, then, would be forensic, epideictic, and deliberative; it would judge the past, honor the good and the heroic, and at least implicitly argue courses for the future. Finally, in the best literary and historical tradition, Hyde expected the history to offer entertainment along with instruction. Several times in his text he emphasized the "pleasure" as well as the "benefit" his reader would receive.[68]

Hyde was not at all hesitant to take contemporary history as his subject. Indeed, when writing about the Elizabethan Earl of Essex years before, he had remarked: "It may be, I have been at my distance too bold an undertaker of these actions, which were performed so many years before my cradle."[69] He considered his intimate participation in the events of the war to be an advantage rather than a handicap, because he believed the historian's personal experience largely determined the value of his work. He wrote in one of his essays that the "genius and spirit and soul of an historian . . . is contracted by the knowledge and course and method of business, and by conversation and familiarity in the inside of courts, and the most active and eminent persons in the government."[70] He agreed with Bacon and Machiavelli that since history was to instruct statesmen, it had to be written by men who understood statecraft.

Despite his own role in events, Hyde hoped to avoid producing either polemic or apologia. "I write with all fidelity and freedom of all I know, of persons and things, and the oversights and omissions on both sides, . . . so that you will believe it will make mad work among friends and foes, if it were published," he explained to Nicholas.[71] He had been Charles I's most effective polemical writer, and at certain levels he understood the distinctions between propaganda and history. In his last major work he observed "how much passion and prejudice" both contribute "to the corruption of history." (Significantly, he added that he believed his observation "will be very unpopular.")[72] At least twice he opposed premature publication of his own history for polemical purposes. In 1647, when Nicholas urged him to release it to defend the King, Hyde declared: "If you think any thing necessary to be said to the vindication of our Master in that point, it ought not to stay for the history, which will require much time before it will be done, and very much time and second thoughts after it is done, before it be published." He then offered to write another "little discourse" supporting Charles I if Nicholas would forward the necessary materials.[73] Again in 1654, when Hyde himself was under attack by dissident Royalists, he was urged either to publish the history "to doe himselfe right, & give others their deserts" or to give the manuscript to others "who will lay all they are at stake to doe him service in that way." Once more he firmly refused.[74]

But if Hyde would not consciously substitute polemic for history, his work would nevertheless carry a Royalist bias. He was convinced that his own side had been the more right in the conflicts, and an accurate account of events as he understood them would necessarily vindicate the King and his supporters. However, his approach was not going to produce exactly the kind of vindication that Charles I must have had in mind when he encouraged his counselor to write. Hyde's partisanship in the history was controlled both by his devotion to historical truth and by his belief that history should instruct. He was painfully aware that the Royalists had made many mistakes, and he considered it part of the historian's obligation to truth to point out and analyze these errors. Moreover, he believed that his party could prosper in the future only if they learned from their past, and he was determined to educate them. He would spare no one. He told Nicholas that even the King would find himself neither "flattered" nor "irreverently handled" in the work, speaking with more tragic irony than he could have recognized in 1646 when he added that "the truth will better become a dead than a living man."[75] Hyde had reason to hope that Charles I might be responsive to the historical lessons he planned to provide. While at Oxford, the King had ordered Davila's history of the French civil wars translated into English for his own use. Charles had read it eagerly—his translators could not keep up with his daily demands for material—and he claimed that an earlier reading might have helped him avoid many of the problems he was facing.[76]

Ironically, Hyde's criticism of his own party, which in certain ways offset his partisanship, at the same time allowed elements of apologia to enter the history. In his view, when Charles I and the Royalists had erred, they had done so because they had ignored the counsel of moderates on their own side—specifically, the advice of Hyde and his friends. These men, who have sometimes been described as "Constitutional Royalists" or "Parliamentary Royalists," had begun their political careers in opposition to the King and turned to support him only when they felt that Parliament had moved beyond necessary reforms to destructive innovations. They constantly tangled with other counselors who advocated royal absolutism. In his history Hyde intended to explain and vindicate his own political views through analyses of the King's successes when he adhered to them and the failures when he followed other courses. Hyde was elaborating a particular way of political thinking, based in English legal, constitutional, and Anglican traditions, showing how policies that evolved from such principles could restore and sustain the monarchy. In this sense, his history was in part a defense of the views of one faction among the Royalists. Although a history designed both to vindicate Charles I and the Royalists and to ventilate their errors could not help but contain contradictory elements, Hyde was unperturbed. In his polemical addresses he had long been accustomed to writing to convince the general public that the King was right and at the same time to try to make Charles himself adhere to a more constitutional position.[77] If this stance was not exactly comfortable, it was at least thoroughly familiar.

Hyde's approach to writing history was an eclectic one. Although in his emphasis on Providential elements, moral and political instruction, and the personal experience of the historian he was reflecting earlier traditions of historiography, he also had some knowledge of the contemporary advances in history made by the antiquarians. John Selden, the noted legal scholar, was one of his closest friends. During the Royalist exile Hyde made great efforts to procure Sir Henry Spelman's writings.[78] In particular, he was well aware of the significance of documentary evidence. He considered "collection[s] of records" and "admission to the view and perusal of the most secret letters and acts of state" as "great and necessary contributions" for the writing of good history.[79] He did his best to collect all the written information necessary for an accurate account of events. Circumstances, however, severely hampered his efforts.

Aside from a few letters, Hyde apparently took no material with him when he fled from England to the Scilly Islands and Jersey.[80] Thus he was entirely dependent on other people to send him what he needed. Cajoling, flattering, importuning, demanding, and bullying, he did all that he could to collect evidence. Intermediaries were enlisted to approach those whom he could not reach personally. Charles I, whose misfortune had always been to trust Hyde with words rather than with policy, personally supported his efforts. Nevertheless, although Hyde received some assistance, the response was generally disappointing. A year after he began, he wrote to his friend John Earle about the history: "Since I find most men so unconcerned to contribute towards it, and some who are very able to satisfy me in what I have desired, so positive against the doing it, contrary to my expectation; I have resolved to lay the task aside, 'till a fitter season, and to employ myself in some study, that I may do myself more good."[81] In fact, he did nothing of the sort. He wrote on, complaining to Lord Digby eight months later that "I often wish I had never begun, having found less assistance from it, than I thought I should have done, as if all men had a desire, the ill should be remembered, and the good forgotten."[82] To the King he apologized for "the presumption I have used in spoiling so much paper upon the stock of an ill memory, refreshed only with some few pamphlets and diurnals."[83]

The failure of his fellow Royalists to supply the materials that Hyde so assiduously sought affected both the content and the form of his history. His writing was constantly interrupted as he waited for materials he knew might never arrive. When he wrote to Earle with questions on the northern campaigns, he complained about "how hard a thinge it is to set asyde that part of the story and proceed with the rest, wch will not only make an hiatus in one place, but perplex the whole beside." He begged for desperately needed background information in order to "forme the current of my story, wch will bee els much interrupted."[84] He admitted to Sir John Berkeley that "for want of informacon & assistancs," he would have to "leave many truths unmenconed."[85] Fortunately, Hyde had never intended to provide comprehensive coverage. In his account of Ireland, he noted that Clanricarde had "left behind so full a relation . . . that I have been the less particular in the account of what passed in the transactions of that kingdom, presuming that more exact work of his will in due time be communicated to the world" (*HR*, 5:272). He deliberately excluded information that he knew was available elsewhere; when he wrote about the Uxbridge negotiations, for example, he explained that "only such particulars as fell out in that time and were never communicated, and many of them known to very few, shall be shortly mentioned" (*HR*, 3:475). Nevertheless, because of the meager outside assistance he received, Hyde was forced to rely more heavily than he wished on his personal experiences. There was much that he had no way of knowing. He had been present at Edgehill—in fact, while attending to the Duke of York and the Prince of Wales, he had almost been captured during that battle—but otherwise he had usually been far away from the more stirring actions of the war. For many of these events, either no source material was available or what Hyde could get was unreliable. Coping admirably, in the history he was forthright about the gaps in his knowledge. His comment on one of the Marquis of Newcastle's marches is typical: "The particulars of all that affair, and the whole transaction of the northern parts, where the writer of this history was never present, nor had any part in those counsels, are fit for a relation apart, which a more proper person will employ himself in" (*HR*, 3:256).

Because of the many problems he faced in writing and because of the kind of work he was determined to write, Hyde very early in the project had resigned himself to the idea that publication of his history would be delayed. He admonished Nicholas: "Therefore you must think in what age my scribble is like to see light."[86] Approaching his task from this viewpoint freed Hyde to write a multilayered work in which he could give primary attention to content rather than to coherence. Thus when Parliamentary forces threatened Jersey in 1647, his instructions for disposing of his papers described his history as "exact memorials of passages . . . [rather] than a digested relation."[87] He also recognized that his devotion to historical truth would delay publication. He explained to Berkeley that because he was absolutely determined that "there shall not be any untruth, nor partiallity toward Persons or Sydes," his frankness would make the work unpublishable "in this Age."[88] He always expected editing, remarking to Nicholas that out of the whole, "enough may be chosen to make a perfect story, and the original kept for their perusal, who may be the wiser for knowing the most secret truths."[89] If he could not structure his work as carefully and completely as he wished, he could at least leave a detailed and honest record from which others could draw. It was the best way he could think of to try to insure, as he wrote in the opening words of his history, "that posterity may not be deceived."

The literary difficulties created by Hyde's situation and materials were to a certain extent exacerbated by his own habits of writing. Early in his career, his political work for Charles I had taught him to compose very rapidly. As an undercover agent left in Parliament to report on its activities after the King had departed from London, he sent his own drafts of royal replies to Parliamentary manifestoes to York so that Charles' responses would be ready almost as soon as the manifestoes arrived. During the Uxbridge negotiations, he stayed up for twenty nights in a row to write summaries of each day's meetings for the King at Oxford and to prepare the Royalist position papers for the next day. Because of the pressures of time, the exhaustive attention to content that most of his writing required left little opportunity for purely aesthetic concerns. This kind of arduous training made him a fluent writer, but not always a careful one.

A manuscript draft of one of Hyde's letters shows Charles II, hardly a grammarian, correcting Hyde's parallelism.[90] The sheer bulk of his extant papers, particularly his letters during the Royalist exile and his manuscripts from his banishment, suggests that revision did not occupy much of his writing time. He was certainly not a Gibbon, who rewrote the first chapter of the *Decline and Fall* three times and the second and third chapters twice before describing himself as "tolerably satisfied with their effect."[91] Hyde tended to let his first drafts stand; the manuscripts of the *History of the Rebellion* show relatively few corrections.[92] Similarly, in the organization of the history, although sections reworked from documentary sources show his skill in abridging materials and his letters indicate his concern about the proportions of his work,[93] traces of carelessness occasionally appear. He cared enough about organization to make preliminary outlines for several books; within these outlines, however, he several times lists the same event twice.[94]

Despite all his personal and situational disadvantages, by early March of 1648, two years after he had begun, Hyde had completed six books of his history, covering events through March of 1644. What he had written constitutes about three fourths of the first seven books of the final *History of the Rebellion*. Those seven books, in turn, represent a little over half the entire work. He had begun the next book when the Queen summoned him in the middle of May to join the Prince in Paris. He put the history aside and did not work on it again for over twenty years. The manuscript was not entirely forgotten. He had a transcript of it made for his own use by his secretary,[95] and within the year he was reminding Prince Rupert to send materials "by which I may be the better able, to remember, what ought not to be forgotten; when I shall have leasure agayne to proceede in that unequall taske."[96] Others occasionally referred to the project. But Hyde was making rather than writing history during this period. He gradually emerged as Charles II's chief counselor during the Royalist exile, and after playing a major role in negotiating the Restoration, he returned home as Lord Chancellor of England and received the title of Earl of Clarendon. His power seemed unlimited and his position unassailable; nevertheless, after seven years he was forced out of office and left in disgrace for exile in France.

Old, gout-ridden, and financially distressed, Clarendon remained indomitable, turning once more to studying and writing. At least initially there could be no question of writing history. The many papers he had so carefully saved over the years had been left behind when he fled from England, and his friends there were forbidden to communicate with him.

Barred from history, he turned to autobiography instead, and in two years (1668–70) he completed *The Life of Edward Earl of Clarendon; From his Birth to the Restoration of the Royal Family in the Year 1660.* This work necessarily differed in purpose and scope from his original history. Although he believed that the story of his political career during the wars and the Interregnum would be useful in supporting constitutional monarchy in England, he was more concerned in this work to vindicate his own conduct and reputation. In addition, he probably cherished other hopes for what the *Life* could accomplish. A well-written presentation of his past services might lead to his recall to office; at the very least, he would perhaps be allowed to return home.

In June of 1671, after Clarendon had been in exile for four years, his second son Laurence finally received permission to visit his father. He brought with him the manuscript of the original history, which Hyde had composed on Jersey so many years before, and also some other materials Hyde had collected for revising and completing it.[97] As soon as his son left, Clarendon gutted what critics uniformly agree is one of the most distinguished seventeenth-century English autobiographies to create another history. He combined sections of the original history he had written on Jersey with parts of the *Life*, adding supplementary sections on public events to broaden the coverage of the later years that the *Life* had treated mainly from a more private perspective. When he had documents or detailed accounts, he followed them carefully and accurately. But, just as with the original history twenty-five years before, Clarendon was still forced to rely heavily on his own experiences and memories. For some periods, particularly for events in England during the Protectorate while he had been in exile abroad, he had little trustworthy information. Without good sources, he refused to speculate. As a result, three quarters of the final *History* focuses on nine of the twenty years it chronicles.[98] The work evolved as a strange and brilliant amalgam, including public history, personal apologia, state documents, polemical vindication, eyewitnesses' accounts, and political and diplomatic analyses. Clarendon used whatever he had. In 1646, for example, he had composed two defenses of himself and other members of the Prince's council in the west, explaining their general conduct of business and specifically their dealings with the Duke of Hamilton. He used these vindications to comprise well over half of Book 9 in the final *History*. Clarendon was in many ways testing the capacity of historical narrative to incorporate diverse materials. He recognized and regretted the inevitable weaknesses in the work; as he noted parenthetically in the dedicatory epistle to his answer to *Leviathan*, his

26

history had been composed, "as far as I am able, without the supply of those Memorials and Records which are fit to be enquired into."[99] Nevertheless, by June of 1672, about a year after he began his second version, the final *History of the Rebellion* was complete.

Clarendon was correct in believing that his work would have to wait for publication. But when it finally appeared from 1702 to 1704, despite the bitter party struggles it fueled, it was widely recognized as a masterpiece.[100] During a crucial time of transition for English historiography, when art was rapidly becoming lost in history as arid fact or unruly life triumphed instead, Clarendon had managed to subsume the major historiographical currents of his age and transform them in his work.

2

Clarendon's Literary Art

As for Language and Style, . . . he who would pen our Affaires in *English*, and compose unto us an entire Body of them, ought to have a singular Care thereof. For our Tongue . . . is very copious, and few there be who have the best and most proper Graces thereof.

> Edmund Bolton, "Hypercritica, or A Rule of Judgement, for writing or reading our History's" (1618?)

Truth does not reside in a collection of facts; truth is shown by the form of their presentation, once their significance has been seized on. In the record, little of all this is *given*. Telling the truth, then, requires sagacity and style, art in composition and skill in exposition.

> Jacques Barzun, *Clio and the Doctors*

Until we submit historical texts to rhetorical analysis, we shall no doubt go on vaguely praising great historians for their 'style' without being able to specify what this 'style' amounts to.

> Hayden White, "Rhetoric and History"

The death which the outmoded historian has to suffer is more complete and pitiful than ordinary death. A man who has written a single lyric may outlast the centuries, living on in perpetual youth; but the author of a hundredweight of heavy historical tomes has them piled upon his grave, to hold him securely down. A mere literary dressing would seem to be insufficient to defend such an author from the ravages of time. The historian who survives seems to be the one who in some way or another has managed to break through into the realm of enduring ideas or gives hints of a deeper tide in the affairs of men.

> Herbert Butterfield, *Man on His Past*

THE LITERARY UNITY OF THE
HISTORY OF THE REBELLION

The most serious obstacle to literary treatment of the *History of the Rebellion* has been the tendency to look at it in terms of its parts, rather than as a whole text. In 1671, when Clarendon received the manuscript of his original history, written years before on Jersey, he turned immediately to recast the autobiography that he had completed earlier in his exile into another history. Most of his best critics have never forgiven him for this decision. On literary grounds the judgments have been particularly harsh. B. H. G. Wormald considered it "a pity Clarendon ever embarked upon this mighty conflation."[1] Leopold von Ranke described the final history as "two different stories," and H. R. Trevor-Roper agreed that it was "not an artistic unit."[2] Sir Charles Firth went so far as to suggest that Clarendon "committed a literary crime when he hacked and mangled" the *Life* to supplement the original history.[3] Historians, consciously or unconsciously resenting autobiographical elements in Clarendon's works as undermining the objectivity ideally associated with history, seem to feel more comfortable with him as an autobiographer; students of autobiography, short of good models in the seventeenth century, are loathe to part with one of the best they have. The consensus has been that of the three narratives, the original history is the most accurate and instructive and the *Life* the most unified and artistic, with the final *History* left as a sort of mongrelized pastiche of the weaknesses of both urtexts without the major strengths of either. The essential unity and the artistic greatness of the *History of the Rebellion* have been obscured by continuing emphasis on the dual texts behind the final work, and particularly on the differences between the original history and the *Life*. However, what is more significant for literary purposes are the remarkable similarities between the two. Given the prevailing attitudes, it is useful to establish at the beginning what these similarities are, and why Clarendon's two works could be combined into a literary whole that is greater than either of its parts.

We do not really need Clarendon's remark that the history of the English civil wars was "the work which his heart was most set upon"[4] to recognize that the *Life* was a compensatory exercise undertaken when his final exile barred him from the materials he needed to write history. His whole approach in the *Life* shows that he was never at heart an autobiographer. Although he opens with details of his family and education, the focus quickly shifts away from himself. Two long series of character sketches of his friends form a prominent part of the account, and even before the end of the first section, he widens the narrative to include commentary on the general state of Europe in 1639 and on the English political situation in particular. By the 1640s, history rapidly subsumes autobiography. Clarendon found a single section of his narrative sufficient to cover the period from his birth in 1609 to 1641; in contrast, Part 2 covers 1641 and 1642, while Part 3 advances the narrative only to 1644. Part 4 of the *Life* exists only in outline, because, as Clarendon explained, "All these particulars are so exactly remembered in those papers, remaining in a cabinet easy to be found, that they will quickly be put into a method."[5] But "those papers," which Laurence Hyde brought to his father on his visit in 1671, were instead put to use in Books 9 and 10 of the final *History*.

Unlike such authors as Richard Baxter, who in his autobiographical writings rigidly separated his accounts of public events from sections on his own affairs,[6] Clarendon sought to fuse both in the *Life* for the sake of a larger historical perspective on his times. Insofar as the *Life* remains the story of Clarendon at all, it is mainly the story of the public servant, not the private man. Even the public man often disappears as Clarendon cannot resist digressing into accounts of events; he frequently apologizes for inserting information that "may not seem precisely pertinent to this present discourse" (*HR*, 1:392). When he writes of Edgehill in the *Life*, for example, he indicates that "the relation of that battle is not proper . . . [in] this place" (*HR*, 2:352). But having mentioned "many notable accidents" connected with the fight that might have changed the course of the war, he proceeds to give what is in essence an abbreviated account of the entire engagement. Indeed, in the final *History of the Rebellion*, the memorial sections commemorating those who fell at Edgehill are taken from the *Life* rather than the original history. Clarendon deliberately widened the scope of his autobiography because, just as he had expected the original history to be read by certain audiences and then edited for others, he clearly hoped that the *Life* at some point would provide historical material that could be used apart from the personal sections. Thus he wrote that "even unawares, many things are inserted not so immediately applicable to his own person, which possibly may hereafter, in some other method, be communicated to the world."[7] At times in the *Life*, the reader can see Clarendon directly instructing future editors, as when he closes the section on his appointment as Chancellor by noting that the account "is only fit to be inserted in these memorials which concern his own life, and will easily be left out of the general history of that time" (*HR*, 6:53).

Whatever his ostensible subject, Clarendon's priority was always the writing of history. Circumstances forced him to rely more than he wished on autobiographical material for both of his historical works. Because other Royalists failed to supply the information he needed for the original history, he had to depend heavily on his own experiences and on personal recall. Similarly, later books of the final *History of the Rebellion*, which come mainly from the *Life*, tend to be more personal not so much because they were originally taken from an autobiography, but because Clarendon was out of England during the period they cover. Most of his accurate information necessarily concerned events among the Royalists in exile. When he tried in 1671 and 1672 to write supplementary sections on public events to incorporate these later books of the *Life* into the final history, he could add very little to his account; he had already written most of the valid public history he knew. The new sections tended to emphasize discourse rather than story. In many ways, the original and final histories were as much autobiographical history as the *Life* was historical autobiography.

Because of his tendency to subsume the private in the public, Clarendon's autobiographical style is not significantly different from his historical prose. Characteristically, he had chosen to write the *Life* in the third person. Since its style was already extremely impersonal, in rewriting parts of it for the final *History*, he altered his expression only in minor ways. What Clarendon recalled while writing the *Life* in 1668, 1669, and 1670 naturally differed from his memories of more recent events in the original history of 1646, 1647, and 1648. But if parallel accounts of the same event in the two texts incorporate different details, they do so in exactly the same style, with similar structures and in many cases direct verbal echoes.[8] Although parts of the *Life* may appear to be written in prose that is less difficult than that of the original history, this impression is actually produced by the content rather than the style. The original history focuses closely on details of Parliamentary and Court debates and policies, and it explores political questions very thoroughly; its content involves more complex issues than the *Life*. In addition, since Clarendon had more information for the period through 1643 covered in the original history, his style in it sometimes becomes more involuted because of his inclusiveness.

The main evidence adduced for literary discontinuities between the original history and the *Life* is that Clarendon's altered purposes in the two works produced substantially different points of view in each. Critics see the *Life* as focusing heavily on a personal vindication of Clarendon's own political career, and hence reflecting much narrower concerns than the history. Significantly, however, on the day after he began to write the *Life*, Clarendon started composing a separate vindication to answer the charges that had led to his banishment.[9] This timing suggests that he perhaps recognized the temptations offered by autobiography, and that he was attempting to separate it from self-vindication. Moreover, although changes in circumstances over twenty years naturally altered Clarendon's authorial viewpoint in certain ways, the changes in the aims of the original history and the *Life* were actually alterations of emphasis rather than substance. Insofar as Clarendon's points of view differed, they were complementary rather than divergent. The larger informing principles that shaped both works remained the same.

The self-vindication that critics connect with the *Life* was already important in the original history, because in it Clarendon was vindicating the principles of his own group among the Royalists as well as the King's position. His principles, based in English legal, constitutional, and Anglican traditions, to which Charles I had given lip service and occasional actual acquiescence, had been eclipsed in Royalist councils after Hyde left for the west with the Prince in 1645 and while he remained in exile in Jersey. Resuscitated briefly when he rejoined Charles II in Paris in 1648, submerged again during his embassy to Spain from 1649 until 1651, by the mid-1650s these policies emerged as dominant when Hyde assumed the central place among Royalist advisers in exile. Although circumstances altered the kinds of actions Clarendon found appropriate at various times to carry out his policies, his basic beliefs never changed. Thus it was this view of politics, based on the same principles he had espoused in 1646 when he began the original history, that triumphed at the Restoration. Significantly, for most of the years covered by the *Life*, events themselves specifically vindicated Clarendon's policies. Alternative recommendations that were tried during that period had failed. If Clarendon had written the *Life* with the hope that it might contribute to his eventual recall from banishment, simply recording those actions as they occurred, as history rather than as polemic, was all that he needed for self-vindication. In contrast, much more effort was actually required to vindicate himself and his policies in the early years covered by the original history. Indeed, it is arguable that adherence to a consistent policy of any kind might have regained the throne for Charles I. Because many insufficiently explored alternatives to Clarendon's position existed during this early period, in the original history he supplied the kind of extensive detail required to show that he and his party had been the most correct in their advice. Thus self-vindication, which is no less a part of the original history than of the *Life*, was in many ways more inherent in the events of the 1650s than in those of the early 1640s.

The purposes of the original history and the *Life* share other similarities. Both works were ultimately written with posterity in mind. In both Clarendon's memorial aim is prominent, for he wished to preserve the memory of those who had participated in great events, particularly the dead on both sides of the conflict. Thus the original history was intended to "serve to inform myself and some others what we are to do, as well as to comfort us in what we have done" (*HR*, 1 : 3). Similarly, the *Life* would comfort himself and his family and supporters, and it too would offer political instruction, although of a slightly different kind than the history. By the time Clarendon began the *Life*, Charles I was of course dead, under circumstances that eclipsed the magnitude of his own errors and ineptitude. Clarendon's emphases altered accordingly; he was naturally less concerned to analyze the mistakes of a royal martyr than of a living king who he hoped would rule again. But though Charles I was gone, there were many others alive to instruct, and Clarendon was throughout his life an incorrigible pedagogue—a characteristic Charles II found harder and harder to tolerate as they both grew older. Thus much general political instruction remains in the *Life*, although its analyses are briefer than those in the original history.

The original history and the *Life* are based on many of the same kinds of materials, are written in the same style, and show aims that are either similar or complementary. Combining two such works could produce a congruent literary whole, and this Clarendon succeeded in accomplishing. The fusion of the two texts was not without certain problems, for some awkward transitions and occasional repetitions were left in the final *History*. Although some of these errors were obviously careless slips, most of what seems to be editorial negligence was probably due in large part to Clarendon's expectation that his work would be edited by others before the general public received it. In any case, despite sporadic difficulties, from a literary perspective Clarendon's various gains from combining his manuscripts usually more than offset his losses.

Clarendon used the similar aims and differing emphases of the *Life* and the original history to enlarge the focus of the completed *History of the Rebellion*. Both the particularity and the generality in the perspectives of each supplemented the other. Causation in the original history had been centered on individuals; the extended character sketches found more often in the *Life* personalize the earlier explanations. Similarly, the general overviews of politics in the first history, especially in the digressions, are balanced by the more anecdotal specificity of the *Life*. The details in the original history, what Clarendon remembered of events in the recent past, tend to be more exact and complete, and they therefore possess one kind of historical accuracy and interest. In contrast, what adheres in the memory over time is in part general impressions, which add depth to the narrative of the *Life* even as factual accuracy diminishes. But if the first account shows the vividness of the immediately exact, another kind of vividness comes from the details Clarendon incorporated into the *Life*. Among the many small particularities of an event, some too insignificant to record contemporaneously, a few will remain embedded in the memory over years. The *Life* includes many of these minor details of personality and circumstance that the history omits; they add their special color to the narrative. The two texts allowed Clarendon various narrative alternatives, and he usually made his choices well. Cutting the original history when its details seemed too minor, omitting parts of the *Life* that were more narrowly personal, preserving sections of general commentary from each, he interwove his two manuscripts to produce a final history that had both coherence and variety in its viewpoint.

The twenty-year interruption of his work was therefore fortuitous for Clarendon. Circumstances helped him to produce the large overview of events that other seventeenth-century historians failed to create. More important, Clarendon took full artistic advantage of his circumstances and used them to improve the literary quality of the final *History*. Literary exploitation of changes over time is characteristic of his narrative. For example, in 1647 when he first described Charles I setting up his standard at Nottingham, he covered the event briefly:

As soon as he came to the town [Charles I] went himself, attended by all the train he could make, to the top of the castle-hill of Nottingham, (which is a place of a very eminent and pleasant prospect,) and there fixed his royal standard; when indeed all the foot which he had yet drawn together were not a sufficient guard to have constantly attended the standard. (*HR*, 2:289)

If the occasion had seemed inauspicious when he depicted it in the original history, by the time Clarendon came to write the *Life*, the raising of the standard had assumed for him a symbolic significance as a pre-

35

figurement of the disasters that came not only in the first civil war, but throughout the entire Interregnum. In the *Life* he added a section explaining why the standard should have been erected at York rather than at Nottingham, using the mistake to foreshadow the action itself (*HR*, 2:284–85). He then wrote his second account of the occasion, the one he chose for the final *History*:

According to the proclamation, upon the twenty-fifth day of August the standard was erected, about six of the clock in the evening of a very stormy and tempestuous day. The King himself, with a small train, rode to the top of the castle-hill, Varney the knight-marshal, who was standard-bearer, carrying the standard, which was then erected in that place, with little other ceremony than the sound of drums and trumpets. Melancholic men observed many ill presages about that time. There was not one regiment of foot yet levied and brought thither; so that the train-bands, which the shrieve had drawn thither, was all the strength the King had for his person and the guard of the standard. There appeared no conflux of men in obedience to the proclamation; the arms and ammunition were not yet come from York, and a general sadness covered the whole town, and the King himself appeared more melancholic than he used to be. The standard itself was blown down the same night it had been set up, by a very strong and unruly wind, and could not be fixed again in a day or two till the tempest was allayed. (*HR*, 2:290–91)

Clarendon adds negative details to lengthen and darken his description of the event. The "very eminent and pleasant prospect" of the castle hill in his first description disappears, and he sets the scene more precisely in the twilight of a blustery day. His development of details of the weather historically reflects his constant metaphorical use of images of storm throughout the *History* in connection with both the disturbances that led to war and also the rebellion itself. The standard, like the House of Stuart, cannot be established until elemental rage subsides. Psychological details parallel physical ones. Low spirits, emphasized by the repetition of "melancholic," blanket the town and extend even to the King himself. Clarendon develops the tone and mood of the incident to produce a somberly effective ending for the fifth book of the *History*.

Like most of the great histories, Clarendon's is a dark one. Much of the sense of tragedy that pervades it comes from his constant juxtaposition of layers of time in the narrative. "Yet" and "now" are important words that recur in his text. Even in the original history Hyde often intermingled past and future with his accounts of events, referring to future

36

Parliaments, to posterity, to roles individuals had played before 1640. The addition of the *Life* further enriched his perspective.

The breadth and variety of narrative perspective in the final *History of the Rebellion* offered something entirely new for English historians and general readers of history. In pre-nineteenth-century English literary historiography, the major advances were made by great individual works, not by theory or by slow accretion. Those who were responsible for theoretical developments, such as Bacon, failed to write good histories. Antiquarian accumulation advanced history technically but not artistically. Practicing historians needed models to show methods of fusing historical evidence and literary art, and Clarendon provided a major one in the *History of the Rebellion*. His *Life* was in this sense worth sacrificing. Clarendon could not have done for English autobiography of the time (arguably even more in need of models, since it lacked the classical examples of the genre possessed by historians) what he did for English history. To progress beyond mere personal chronicle, straightforward diary or memoir, seventeenth-century autobiography needed writers with the kind of increased self-consciousness that would demand new ways of recording the self.[10] But it was precisely this kind of imaginative approach to autobiographical material and form that Clarendon could not provide. He lacked the literary interest in the subjective, the commitment to the portrayal of personal identity rather than deeds, which has been crucial to autobiography as a genre. However, for Clarendon autobiographical weakness translated into historical strength. In combining his original history and his *Life* into an artistic unit in the *History of the Rebellion*, he showed how to create the enlarged historical and literary scope that seventeenth-century English histories had so far lacked.

CLARENDON'S HISTORICAL PROSE

Clarendon was in certain ways typical of his age in emphasizing historical matter over manner. He described his original history to one correspondent as a "plain, faithful narrative" and promised that his own style would not "defraud" accounts of the northern campaigns "of their due integrity, which will be ornament enough."[11] He shared the seventeenth century's general dislike for rhetorical elements in history, writing in one of his essays that in European histories of the past hundred years, rhetorical and oratorical elements had been employed to misrepresent events and mislead readers. Like Milton, he especially censured the "mixture of oratory and rhetoric with history." [12] In politics Clarendon had repeatedly seen language used to deceive—he noted parenthetically in a letter to Hopton that "a little logick or rhetorick will make every great and notable conveniency look too like necessity" [13]—and he came to distrust stylistic ornament generally. His answer to Hobbes' *Leviathan* sums up his attitude toward the dangerous potential that effective styles have for misuse: "Those Books have in all times don most mischief, and scatter'd abroad the most pernicious errors, in which the Authors, by the Ornament of their Style, and the pleasantness of their method, and subtlety of their Wit, have from specious premises, drawn their unskilful and unwary Readers into unwarrantable opinions and conclusions." [14]

Although Clarendon reflected the general seventeenth-century reaction against rhetoric in history, he nevertheless expected history to be written in prose that was effective and interesting. Unlike too many of his contemporaries, he never confused rhetoric with good writing. He appreciated the antiquarians' contributions to historical studies, but he disliked their neglect of literary art. His remarks on his good friend John Selden, that *locus classicus* of the seventeenth century's tendency to prefer scholarship to style in history, reveal Clarendon's priorities: "His style in all his writings seems harsh and sometimes obscure; which is not wholly to be imputed to the abstruse subjects of which he commonly treated, . . . but to a little undervaluing the beauty of a style, and too much propensity to the language of antiquity" (*Life*, p. 26). He similarly mentions stylistic beauty in connection with the failings of early English historians, whose "obscure truths" are "so blindly and lamely set down and described, that a history compounded out of them can have very little beauty." [15] Clarendon wanted his readers to be instructed, but he felt that the way historical truth was conveyed was also important. He condemned ecclesiastical histories, for example, for yielding the "least credible information, and least pleasure to the reader, in the importance of the subject, or in the acuteness of the delivery." [16]

In creating a style that would have literary merit and yet not be overly rhetorical, Clarendon was guided by his sense of what history should do and be. His historical priorities limited the kinds of literary effects he would incorporate into his writing; he deliberately chose not to exploit certain literary abilities he had, in order to write a particular kind of history. For example, the *History* offers scattered evidence of a visual sense that shows Clarendon did not lack pictorial ability. Thus in relating the

Battle of Lansdown, he assembles geographic details scattered through two other accounts and renders a much clearer description of the topography of the engagement than either of his sources.[17] However, he remains the least pictorial of the great English literary historiographers.

More telling in terms of literary conventions for history, throughout the *History of the Rebellion* Clarendon shows no interest whatsoever in the dramatic development of important events. It is not in his work that we see the great scenes of the period: Strafford on the way to his execution pausing beneath Laud's prison room in the Tower to receive his old friend's final blessing; Charles I, stepping forth from the Banqueting Hall before the hushed crowd, noble in the moments before death as he had seldom been in life; Charles II, landing at Dover and lifting Monck from his knees to embrace the man whose arms had returned the kingdom to loyalty. Dramatizations were an established literary convention in classical and Renaissance historiography, and despite early English commentators' limited interest in historical style, they retained this emphasis on dramatic verisimilitude.[18] The opening of Clarendon's dialogue on old age indicates that he had some skill in dramatic depiction when he wanted to use it. But he disliked rhetoric in history in part because it could "artificially . . . work upon the affections, and even corrupt the judgment of the reader,"[19] and he recognized that dramatizations could function similarly. In one of his commonplace books he recorded Hobbes' explanation of why he had not wanted to publish his translation of Thucydides:

I saw for the greatest part, men came to the reading of History, with an affection much like that of the people in Rome: who came to the spectacle of the gladiators, with more delight to behold their blood, than their skill in fencing. For they be far more in number, that love to read of great armies, bloody battles, and many thousands slain at once, than that mind the art by which the affairs both of armies and cities be conducted to their ends.[20]

This was precisely the taste that Clarendon had no intention of satisfying in his own history.

Ben Jonson commented that "Daniel wrott civill warres, & yett hath not one batle jn [*sic*] all his book."[21] Like Daniel, Clarendon was more interested in analyzing than in depicting events. He himself had been appalled and frightened by what had happened during the civil wars, and in the *History* his expressions of outraged incredulity recur: "It can hardly be imagined"; "It is not easily believed"; "It can never be enough wondered at" (3:362; 2:296; 4:295). Just before the Restoration, he notes that Englishmen brought gifts to Charles II in Breda to supply "his necessities; which had been discontinued for many years, to a degree that cannot be believed, and ought not to be remembered" (*HR*, 4:226). In a real sense, Clarendon was not concerned that details of specific events be remembered. He was writing history to help readers learn enough from his analyses of the actions of a terrible era so that nothing similar would happen in England again. Thus he structured his prose to appeal to the reader's mind rather than his feelings. He avoided the emotional immediacy of dramatized episodes and other colorful writing so that readers would evaluate rather than participate vicariously in the events he depicted. As a statesman Clarendon's best efforts had always been directed toward calming the emotions aroused by England's political and religious struggles so that reason could prevail. Similarly, in writing his *History* he sought to objectify the nation's searing experiences during the civil wars in order to analyze and understand them.

To shape a historical style appropriate for showing the significance of events, Clarendon relied on a simple and straightforward vocabulary. In this avoidance of the elegant and ornamental, he reflects the post–Restoration movement toward a more utilitarian prose, although no evidence directly connects his practice with Thomas Sprat and other apologists associated with this aim.[22] Clarendon did not lack metaphorical and descriptive abilities—in 1641 Parliament was "that warm region where thunder and lightning was made"; Lord Herbert's "mushrump-[mushroom]-army" was collected and annihilated almost overnight; Cromwell's agitators were to avert inconveniences from "the drowsy, dull, presbyterian humour of Fayrefax" (*HR* 1:390–91; 2:483; 4:275). However, in the *History* he employed such expression sparingly. His most characteristic metaphors, mainly those connected with storm, fire, and disease, are conventional ones found in every seventeenth-century historian from Bacon to Burnet.[23] By Clarendon's time they had largely lost their impact as images. With many abstract nouns and few adjectives, his style deliberately sacrifices vividness to exactness. The power of Clarendon's phrasing comes in part from its precision, especially reflected in the careful differentiations that mark his writing. When the Earl of Northampton was killed at the battle of Hopton Heath, "a greater victory had been an unequal recompense for a less loss"; Sir Philip Stapleton appeared "to be rather without good breeding than not capable of it"; Queen Henrietta Maria's graces "were still more towards those who were like to do services than to those who had done them" (*HR* 2:477; 1:393; 5:14). The vocabulary Clarendon employs in the *History*, which is particularly suitable for the analysis he favored, in general reflects the separation of poetic and historical language that prevailed at the time.

Clarendon structures his chosen vocabulary formally. Because in certain sections of the *History* he followed his sources so closely, it is easy to see his characteristic methods for producing the elevated expression he preferred. The examples below are from Sir Edward Walker's narrative of Charles I's activities in 1644, from which Clarendon drew heavily, and also from the accounts by Sir Ralph Hopton and Colonel Walter Slingsby on which he based his depiction of military affairs in the west. Clarendon raises the level of language and formalizes the syntax of his sources to produce a more dignified impression. His tendency to employ nouns and nominal constructions adds weight and dignity to his style:

WALKER: Waller was "to go into the West"
CLARENDON: Waller was "to attend the service of the west"[24]

WALKER: "Yet *Waller*, seeing no Remedy, actively pursued his Employment, and presently marched. . . ."
CLARENDON: "When Waller found there was no remedy, he obeyed his orders with much diligence and vigour, and prosecuted his march. . . ."[25]

Removing direct agents, he uses "it was" or "there was":

HOPTON: "They had by the next morning fifteen hundred waight of that sort of match in store which served the turne"
CLARENDON: "There was by the next morning provided fifteen hundred weight of such serviceable match. . . ."[26]

He prefers passive verbs in his sentences:

SLINGSBY: "Our ffoote leps into their brestworks"
CLARENDON: The Royalists "became possessed of their breast-works"[27]

Speech is usually reported in indirect discourse:

SLINGSBY: The Cornish troops "desir'd to fall on and cry'd lett us fetch those cannon"
CLARENDON: The Cornish troops "desired to fall on, and cried out, 'that they might have leave to fetch off those cannon'"[28]

The formal and impersonal prose produced by these stylistic methods predominates in the *History of the Rebellion*. Because history for Clarendon was not the linguistically immediate, the major effect of his style is to remove direct action from the narrative. As he deliberately distances experience with the structure of his expression, interpretation and analysis tend to dominate. The aesthetic distance which Clarendon creates stylistically renders the impression of authorial detachment and objectivity that is crucial for a historian.

Clarendon's ability to sustain a high level of rhetorical impersonality was a remarkable stylistic achievement for a committed partisan who had personally participated in many of the actions he recorded. But if distanced and formal language predominates in the *History*, the texture of the prose shows that this level was not maintained without a struggle. Clarendon's frequent employment of litotes and understatement suggests the restraint that was required. Moreover, because not all of the original history or the *Life* was intended for a public audience, in certain sections Clarendon felt freer to express himself more directly or forcefully. Too much impersonal prose would have been bland. In his constant movement toward public expression of the personal, Clarendon's middle course between the overly formal and the overly immediate is enhanced by his deviations on both sides.

In addition to his general dislike of rhetoric in history, Clarendon was an astute enough politician to recognize that the case he was presenting in the *History of the Rebellion* would be better served by historical discourse than by declamatory and rhetorical language. But because the history was a record of frustration, defeat, endurance, and triumph in many ways deeply personal, he did not totally succeed in banishing rhetoric from it. Clarendon was a man of strong emotions who struggled throughout his life to control what he termed "that heat and passion, he was naturally inclined to be transported with" (*Life*, p. 25). In spite of his best efforts to maintain narrative detachment, his feelings sometimes erupted into his account—sentiments he of course knew that his private audiences of Royalists and his family and friends would share. Weighted adjectives occasionally reflect his biases. "Monstrous" is a favorite, but others express his outrage at Presbyterians, Scots, Irish, Independents, and almost everyone else who thwarted the Royalists. Lawyers in Parliament who sought popular applause were guilty of "cheap and vile affectation"; quotations from seditious sermons showed "impious madness"; the Scots were dominated by "their senseless and wretched clergy"; "brutish behaviour" and "sottish lethargy" characterized the Irish rebels

(*HR*, 1:404; 2:321; 4:304; 5:215). An occasional wistful "Alas!" escapes into his text. His years of legal pleading and Parliamentary speeches are reflected in some oratorical echoes in the text, and, very rarely, fullblown declamatory rhetoric enters the *History*. Rhetorical denunciation heavily colors his portrayal of the last days of Charles I, from the occupatio with which he treats most of the trial and the execution of the King to the anaphora at the end of Book 11 condemning 1648 as a year of infamy. He also draws heavily on rhetorical devices in other sections in which his feelings were deeply involved, such as his character of Falkland and his tributes to Oxford.

Although Clarendon's career shows his adeptness at the florid speeches and elaborate ceremonial compliments characteristic of his age, he was equally able to employ what, in describing one unfortunate encounter with Charles II, he termed "some other, too plain, expressions, which it may be were not warily enough used" (*CL*, 2:285). Similarly, at times in the *History* more colloquial language reflects Clarendon as harassed participant remembering rather than as detached historian recording. In early 1660, Monck's march gave Charles II "some faint hope (and God knows it was very faint)" (*HR*, 6:163). Or, after Cromwell informed Falkland that he would have emigrated if the Grand Remonstrance had failed to pass, Clarendon cannot resist interjecting: "So near was the poor kingdom at that time to its deliverance!" (*HR*, 1:420). Sometimes colloquialisms reflect the immediacy of his memories, as when the Duke of Lorraine "received great sums of money yearly from the Spaniard, and was, sure, very rich" (*HR*, 5:45). In sections intended primarily for his Royalist friends, his expression occasionally becomes conversational in reminiscence: Henry Burton, John Bastwick, and William Prynne were tried "in as full a court as I ever saw"; Sir Richard Grenville's letter to Sir John Berkeley was "so full of ill language and reproach, as I have never seen the like from and to a gentleman" (*HR*, 1:267; 4:30). Other colloquial elements reflect his strong aural predispositions, for Clarendon tended to tell stories more effectively when he had heard them originally from master storytellers. Such accounts as Charles II's escape after Worcester and Charles I's and Buckingham's plans to visit Spain contain many colloquial elements that he undoubtedly picked up in this way. Because of their vividness, these undertones of colloquial immediacy, along with the moments of rhetorical eloquence, add richness and variety to his prose.

Clarendon's use of irony in the *History* also reflects how he stylistically transmutes personal experience and observation into impersonal historical record, with personal traces remaining which add variety and interest to the narrative. Events themselves insured that irony would necessarily be present in any accurate account of England from 1640 to 1660, when putative rulers successively rose to be displaced by the very individuals or groups whom they had called forth to consolidate their own power. Parliament overcame the King, only to become subject to its own army, which in turn was conquered by its greatest leader. In the *History*, the bulk of Clarendon's irony is straightforwardly situational: Strafford was destroyed "by two things that he most despised, the people and sir Harry Vane"; Fairfax "wished nothing that Cromwell did, and yet contributed to bring it all to pass" (1:342; 4:275). However, presenting without comment the many incongruencies inherent in the historical record would have been difficult for any contemporary, and Clarendon was a man who appreciated wit. Although he commended Pascal's *Provincial Letters* for their "most natural wit," his general taste in irony is better shown by his enthusiasm for the polemical tract *Killing No Murder*, in which the wit is mainly heavy and unsubtle sarcasm.[29] Clarendon's letters during the Royalist exile show his tendency to use this kind of irony to control his personal outrage at various political developments. In 1653, angry that Sir Marmaduke Langdale was to join their council, he commented to Secretary Nicholas: "I have been long acquainted with Langdale's opinions, this day for the Presbyterians and the next for the Catholicks and for cordially joining with either, so that I am very glad we shall have his assistance shortly here."[30] A month later, furious at Buckingham's machinations, he tells Nicholas that the Duke "without doubt will marry his [Fairfax's] daughter or be Cromwell's groom to get his estate."[31]

Clarendon occasionally flares into similar sarcasm in the history of what he once termed in a letter to Nicholas "this most lovely Rebellion."[32] When Parliament in 1641 abolished the High Commission Court, it left "adultery and incest as unpunishable as any other acts of good fellowship" (*HR*, 1:373). Although his irony can be lightly humorous— orthodox divines in 1642 were "discountenanced, imprisoned, or forced to a long attendance upon committees or the House, (which was worse than imprisonment . . .)"—it is often disdainfully judgmental. For example, he notes that many who accompanied Charles II to Germany in 1659 "thought of providing a religion as well as other conveniences for their journey" (*HR*, 1:591; 6:123). Ironical comments enliven the *History* because Clarendon employs them sparingly. Bishop Burnet wrote that as a statesman, Clarendon "had too much levity in his wit, and did not always observe the decorum of his post";[33] in contrast, as a historian he carefully controlled his irony. Because his characteristic modes are understatement and sarcasm, both of which are considered relatively early and obvious ironic forms,[34] he is always overt, never employing irony to undermine unfairly and never allowing it to dominate his narrative. Like the rhetorical and colloquial elements, irony helps Clarendon to produce an effective historical style, thoroughly magisterial in its formality without becoming dull.

Like the language, the syntax of the *History of the Rebellion* shows both variety and tension. Faced with complicated historical events and a prose with no one syntax adequate for depicting them, Clarendon, like many of his contemporaries, simply drew on all the available syntactical resources. He begins the *History* with a sentence imitating Richard Hooker's stately periodic opening for *Of the Laws of Ecclesiastical Polity*, and he often employs the Ciceronian period:

What seeds were then sown for the rebellion, which within a year after brake out in Ireland, by the great liberty and favour that committee found, who, for the good service against that lord, were hearkened to in all things that concerned that kingdom, shall be observed and spoken of at large hereafter. (*HR*, 1:286)

So that, between those that loved them and those that feared them, those that did not love the Church and those that did not love some churchmen, those whom the Court had oppressed and those who had helped the Court to oppress others, those who feared their power and those who feared their justice, their party was grown over the kingdom, but especially in the city, justly formidable. (*HR*, 2:74)

At other times, his informal loose style approaches Drydenic speed and smoothness:

Nor was it more in his [Buckingham's] power to be without promotion and titles and wealth, than for a healthy man to sit in the sun in the brightest dog-days and remain without any warmth. (*HR*, 1:43)

He [Pym] died towards the end of December, before the Scots entered, and was buried with wonderful pomp and magnificence in that place where the bones of our English kings and princes are committed to their rest. (*HR*, 3:324)

More rarely, his prose shows traces of the antithetical wit associated with Senecan style:

He [Arundel] resorted sometimes to the Court, because there only was a greater man than himself; and went thither the seldomer, because there was a greater than himself. (*HR*, 1:69)

Clarendon's strength is in his combination of syntactical modes.[35] Typically, he joins individual periodic units linearly, with weak subordination, following psychological or conversational order to produce the trailing structures characteristic of much of the prose of his time:

And in this manner, and with so little pains, this extraordinary man [Cromwell], without any other reason than because he had a mind to it, and without the assistance, and against the desire, of all noble persons or men of quality, or of three men who in the beginning of the troubles were possessed of three hundred pounds land by the year, mounted himself into the throne of three kingdoms, without the name of king, but with a greater power and authority than had been ever exercised or claimed by any king; and received greater evidence and manifestation of respect and esteem from all the kings and princes in Christendom than had ever been shewed to any monarch of those nations: and which was so much the more notorious, in that they all abhorred him, when they trembled at his power and courted his friendship. (*HR*, 5:287–88)

Clarendon's characteristic syntax blends the periodic and the loose, and its literary effectiveness derives from the mixture. Slow and weighty periodic elements produce an impression of nobility and amplitude, while ease and fluidity result from the forward propulsion of the more direct loose style. Grandeur and sweep, strength and rapidity are in this way combined in the long sentences in which Clarendon usually works. Through them he can effectively manipulate his varied syntactical constructions to control the pace of his narrative. At its best his syntax mingles flux and stasis, the simultaneous depiction of life and evaluation of life that is necessary for truth of historical presentation.

Clarendon's achievement in prose style was to find a level of language and a syntax suitable for historical discourse at a time when English prose was in transition and when other historians were unconcerned about or negligent of literary art. In the works of his contemporaries, the strength and authority of the periodic style become lost amid the syntactic chaos of loose constructions, while simultaneously sabotaging the rapid movement and clarity that gave the loose style its power. Clarendon managed to synthesize the old and the new, the traditional periodic and the evolving loose, holding together disparate prose elements to exploit the strengths of each syntax. In addition to finding a functional syntactic compromise for history, he consistently maintained that middle stylistic level between the overly poetic and the overly prosaic that commentators on history had traditionally demanded. He never makes history into poetry. At the same time, his general practice, particularly illustrated by his elevation of the language in his sources, reveals his conviction that history requires a certain formality of diction. His vocabulary and occasional colloquial insertions show a directness of expression that reflects the later seventeenth-century movement toward a plain style. But these more modern elements are most apparent when he is compared to his predecessors; from the vantage point of the early eighteenth century, his language is quite elevated. Clarendon consciously retained elements of earlier, more formal seventeenth-century styles that were not current when he was writing. Gilbert Burnet, the next significant figure in English literary historiography, wrote entirely in the looser and lower style more characteristic of post–Restoration prose. Like Clarendon, Burnet wrote history as a participant and as an author with considerable literary experience. Yet his *History of My Own Times* lacks the literary stature of the *History of the Rebellion*. Although Burnet's poor organization, his gossipy content, and the inferior quality of his thought account in part for his diminished achievement, the level of his language also contributes significantly. The increasingly informal prose of the Restoration period, which would develop into a vehicle ideal for the more private genre of the novel, lacked the weight and authority required for historical narrative. Clarendon remains the only English historian until Hume who could sustain the middle style considered appropriate for history. His achievement came at a crucial time for English historiography. For half a century, his work provided the only major model of readable historical prose that did not sacrifice dignity and nobility.

In both its level and its structure of language, Clarendon's prose style was difficult to sustain. His mixture of the periodic and the loose was a volatile one, especially when combined with his tendency toward formal and impersonal language. If his vocabulary was simple, his structuring of the words could be awkward, and verbosity sometimes resulted when long sentences exceeded the bounds of syntax and of the reader's comprehension. These problems in Clarendon's prose stemmed directly from his historical priorities.

Clarendon described his original history as "*exact* memorials of passages," and during his final exile he worked to make English history "more profitably and *exactly* communicated than it hath yet been" [italics mine].[36] His concern for exactness pervades his prose style. For example, the description of his father's final illness in the *Life* is so detailed that it appears in a modern collection of *Classic Descriptions of Disease* as the best early account of the symptoms now diagnosed as angina pectoris.[37] This kind of precision in expression, in many ways useful for a historian, can create stylistic difficulties, particularly because of Clarendon's related tendency toward inclusiveness in content. Clarendon was at no time a man of few words. He explained to Sir John Berkeley that in debates he disliked leaving "any thing unsaid, which in my judgment is of weight towards the decision of the matter in question."[38] He wrote similarly, for he wanted his readers to have all the information available in order to understand events. Indeed, he seems to have believed that completeness of explanation directly correlated with length. Although he admitted to Nicholas (who accused him of having "an itch . . . of writing") that he was "generally accused . . . of enlarging more than is necessary" in his letters, he informed his friend that people who disliked long letters "care neither to understand business nor to make others understand."[39]

In writing history, Clarendon had no intention of simplifying or abridging; his goal was to tell not only the truth, but the whole truth. Eager to present all that he knew, he at times seems more concerned to insert every detail than to incorporate his information grammatically into an ordered account:

The King [Charles I], who was excessively affected to hunting and the sports of the field, had a great desire to make a great park for red as well as fallow deer between Richmond and Hampton Court, where he had large wastes of his own and great parcels of wood, which made it very fit for the use he designated it to: but as some parishes had common in those wastes, so many gentlemen and farmers had good houses and good farms intermingled with those wastes, of their own inheritance or for lives or years; and without taking in of them into the park, it would not be of the largeness or for the use proposed. (*HR*, 1:132–33)

The color of the deer, the existing distribution of the area, and the tenures of the landholders take precedence as Clarendon repeats adjectives and nouns and employs awkward phraseology. When his antiquarian desire to assemble factual information overwhelmed his literary control, lengthy sentences, in a complicated relationship of cause and effect, both produce and are produced by verbosity and awkward syntax.[40] That such stylistic difficulties represent in part the integrity of the historian facing his material is shown by the fact that Clarendon's prose becomes less complex whenever he lacked detailed knowledge of events. Sections of the final books of the *History*, for which he was able to gather less information, are written with more smoothness than earlier volumes.

Much of the power of Clarendon's prose results from the stylistic tensions it embodies. Whether or not he completely controlled his expression, his style always conveys to the reader a continuing sense of intellectual process. His sentences evolved as an active mind forged ahead, thinking in individual periodic units, piling clause upon clause, inserting qualifications, interjections, and afterthoughts just as they occurred. Rhetorical order necessarily gave way to psychological order. In most cases, the stylistic successes of this play of mind outweighed the failures. Clarendon created a prose appropriate for the story he had to tell, writing in the only way that he could in order to be true to his own understanding of events, while implicitly recognizing that the very nature of the historical period he was depicting precluded final resolution and explanation by any contemporary. Because he refused to simplify stylistically the texture of reality, the prose itself reflects the complexity and variety of a tumultuous period when no one individual or group in England could long control the momentum of events. Clarendon's style thus became a direct expression of his historical integrity. As he constantly strives for precise statement and complete information, despite occasional grammatical failures, the reader sees the struggle toward truth. Indeed, the style itself forces readers to participate in the search. Never abandoning efforts to order his material, and yet never allowing stylistic order to become an end in itself, Clarendon created a prose that made his history a unique blend of process and product. T. H. Lister has noted that Clarendon is not a writer well served by short excerpts because, despite "defects which a minute criticism notes with ease," his prose is truly impressive "by the aggregate."[41] It is the constant sense of intellectual process reflected in his prose style, complete in some sentences and incomplete in others, that makes the *History* a satisfactory stylistic whole.

Clarendon's prose is in many ways a transitional style, a temporary solution to the problems of historical prose at one particularly difficult time in England. His achievement can be evaluated fairly only within this context. The demands of his subject, the kind of world he was depicting, were at variance with the prose styles of his age. In addition to syntactical limitations, G. M. Trevelyan points out that by the middle of the seventeenth century, the English language was proving insufficient in other ways: "Its fault . . . is want of exactness and of complexity in ideas, that renders it unfit for psychology or for close analysis of things either mate-

49

rial or spiritual."[42] Writers on theology, political theory, science, and literature shared these linguistic difficulties, but for historians, faced with different kinds of insights and evidence from more sophisticated methods to incorporate into their works, the problems were particularly acute. Clarendon's triumph was to be able to recognize which elements of existing styles could be useful for his own purposes and then to combine them effectively. He writes a prose that is capacious because of its interplay of diverse elements—loose, periodic, and Senecan syntaxes; simple vocabulary; colloquial and rhetorical interjections; understatement and sarcasm—held together within his formally impersonal dominant style. Poised between the prose of the Renaissance and that of the Restoration, Clarendon looks simultaneously to the present and the past to synthesize the best in both so that historical evidence and literary art can merge.

NARRATIVE STRUCTURE IN THE *HISTORY*

In structure, just as in prose style, Clarendon adapted the prevailing forms of his era for his own purposes. Various remarks show his awareness of the structural problems that were created in contemporary historical writing by both antiquarian accumulation and annalistic chronology. To avoid the overinclusiveness characteristic of the chronicler and the antiquarian, he carefully restricted his focus, limiting the amount and the kind of material he incorporated into his text. Several times in the *History* he emphasizes his exclusion of trivial information—"I . . . shall no otherwise mention small and light occurrences than as they have been introductions to matters of the greatest moment . . ."—as well as his omission of concerns extraneous to his main themes: "But in this discourse of Ireland, it cannot be imagined, nor do I intend, to mention any of the memorable actions, . . . or other transactions within that kingdom; but shall remember no more of that business than had immediate reference to and dependence on the difference between the King and the two Houses of Parliament" (*HR*, 1:3; 2:485). Annals Clarendon considered "an imperfect kind of history, and rather memorials for history than history itself."[43] Although he employed annalistic organization for five of the *History*'s sixteen books (7–9, 11, and 12), he used the mode with flexibility, altering it in accordance with the materials he had and his literary priorities.

Clarendon found various ways to modify the overly chronological approach that inhibited narrative development in other seventeenth-century histories. He recognized how certain chronological blocks could form effective units of story. At the end of Book 10, for example, he explains that "contrary to the order formerly observed" in the work, he has "crowded in all the particular passages and important transactions of two whole years into this book, that I might not interrupt or discontinue the relation of the mysterious proceedings of the army . . . towards the King and his party, . . . with the vile artifices of the Scots' commissioners" (*HR*, 4:314). In several of the early books of the *History*, which cover less than a year, narrative time (the time required to read the account) markedly exceeds chronological time (the duration of the actual events covered in the text)[44] because Clarendon had a great deal of information and included extensive analyses. After Book 12, which surveys the year 1649, Clarendon abandons annals entirely. Because he saw this period as a time when the Royalists were required to wait passively rather than to act, events themselves become less important in the text and chronological time is accordingly much greater than narrative time. Individual books cover periods from two to four years, and within books Clarendon also shows himself no slave to strict chronology. His comment in writing of one of Digby's forays is typical: "Because this expedition was in a short time at an end, it will not be amiss to [finish] the relation in this place, there being no occasion to resume it hereafter" (*HR*, 4:120). Finally, to add coherence, Clarendon occasionally replaces chronology with geography as a structuring device. His separate surveys of events in each area of England are an important source of narrative continuity, and they are historically effective because in certain ways the war was as much a series of local conflicts as a national phenomenon. Similarly, the affairs of Scotland and Ireland are usually treated in sections that are set apart.[45]

In structuring the narrative perspective of the *History*, Clarendon also carefully controlled the personal elements that marred most contemporary accounts. The position he created for his narrator, like his prose style, distanced the depiction of events in his text. Although Robert Scholes and Robert Kellogg have noted that from ancient times third-person rather than first-person narrative was traditionally associated with historical writing, Clarendon apparently connected first-person narration with history.[46] He wrote in the first person not only in the original history, where some of his expression might be expected to be more personal because of his private Royalist audience, but also in the supplementary sections he composed in 1671 and 1672 for the final *History*.

However, even in the more personal sections, Clarendon ultimately maintained his authorial distance. He separates the narrator from himself to produce a rhetorically objective perspective: "I remember . . . many of those who had during the debate positively argued against the thing were called upon to be of that committee, and amongst these, the lord Falkland and Mr. Hyde" (*HR*, 1:402). The third-person narrative of the *Life* was more impersonal in surface rhetoric than the histories. Acutely sensitive to autobiographical elements in history, Clarendon placed even more emphasis on rhetorical distance when his material came from the *Life*. In reworking sections of it for the final *History*, he often removed even the references to himself in the third person. For example, "This caused some debate, and Mr. Hyde . . . told them" became "in the debate, it was told them"; "The Chancellor was appointed to prepare the letter, which he did" emerged as "A letter was prepared accordingly" (*HR*, 1:492; 3:257). Clarendon's changes further camouflage his own role, and on historical grounds the revisions are less exact in the information they convey.[47] Nevertheless, they highlight his determination to create a distanced position for the narrator by rhetorically obliterating himself as much as possible from the text.

In other ways, Clarendon showed considerable literary skill in exteriorizing the third-person references to himself. When he discusses plans for his private meetings with the Duke of Hamilton in 1649, for example, he writes: "The other [Clarendon himself], who indeed had an esteem for the duke, seemed very desirous of it" (*HR*, 5:20). The kind of expression represented by Clarendon's use of "seemed," which precludes grammatically replacing the third person with the first person in the sentence, is the basis on which Roland Barthes distinguishes apersonal from personal narrative.[48] Barthes has also pointed out that in historical narratives written in the third person by participants, the "choice of the apersonal pronoun is only a rhetorical alibi, and . . . the true situation of the narrator is manifest in the syntagms he chooses to express his past acts." Using the Caesarian "he," Barthes analyzes how the narrator reveals himself in the language that he chooses to depict his role in events (in the case of Julius Caesar, through expressions Barthes describes as "syntagms of leadership").[49] Clarendon's extreme narrative impersonality is shown by his ability in the *History* to integrate his own role rhetorically with the roles of others, making his situation virtually indistinguishable in the text from theirs. The syntagms associated with "Mr. Hyde" or "the Chancellor" are, for obvious reasons, syntagms of counsel—"speaking," "writing," "persuading," "conferring," "informing," along with expressions connected with dutifulness and submissiveness in responsibilities. But the very same syntagms are used with others in Clarendon's circle (the Marquis of Ormonde and Lord Falkland, for example) who held positions of trust among the Royalists. Thus, although Clarendon's references to himself in the third person identify him as a knowledgeable Royalist insider and associate him with one particular Royalist faction, they do not conclusively differentiate him from certain other characters.

Insofar as the Clarendonian "he" can be established as the narrator of the *History* at all, it would have to be mainly on grounds involving exterior considerations of context rather than interior ones of form: the amount of information about events in certain out-of-the-way areas (Jersey, Spain, local disputes in the west of England) that suggests the narrator's presence on the scene, or transcriptions of private conversations so detailed that they imply the narrator's participation. Such contextual identification can be misleading, however, because of Clarendon's wide circle of acquaintances and knowledge of events. For example, the *History* includes many long conversations at which he was not present but which he presumably learned of from participants. The distanced narrative perspective that Clarendon created in the *History* was one of the reasons why, before all of his manuscripts were available, those who attacked his work found it difficult to prove his biases from the text itself. In structuring the narrator's position, Clarendon was able to subsume personal elements and convey detachment and historical objectivity through his literary art.

To shape his narrative, Clarendon blends story and discourse to create an enlarged context for the events he depicts, establishing both the significance of each individual action and overall continuity. One historical incident that provides a useful point of reference for discussion of his methods is Queen Henrietta Maria's attempt during the Royalist exile to convert her third son, the Duke of Gloucester, to Roman Catholicism. Clarendon's account of the conversion crisis is brief—it covers only three pages (sections 117 through 119) in Book 14—and is also methodologically typical. It succinctly illustrates his most characteristic structural techniques throughout the *History*.

In late October of 1654, Charles II and his little Court at Cologne learned that the Queen in Paris was pressuring the Duke to become a convert to her religion. She had discharged his Anglican tutor and had sent her son to the Abbey of St. Martin's near Pontoise, where her confessor, Walter Montagu, the English convert who was its abbot, was aiding her schemes. The King was furious, recognizing the adverse effect such a conversion would have on English public opinion; at the same time, he knew that he had little leverage either in the French Court or among the English Royalists in Paris to stop his mother. Letters flew between Cologne and Paris as everyone who thought they had any interest in the affair, from Gloucester's tutor and Lord Jermyn to the Princess of Orange and the Queen herself, entered the fray.[50] Hyde told several correspondents that he had never seen the King so disturbed and that Charles had— the implication is for once—needed no one's advice to deal firmly with the crisis.[51] (He prudently omitted these observations from the *History*.) Charles' seriousness is also suggested by the fact that the drafts of most of his letters on the matter are in his own hand, rather than, as was more usual, in Hyde's.[52] In mid-November the Marquis of Ormonde left for Paris as the King's emissary to deal with the crisis; on December 2, he notified Charles that Henrietta Maria had capitulated and that the Duke was safely with him. The way in which Clarendon structured his depiction of this incident is presented in outline form in Figure 1. Italics indicate those parts of the narrative that are predominantly discourse (historical explanation or analysis), to distinguish them from sections focused primarily on events or actions (the story).

Clarendon's account of the attempted conversion covers 104 lines in the text. Of these, 46 lines (44 percent of the total) are predominantly discourse, while 58 lines (56 percent) relate the story. Clarendon thus anchors the actual events he relates in a rich interpretive context; like his prose style, his narrative is structured to show the significance of actions rather than simply to depict them. The major action that initiates the resolution of the crisis, Ormonde's mission to Paris, is not introduced until line 60, and of the 59 preceding lines that set up the conflict, 46 are mainly discourse. Thus the precipitating event occurs in the text only after its antecedents and current contexts have been delineated at length. The remainder of the account is story. Clarendon deploys discourse and story to provide a full analytical context and then maintain forward propulsion in his narrative. He also mingles contextual and connective discourse effectively. He had thoroughly prepared for the introduction of the conversion crisis, mentioning it initially in connective discourse four books earlier, when he first discusses the Duke of Gloucester in the *History* (4 [Book 10]: 253). In his account of the crisis itself, the opening line of connective discourse also ties the incident to two earlier foreshadowings of it in the book in which it occurs (5 [Book 14]: 337, 339–40). Both the Queen's and Duke's arguments and the King's ruminations are primarily contextual discourse, with some connective discourse.

Clarendon's emphasis in his narrative of the conversion crisis on dis-

Figure 1. THE ATTEMPTED CONVERSION OF THE DUKE OF GLOUCESTER BY
THE QUEEN (*HR*, 5:361–64)

117.	The King hears of the Queen's action	5 lines
	(FLASHBACK)	
	Explanation of why Gloucester is at Paris	*1 line*
	Summary of the Queen's arguments to Gloucester	*19 lines*
	Summary of Gloucester's arguments to the Queen	*10 lines*
	The Queen's action	8 lines
118.	*The King considers the ramifications of the case*	*16 lines*
	The King's actions: Ormonde dispatched to Paris	4 lines
	Letter to the Queen	6 lines
	Commands to the Duke	4 lines
	Commands to Montagu and others	5 lines
119.	Actions at Paris: Ormonde's behavior	1 line
	The Queen's behavior	6 lines
	The Duke's behavior	1 line
	The behavior of Montagu and others	3 lines
	The Queen gives in	6 lines
	The Duke and Ormonde remove to another house in Paris; Ormonde seeks travel money; both journey to the King at Cologne	6 lines
	(SUMMARY OF RESULTS)	
	The King is happy with Ormonde's success	1 line
	The Duke remains with the King until the Restoration	1 line
	The Queen is unhappy	1 line
		104 lines

course as an element almost as important as story is characteristic of the
History of the Rebellion as a whole. Because he was more concerned with
political instruction and had more information to analyze in the original
history than in the *Life*, he tends to use discourse somewhat more often
in the earlier work. Nevertheless, the *Life* (from which the account of the
conversion is taken) does not slight discourse for story. Clarendon's con-

cern for discourse is particularly apparent whenever he is reworking other sources to write the *History*. Hopton's and Slingsby's laconic, factual accounts of the war in the west are almost entirely chronicle; the two officers focus on battles, portraying each as a discrete action. When Clarendon adapts Slingsby and Hopton, he does some restructuring for the purposes of story, to develop each action as an aesthetically satisfying whole. However, his major changes are in adding sections of contextual and connective discourse to show individual engagements as part of a larger complex of historical events. As he assesses the relationship between the western campaigns and other Royalist military maneuvers, his connective discourse conveys a sense of general military strategy that Hopton lacks entirely, even though Sir Ralph had for a time been Charles I's commander in the west and was writing his account long after the actual fighting was over. In contextual discourse which explains administrative details and personnel problems, Clarendon superimposes the view from Royalist headquarters at Oxford onto the commander's story (despite the fact that he had been in the west himself for part of the period, away from the Oxford councils). Throughout the *History of the Rebellion*, by blending story and discourse and incorporating both contextual and connective discourse, Clarendon creates a unified literary narrative that sacrifices neither historical action nor analysis.

A second of Clarendon's characteristic narrative methods is his tendency to structure in terms of what might be described as an abbreviated dialectic. Clarendon always loved argument. He admitted that he was naturally inclined to "a humour between wrangling and disputing very troublesome" (*Life*, p. 58); his legal training and theological interests, as well as his positions as a member of Parliament and a royal counselor, had saturated his life with debate. He came to see this kind of interchange as the best way to learn, describing "disputation in conference" and "writing in the way of controversy" as "the best, if not the only, remedies and expedients for the discovery of error, and for the establishment of truth." [53] This belief is embodied in all his historical writings; from his youthful comparison of Essex and Buckingham to his final discussion of the temporal powers of the papacy, each of his historical works shows an interest not so much in history for its own sake as in a kind of argumentative history written to prove various points. Clarendon's belief in the educatory powers of argument also became a major structural principle in his depictions of individual events in the *History*. To develop the conversion crisis, he establishes its background by juxtaposing summaries of the Queen's and the Duke's arguments to each other. The King's deliberations are also organized in terms of arguments for and against his various options. In this way, Clarendon's abbreviated dialectical organization places the incident itself within a fully developed intellectual matrix.

Throughout the *History*, Clarendon uses his abbreviated dialectic to show how historical events develop through a combination of accident, necessity, and conscious and unconscious choices. He juxtaposes conflicting ideological principles and circumstantial considerations at important points in order to analyze how actions evolved. As the *History* progresses, political positions are defined and redefined; Clarendon's dialectical structure rhetorically reflects the give-and-take of the political process itself. He alternates summaries of Charles I's positions with those of the Parliament, illumines internal divisions among Royalists and Parliamentarians by outlining the arguments of contending factions, weighs the proposed strategies of different military commanders, and balances claims for and against French, Spanish, and papal interventions in English affairs. He is especially effective in geographically structuring such exchanges, pitting the King in York or Oxford against the Parliament in London, or juxtaposing the views of the Royalist exiles in Paris with those scattered elsewhere. This ability to deploy an abbreviated dialectical structure also explains why many of Clarendon's most effective depictions are of official occasions: state trials, Parliamentary debates, or diplomatic negotiations and conferences. Comparison of his and Bulstrode Whitelocke's accounts of the treaty at Uxbridge, for example, shows how ably Clarendon can recreate the complexities of the political world he knew so well when he develops it in terms of the argumentative structure congenial to his mind.[54] Finally, Clarendon's dialectic becomes a major source of structural continuity in the *History* because he is always concerned not only with the particular issues that give significance to each individual event, but also with the ways in which these issues reflect the larger ideological conflicts of the period. In his depiction of the conversion crisis, he uses the Queen's and Gloucester's interchange and the King's ruminations to illumine several long-term problems: the attitudes of the English people toward the religion of their rulers; the Royalists' ability to procure Catholic assistance; and the desirability of any foreign involvement in restoring the Stuarts. Thus, although contextual discourse in the *History* is heavily based on abbreviated dialectic, connective discourse also occasionally reflects it.

Whenever he can, Clarendon structures his story so that it directly mirrors the dialectical exchanges of his discourse. In the account of the attempted conversion, the King's actions are exactly juxtaposed with corresponding reactions at Paris not only to establish their relationship of cause and effect but also to show them as natural extensions of the ideological dialectic. Clarendon is not always lucky enough to find such correspondences between intellectual and physical action, and he is too good a historian to impose structural correlations between discourse and story that are not inherent in the chronicle as he understands it. However, his narrative usually gains because of his alertness to the structural potential of such correspondences. (An exception is his predilection for inserting the manifestoes exchanged between Parliament and Charles I directly into his text; at these points the amount of discourse overwhelms the story, and narrative continuity suffers.) As issues are juxtaposed dialectically throughout the *History*, Clarendon develops the entire period in terms of ongoing ideological conflicts.

Augmenting the intellectual context that Clarendon's abbreviated dialectical structure produces for events is the psychological context he creates by personalizing ideological issues and sometimes the narrative point of view in the *History*. For him, political and personal forces were inextricably merged. He carefully develops certain characters throughout the narrative as representatives of political stances: Prince Rupert comes to stand for unfettered militarism, Lord Falkland for political idealism, George Goring for unprincipled opportunism, and so on. At the same time, Clarendon never slights the complexities of individual personalities. The conversion crisis evolved not only because of the beliefs that Henrietta Maria stood for (the Roman Catholic and French influences that Clarendon opposed as alien to English political and religious traditions) but also because of what she was as a person—a stubborn, limited, frivolous woman, seemingly determined to compensate for her years of playing second fiddle to the Duke of Buckingham early in her marriage by meddling at will in state affairs for the rest of her life. Keenly aware of the psychological forces that drive individuals, Clarendon structures his narrative to highlight the play of personal wills behind clashes of conflicting ideologies.

As Clarendon writes of the deliberations that lead to decisions and actions in the *History*, he often moves his narrative point of view among the characters concerned, interiorizing the narrative to reveal different perspectives and motivations. Gérard Genette has described this type of narrative as showing "variable internal focalization": the narrative is "internally focalized" because the narrator limits his account to what one character knows, and the interior focalization becomes "variable" when the text includes more than one focal character.[55] Clarendon often employs this kind of focalization to structure his discourse. He moves into one character's mind—or into the minds of a series of characters—and develops his abbreviated dialectic in terms of their personal assessments of situations. In the conversion crisis, the only internal focalization occurs when the King weighs his options, but usually more characters are included. When Clarendon explains the complicated dispute over the governorship of Bristol, for example, he develops his narrative through a group of focal characters. Opening with Princes Maurice and Rupert and the Marquis of Hertford, he moves to Charles I, then takes up the Royalist Court and Council, returns to the King, and finally concludes with Sir Ralph Hopton (*HR*, 3:120–26). As he focalizes this account to render a sense of the way events develop from the personal reactions of individuals, he produces a wide historical perspective through his literary manipulations. The narrative interiority that Clarendon creates using variable internal focalization also enhances the rhetorical impersonality of the narrator. In particular, this kind of perspective allows for subtler forms of didacticism, since authorial views can be presented through the perspectives of others. Genette's caveats on internal focalization—that it is "rarely applied in a totally rigorous way" and that "the commitment as to focalization is not necessarily steady over the whole length of a narrative"[56]—definitely apply to Clarendon. He will, for example, sometimes point up what a character did *not* see or recognize; in addition, many sections of his narrative are nonfocalized. His historical success with this literary method is, of course, limited by his own knowledge of the people he depicts and particularly by his understanding of certain kinds of motivation. Firth has emphasized Clarendon's failure to recognize the genuine religious fervor inspiring the Puritans, and Hill his problems in evaluating the lower classes.[57] His insistence on a conspiracy theory to explain the actions of the leaders of the Long Parliament[58] at certain points limits the effectiveness of his interpretations of them. But in general, because Clarendon's positions had given him detailed knowledge of most of the characters he treated in depth, and because he was able to choose his focal characters well and manipulate them adroitly, his focalization of discourse adds substantial psychological reality and literary interest to his narrative.

Just as Clarendon personalizes his discourse with variable internal focalization, he also manipulates his story to highlight the conflicts of personalities that mold events. Wherever possible, he juxtaposes individuals to develop his narrative: Essex and Waller after the Parliamentary defeat at Roundway Down; the Earls of Portland and Holland in the power vacuum following Buckingham's death; Rupert's and Newcastle's maneuvers at the time of Marston Moor; Montrose's opposition to Lauderdale, Hamilton, and Argyle in Scottish affairs. His treatment of the Marquis of Ormonde's role in the conversion crisis is an excellent example of this kind of narrative structure. In the incident as story, the key figure in resolving the crisis is the faithful and ever-resourceful Ormonde. Few of Charles II's followers could have negotiated the difficulties as successfully; one has only to think of the disastrous possibilities if Digby, Colepeper, Ashburnham, or practically anyone else had been Charles' emissary. (Even Hyde, usually an able diplomat, would have been useless because of Henrietta Maria's enmity toward him.) Yet Clarendon carefully structures his account to downplay Ormonde's part, limiting his depiction of Ormonde's negotiations to one line of generalized summary: "The marquis behaved himself with so much wisdom and resolution" (*HR*, 5:363). Rhetorically, Ormonde becomes in the text an inert pivot rather than an active agent in events. In this way Clarendon is able to center his account on the conflict between the King and his mother, with the conflict between the Queen and Gloucester functioning as a complementary subset. Thus he not only emphasizes the psychological deep structure of the incident itself, but he also identifies it as one skirmish in the running battle in the *History* between Henrietta Maria and the men in her family. The Queen had inadvertently done all in her power to help Charles I lose his throne, and she remained an impediment to Charles II's efforts to regain his. Control of her influence over her husband and sons and over Royalist activities in general is a major ongoing problem in the *History*. Clarendon structures the ending of his account to relate the conversion crisis to this long-term psychological conflict. The initial reference to the King's pleasure emphasizes his status as the victor in this skirmish, while relating this happiness to Ormonde's success gives Ormonde the credit that is understated by the structure of the story. Charles' keeping Gloucester with him until the Restoration emphasizes that this particular problem has been settled for the foreseeable future. The verbs in these descriptive clauses are in the past tense—"was" and "kept"—but Clarendon's final words are of Henrietta Maria, and he uses a present participle: "the Queen remaining as much unsatisfied" (*HR*, 5:364). The end of the conversion crisis has resolved only one aspect of an Oedipal battle that would continue unabated to the Restoration and beyond.

Thus Clarendon in the *History* creates a rich ideological and psychological context for events, as well as continuity in his narrative, by balancing discourse and story and by structuring both in terms of dialectical and personal conflicts. His emphasis on discourse distances his depiction of events at the structural level of the narrative just as his prose style does at the grammatical level. However, his other structural techniques add a different type of action to the *History*. As the play of personalities reflects and complements the play of issues, the kind of drama created by psychological and intellectual immediacy enters the account. With these literary manipulations Clarendon compensates for his intentional underdevelopment of physical action in the narrative as he focuses his conflicts at those levels where he believes his readers can learn the most about why historical actions evolve. Moreover, the literary methods that center his narrative on people and ideas are not restrictive. They allow for coverage of other historical concerns. Critics have pointed out, for example, that Clarendon shows some sensitivity to the roles of social and (to a lesser extent) economic forces in history.[59] In the narrative these factors generally emerge in connection with his dual emphasis on ideology and personality. For example, his ubiquitous concern with rank—most of the participants in Barebone's Parliament were "inferior persons, of no quality or name, artificers of the meanest trades, known only by their gifts in praying and preaching"; "The officers of the enemy's side were never talked of, being for the most part of no better families than their common soldiers" (*HR*, 5:282; 3:437)—is usually related to the susceptibility of certain classes to Parliamentary or Royalist ideology. Clarendon's dialectical and personal structural techniques produce a capacious narrative that renders a very full sense of the complexities of historical events.

One final contribution Clarendon made in advancing the literary structure of seventeenth-century historical narrative was his integration of related literary forms into his *History*. Just as he recognized the potential of autobiography for historical purposes, he could exploit other genres. The character is obviously the best example; Clarendon took a widely used contemporary form and made it an integral part of the *History*. Character sketches had, of course, appeared in both classical and earlier English histories. But before Clarendon, only Tacitus had managed to integrate the form so completely into his narrative. Suetonius and other early biographers were the major inhibitory models, for their works had tended to separate action from personality, often surveying the events of a man's life first and then summarizing his character in closing. Most historians followed the biographers' example. In England, Polydore Vergil reserved biographical details of important figures to conclude each book; Camden placed a set of obituary characters after each year in his *Annals*.[60] Bacon ends his history with a separate character sketch of

Henry VII, which is in effect detachable from the narrative. In contrast to these narrative interruptions, Clarendon incorporates rather than inserts his characters into his *History*. Juxtaposing one character with another to explain why given events occurred, grouping characters of opposing parties to form the historical equivalent of epic roll calls, he uses this material to advance his story. He similarly integrated other forms into the *History*. Many of the general political analyses in his discourse could stand as independent essays, while his account of the Spanish embassy in Books 12 and 13 is in essence a travelogue. With his extended character sketch of Falkland, Clarendon showed how short biography could enhance history.

Clarendon managed to employ literary genres to historical advantage because he carefully tailored the forms to serve historical purposes. Unlike the digressions of Raleigh, Milton, and other seventeenth-century English historians, Clarendon's material includes only information that directly reflects thematic or other concerns in the narrative, and his inclusions are painstakingly justified in accordance with the historical context. The account of his and Cottington's fruitless embassy to Spain in 1649 and 1650 shows his approach. Always uneasy with the directly personal, Clarendon twice explains why he has inserted this story. At one point he indicates that although the Spanish travelogue might "seem foreign to the affairs of England," it was actually "the first and only embassy in which his majesty's person was represented until his blessed return into England." For this reason an account of it could reveal "what sense other kings and princes had of those revolutions in England, and of the miserable condition to which this innocent young prince was reduced." He promises that "every circumstance" of the ambassadors' "reception and treatment serves to illustrate those particulars" (*HR*, 5:84–85), and his alterations show that he deleted all details of the sojourn that were irrelevant to these concerns. He is similarly careful in his placement of such material, often using it to enhance narrative continuity. He prefaces the account of the Spanish embassy by noting that during that period Charles II remained in Jersey "for many months, waiting such a revolution as might administer an opportunity and occasion to him to quit that retirement, in all which time there was no action or counsel to be mentioned at present" (*HR*, 5:84). Whether or not this conclusion is entirely justifiable on historical grounds, Clarendon uses it to provide a literary opportunity to adapt his experiences in Spain for historical purposes so that gaps in his knowledge will not damage the continuity of his work.

In converting literary forms to historical use, Clarendon had thought carefully about what historical narratives could properly include. In a letter to John Earle, he worried over his biographical account of Falkland: "It may be I have insisted longer upon the argument than may be agreeable to the rules to be observed in such a work." He wrote that he wished Earle could read the section, because if his friend "thought it unproportionable for the place where it is, I could be willingly diverted to make it a piece by itself, and inlarge [*sic*] it into the whole size of his life."[61] Clarendon recognized which genres could be appropriated for history and which would be unsuitable. Despite his irony, he never deviates into actual satire in the *History*. Although he wrote to Secretary Nicholas that Wogan's march into Scotland was "as great a Romance as hath been acted in our time,"[62] his description of it in the *History* carries no such overtones. Indeed, Charles II's escape after Worcester is the only incident that Clarendon tinges with romance, and even then, when events themselves demanded such treatment, he subdues the miraculous within a heavily Providential context. By using literary genres in ways that enhanced rather than disrupted narrative, Clarendon significantly enlarged the literary bounds of history.

In order to go beyond chronological accumulations of fact and produce histories with literary value, seventeenth-century historians needed more sophisticated narrative techniques to organize and evaluate the events they depicted. Earlier English historians, particularly those writing for political or moral purposes, had, of course, in some instances provided analytical contexts for individual events. Clarendon's significance is in the comprehensiveness of the context that he creates and also in his use of this context to give continuity in his *History*. His literary methods of structure—the manipulations of story and discourse, the use of abbreviated dialectic and variable internal focalization, and the generic inclusions—created in the *History of the Rebellion* a historical narrative with new kinds of depth and scope.

THE *HISTORY'S* THEMATIC ELEMENTS OF STRUCTURE

Clarendon's literary style and his deftness in handling narrative structure surpassed the abilities of most of his contemporaries, but what makes his *History* a work of literary art—although an imperfect one—is the imagination he brought to bear on the matter of history, thereby giving coherent value to particular events and larger thematic structure to the narrative. From his knowledge of his own and others' experiences, his careful use of documents, and his objective examination of the evidence he had, infused with his own creative imagination, evolved a complex conception of what for him was the true nature of the civil wars and their significance to the English nation. Shaping his account is this personal vision of Englishmen engaged in a struggle to achieve a just and ordered society, with a stable government firmly established on laws and on English constitutional traditions that would protect and enhance the freedom of every individual citizen in the state. Guided by this imaginative referent, Clarendon structured his *History* in terms of the political, psychological, and moral forces that he saw as dominating the conflicts, and he produced a narrative that could evolve naturally through particular events to universal significance.

Clarendon's conception of the purposes of the struggle of course included the kind of government he believed Englishmen were trying to achieve out of the chaos they had faced at midcentury. A parliament and a king, respecting each other's prerogatives, would share power and work together with the aid of a strong privy council in order to insure the good of the nation and the rights of all its people. The goal was a society built on the mutual cooperation of all classes, in which hierarchical allegiances and loyalties would flourish. Integral to the unified nation that Clarendon saw at stake in the civil wars was a single established church, because he believed that a kingdom "is very seldom unprosperous, never unfortunate, whilst the Church continues united in her Devotions and Intercessions."[63] The Anglican church was in his view the most satisfactory for the English people, on political as well as doctrinal grounds. He pointed out that Anglican discipline and government were "more agreeable" not only "to the word of God" and "to the propagation and preservation of the Christian Religion," but also "to the honour, peace, happiness, and tranquillity" of the kingdom, than any other religion that could "be settled in the place of it."[64]

Politically, Clarendon's vision is a conservative one, rooted in the traditions of the English past—"the good old frame of government," as he describes it in the *History* (1:430). But these political ideals appear in all of Clarendon's writings, with different details emphasized according to the subjects of the various works. His declarations and speeches for Charles I focus on the relationship between king and parliament, while his answer to Hobbes considers general principles of government. The essays and the commentaries on the Psalms stress the duties of a loyal subject. The political role of religion is considered both in *Religion and Policy* and in his defense of Stillingfleet. Even Clarendon's dialogues, his least overtly political writings, discuss citizenship and state service. What separates the *History of the Rebellion* from these other works is the more comprehensive context in which such specifically political elements are embedded. Only in the *History* did he find the scope necessary to embody a more complex vision of England's past and present effectively in literary form.

Clarendon's imaginative referent establishes the historical reality of the civil wars in terms of a deeper truth than a mere power struggle between Parliamentarians and Royalists for control of government and religion. The personal characters and the perspectives of individuals were crucial factors in determining the kind of nation Clarendon believed could have emerged from the midcentury conflicts. As he explains in the *History*, one of the problems in the period between 1629 and 1640 had been that:

All these blessings could but enable, not compel, us to be happy: we wanted that sense, acknowledgment, and value of our own happiness which all but we had, and took pains to make, when we could not find, ourselves miserable. There was in truth a strange absence of understanding in most, and a strange perverseness of understanding in the rest. (1:96)

Integral to Clarendon's imaginative vision of the significance of the civil wars was a conception of individual Englishmen, which served and complemented the larger perspective. On the political level this personal emphasis is particularly clear. For example, a king and a parliament who were both reasonable and generous were necessary if the legislative and executive branches were to cooperate rather than clash. The kind of governmental system Clarendon envisioned was essentially a series of reciprocal processes that depended for success not so much on legally defined responsibilities as on personal relationships. His emphasis on the importance of the privy council reflects the personal elements required for the state to function; as mediating agents these men could compensate for individual shortcomings on either the royal or the parliamentary side.[65] Thus his description of the kind of men who should serve is not primarily concerned with their political skills. In discussing the attributes of the ideal privy councilor, Clarendon includes qualities such as judiciousness, efficiency, dedication, and practical experience, but he ends with "and integrity above all" (*HR*, 1:261). Here, just as in his narrative structure, he thematically merges political concerns with personal ones; in addition, he seeks to establish both within larger moral contexts.

To Clarendon, personal character was the crucial index of national character. For this reason he presents the civil wars as destroying "the courage and conscience and the old honour of the English nation" (*HR*, 1 : 349). In his view, the conflicts revealed the loss of the kinds of attitudes that every citizen needed if a healthy society was to be maintained. From such a perspective, as he traces individual characters over time, larger historical patterns in the *History* come to reflect general patterns of human interaction: the many ways that friendships grow or disintegrate, the various forms of healthy or destructive paternal relationships, the different bonds with his people that can sustain or destroy a king, the subversion of success by individual weakness or perversity of character. Thus, for example, when some members of Parliament early in 1660 misread General Monck's acquiescence in certain orders as total capitulation to their will, Clarendon immediately translates their political misjudgments into psychological and moral terms: "But they were so infatuated with pride and insolence, that they could not discern the ways to their own preservation" (*HR*, 6 : 170).

Clarendon's conception of the struggle in which the English people had been engaged and its potential significance was precisely the kind of imaginative referent that could add literary scope to seventeenth-century historiography. His referent was integrally enough related to the actual course of events to be viable for historical use. Indeed, in the early 1640s Clarendon himself had believed that most of the purposes of the conflict had been achieved and that the kind of nation he envisioned would become a reality as soon as the King and Parliament could be reconciled. He closes the third book of the *History* with a survey of laws passed by the Long Parliament from which "the kingdom might have received ample benefit and advantage" (1 : 371). One of the tragedies of the civil wars which Clarendon emphasizes was that despite the efforts of moderates on both sides, extremists refused any viable solutions. Government by Parliament alone could not—and did not—insure the freedom of every man, any more than royal power had previously done so. Clarendon's conception of what the outcome of the civil wars could have meant for England and Englishmen remained only an ideal not so much because it had not been realized during the period between 1640 and 1667, but because it could not at any time have been realized. Certain elements of it were untenable in practice. What Clarendon apparently never recognized or never faced was that his ideas demanded a public and private altruism beyond the capacities of most men. Even had human beings actually been as noble as Clarendon thought they could be, administering the increasing complexity of seventeenth-century society required a more formally structured government with greater delegation of powers and a larger bureaucracy than his conception could provide. His vision of the English struggle and its meaning was thoroughly enough embedded in the realm of the imagination so that a history written in terms of it could not become formulaic, nor could a chronological accumulation of facts adequately accommodate such a referent. Circumstances prohibited both alternatives.

Clarendon had an imaginative referent, and he had a course of events to relate, but there were serious discontinuities between the two. Had he written the entire history in 1660, his literary course would have been easier—although even then he would have encountered some problems. But at least his story could have settled into conventional thematic patterns of narrative. From 1641 on, he could have presented an English fall from grace, a gradual recognition of errors, and a return with new knowledge: the Long Parliament begins destroying essentials of English government; the Presbyterians, Independents, the Army, and the Cromwellians compound the damage; the English over years of misrule slowly learn to respect their older political and religious traditions; finally, with Charles II's restoration, a new monarch, ruling according to the early reforms of the Long Parliament, inaugurates a new era for the nation. Like the erring Israelites of the Old Testament or the Prodigal Son in the New, the English saga could have been depicted as a straightforward one of loss and redemptive reinstatement for the nation and for individuals. Unfortunately, such a plot in no way accorded with history as Clarendon had experienced it since the Restoration. His Englishmen had finally abandoned false gods only to follow other idols; the prodigals had returned to degenerate rather than regenerate.

Like Milton, Clarendon had watched every opportunity for establishing the kind of nation he desired neglected until no hope remained. He had devoted his career to making his conception of the nation's potential a reality; he was not the man to admit at the end that his life's work had been dedicated to a political chimera. But as a pragmatic politician grounded in the actual, Clarendon, unlike Milton, was incapable of turning to the fictions of poetry to embody his beliefs. He instead chose historical writing as his last chance to serve, by recreating his ideals in lasting forms for others. He would not violate the facts of the actual past as he knew them, but at the same time he would infuse his knowledge of the past with his vision wherever he could.

Clarendon's *History* becomes most effective as literature when the events he records can be related in some way to his larger conception of the significance of the struggle for England and its people. Wherever he sees the political, social, personal, or moral values central to it reflected in the actual past, his imaginative referent enhances his selection as well as his presentation of evidence. He moves with assurance among details, marshalling only the most relevant and using all his literary skill to portray them effectively. Because he sees so clearly, he can write without stumbling. Dialectical exchanges, whether between the King and Parliament or between warring Royalist factions in councils, are effectively structured as narrative because the interplay of ideas directly reflects the larger political principles with which Clarendon was concerned. His digressions work well within his text because they allow him to elaborate on the meaning of historical circumstances in relation to his own vision. His prose is succinctly masterful in the character sketches of men whose personal qualities have a significant relationship, whether positive or negative, to the developing struggle and the ends he saw for it. Thus his portraits of his enemy Oliver Cromwell and his opponent John Hampden come alive as surely as the portrayals of his close friends Lord Falkland and Lord Capel. In contrast, his series of character sketches surveying the Spanish court and ambassadors to it are relatively ineffective, for these men were not important to the main themes of his narrative. The early books of the *History* are superior to the final ones not only because they are more accurate and contain more information, but also because the loss of the kind of nation Clarendon wanted was easier to highlight within the events of the period they cover. In contrast, during the exile, the only way to further his national goals was to sit still without compromising; this less overtly active assertion of an ideal over time was more difficult to depict in an interesting way.

At points where events seem to have little connection with his imaginative referent, when the historical evidence seems unrelated or unimportant to what he saw as the ultimate meaning of the struggle, Clarendon writes ineffectively. He has no interest in battles as such, only in their results. His focus sometimes wavers in describing many of the events in the west, and when he fails to show the larger issues behind local conflicts, they emerge simply as petty squabbles. Significantly, he is at his literary worst when he is poorest as a historian. In recounting some of Charles I's more flagrant misdeeds—notably the abortive arrest of the five members, the attempts to capture Hull, and the efforts to control the Tower of London, all of which Hyde as a royal adviser had opposed when they occurred—he becomes more of an apologist than a historian. He tries to palliate the King's offenses, misrepresenting and underplaying both their causes and effects. The result is awkward prose and a narrative often incoherent. For similar reasons, it is impossible to reconstruct from Clarendon's account what actually occurred during the famous Scottish "Incident" or what the Army Plot of 1641 really involved.

The ending of the *History* reflects Clarendon's problems with the dichotomy between his imaginative referent and the course of events. After sixteen books and well over twenty-five hundred pages of history,[66] he finally reaches Charles II's triumphal entry into London for the Restoration. However, the entrance itself is covered in one short paragraph. It is not from Clarendon that we learn of the conduits running claret wine, the trumpets, bells, and bonfires, and the flower-strewn streets decorated with tapestries. Characteristically, he avoids developing visual and dramatic elements of the scene, particularly since other published accounts covered the more spectacular aspects.[67] It is also characteristic that he never mentions himself in the account of Charles' return, although he had been its chief Royalist engineer and was at the center of events. Never one to stress his own achievements, he was in addition probably unsure that he wanted to claim credit for this particular one. Then he writes a peculiarly unsatisfactory final paragraph:

In this wonderful manner, and with this miraculous expedition, did God put an end in one month (for it was the first of May that the King's letter was delivered to the Parliament, and his majesty was at Whitehall upon the 29th of the same month) to a rebellion that had raged near twenty years, and been carried on with all the horrid circumstances of parricide, murder, and devastation, that fire and the sword, in the hands of the wickedest men in the world, could be ministers of, almost to the desolation of two kingdoms, and the exceeding defacing and deforming the third. Yet did the merciful hand of God in one month bind up all these wounds, and even made the scars as undiscernible as in respect of their deepness was possible. And if there wanted more glorious monuments of this deliverance, posterity would know the time of it by the death of the two great favourites of the two Crowns, cardinal Mazaryne and don Lewis de Haro, who both died within three or four months, with the wonder, if not the agony, of this undreamed of prosperity, and as if they had taken it ill that God Almighty would bring such a work to pass in Europe without their concurrence and against all their machinations. (*HR*, 6:234)

Commentators have noted Clarendon's heavily Providential emphases in the last books of the *History of the Rebellion* and his treatment of the Restoration as an Anglican miracle of sorts.[68] Certainly the speed with which the long turbulence was suddenly settled must have made the event seem miraculous to him. But Clarendon tended to invoke Providential explanations to assist him in coming to terms with any difficult or ambiguous circumstances; throughout his commentaries on the *Psalms*, for example, he refers to his banishment in such terms.[69] He may have treated the Restoration similarly because of his recognition of the disparity between his concept of the potential purpose and meaning of the civil wars and the actual course of events after 1660. Straining, almost overwriting, for effect, he indulges in violent declamatory language in the long first sentence surveying the horrors of the wars. But even in this rhetorically charged context, his tendency toward exactness remains (the precise dates of the "one month"; two kingdoms "almost" desolated), and in the much shorter second sentence on the immediate past which follows, his precision stems rhetoric with realism as he describes the scars. As if in reaction to this recollection, he switches in the third sentence of the paragraph, the last one in the *History of the Rebellion*, away from Charles II's return itself to the future. Incongruously enough, Clarendon, the most English of Englishmen, who even when his *History* centers on events abroad never loses his home focus across the Channel, closes with a Frenchman and a Spaniard. As the final sentence of the *History*, the statement lacks both literary and historical impact, particularly when contrasted with the magnificent first sentence of the work, one of its most frequently quoted passages.

The ironies multiply at every level. First of all, Clarendon mistakes his dates, for Mazarin died over nine months after the Restoration and de Haro two and a half years later (*HR*, 6:234, n. 1). Thus what Clarendon presents as situational irony becomes, because of his inaccurate dating, an irony at his own expense—as the entire Restoration turned out to be. The misdating is not, however, the crucial factor, since in the *History* Clarendon errs on dates that he should have recalled much more easily than these two. And even had the men died when Clarendon thought they did, their deaths would hardly have counted among the "more glorious monuments of this deliverance." Despite many attempts to meddle, Mazarin's and de Haro's influence on England during the period of the civil wars was not finally the determining factor in the conflicts. Disturbances began when the English people were dissatisfied, and ceased only when the nation as a whole decided, without outside intervention, that a Stuart monarch alone could bring peace. The reference to the two men is partially explicable in terms of Clarendon personally, for he was always intensely interested in the affairs of men who held positions analogous to his. His letters during the Royalist exile show a great deal of purely personal curiosity about Thurloe, while after the Restoration his communications show considerable empathy with French officials. Moreover, during the Interregnum he had many frustrating dealings with Mazarin and particularly with de Haro, from whom he sought help for Charles II in vain. He was undoubtedly pleased to remember that he had bested them at last, by engineering a Restoration on his own terms without their aid. But outmaneuvering two foreigners despite diplomatic games was hardly Clarendon's real achievement in 1660. Furthermore, if he had outplayed de Haro and Mazarin once, he still had never come to exercise ministerial power in England as both of them had in Spain and France. Thus even in personal terms the references to the two foreigners celebrates only a temporary and evanescent victory.

Clarendon's loss of focus in his ending suggests that he had to look away from England in order to conclude the *History* on a positive note. Charles II's triumphal restoration had ended the rebellion. It had also, Clarendon had come to know in retrospect, destroyed any chances that his own conception of England would become a reality, because of human frailties in general and Charles II's own character in particular, and also because the personally based government Clarendon envisioned could not be a permanent political solution for the nation. In the *History of the Rebellion* Clarendon had tried to show this vision, but he could not with any honesty connect it to the Restoration. His ending thus lacks literary interest and impact—and again, significantly, his literary failure occurs in a section where there are serious historical inaccuracies.

Although Clarendon's ending is disappointing, it shows his historical integrity. He would not simplify history for literary effect by depicting as a triumph an event that in his view had been a bitterly illusive success. The Restoration of the Stuarts, which he had hoped would inaugurate a new era based on old traditions reformed, had turned out to be merely a temporary reconciliation, swiftly dissolved by factionalism. Most of the political, social, and religious issues that had sparked the civil wars remained, and the Restoration was only an initial step toward settling them.

Early in the *Continuation of the Life*, Clarendon emphasized that at Charles' return, "the King was not yet the master of the kingdom, nor his authority and security such as the general noise and accclamation, the bells and the bonfires, proclaimed it to be" (*CL*, 1:9). In this context, his underplaying of the event is more historically accurate than a satisfactory rhetorical climax would have been.[70]

In closing the *History* at 1660, Clarendon showed literary as well as historical integrity, the sense of what would make the best story he could tell with the materials he had. He could have continued his work through 1667, the year in which he left England for his final exile. But unlike most historians of his era, Clarendon had always done his best not to allow his own story to become the major organizing principle of his works; he had tried to subordinate himself to the events of his time. Thus he reserved his account of the years from 1660 to 1667 for another work, the *Continuation of the Life*, which is focused around his own attempts to unite constitutionalism and the Stuart monarchy. A strong defense of his conduct as Chancellor, it is narrower and much more personal in scope than the original history, the *Life*, or the final *History of the Rebellion*. Clarendon had recognized that his original history and his *Life* could be combined into a satisfactory literary and historical whole. Ever sensitive to the differences between history and autobiography, and dedicated above all to history, he realized that the years after the Restoration formed an entirely different story, which needed to be told in another way. He accordingly separated this more self-interested account from the *History of the Rebellion*. Closing the *History* at 1660 was the best way to articulate his conception of the meaning of the civil wars for England as a nation in effective literary form. Although at certain points his historical evidence could not be shaped in terms of his imaginative referent, the *History* provided many more opportunities to do so than the account of his chancellorship, which, as a story of increasing failure and final isolation, was hardly one in which his ideals could be effectively embodied. If he could not show the historical realization of his vision, closing his work at 1660 at least allowed him to depict the destruction of one set of threats to it. Hayden White has suggested that narrative closure consists of "the *passage* from one moral order to another."[71] Although his description is on the whole too restrictive, it works very well for Clarendon. At the moral level, the year 1660 provides a decisive dividing point in the history of England; between the years of Cromwell and the years of Charles II, the moral order of the nation altered irrevocably.

Clarendon's position in English political life had given him a unique perspective on events, but all of the participants in the civil wars who wrote had viewpoints that were in various ways uniquely their own. What set Clarendon apart was his ability to synthesize so much more effectively than the others, an ability that was directly related to the imaginative referent that molded the form of his work and its themes. This referent led naturally to the kinds of general insights into human nature and the human condition that the great literary historiographers have traditionally provided. Clarendon in effect juxtaposes two worlds in the *History of the Rebellion*, one the depiction of actual events in England from 1640 to 1660, and beyond that his own commonwealth of the imagination. The political systems he depicts are long outmoded, but his presentations of political behavior in social, psychological, and ultimately moral contexts retain lasting validity. Clarendon's two worlds allowed him to show the actual without neglecting the potential. He knew what England and Englishmen had been from 1640 to 1660, and he portrayed the era well. But he also knew what the nation and its citizens could have been during that period, and his acute awareness of this potential at one particular time in the past shows readers of any era a good deal about human beings and human values.

3

The Man Behind the Historian

So that a man had need, if possible, to know somewhat of the temper of his Historian, before he know what to think of his relations.

Meric Casaubon, *Of Credulity and Incredulity*, 1668

The 'facts' of history do not exist for any historian until he creates them, and into every fact that he creates some part of his individual experience must enter.

Carl Becker, "Detachment and the Writing of History"

Historical knowledge is dead and worthless that has not as its sounding-board and its measuring-rod the historian's personal intellectual and spiritual life.

Johan Huizinga, "The Idea of History"

How was it such noble minds were generated in those times? I know not but think it well worth inquiring into.

Thomas Carlyle, *Historical Sketches*

SOME CIRCUMSTANCES OF
CLARENDON'S LIFE

Just as before the mid-twentieth century, most of the famous definitions of style—*Oratio vultus animi est*, for example, or *Le style, c'est l'homme même*—focused on the writer rather than on technique, studies of the writing of history since Lucian have centered on the character of the historian. Bodin is typical of early critics in his warning that "the cautious reader of history . . . will not form an opinion concerning the work until he has understood clearly the character and the talent of the historian."[1] Clarendon's own most extended discussion of historical writing considers mainly the experiences and characters of individual historians, weighing "the different value of histories, according to the qualifications of the persons who write them."[2] Although recent literary critics, reflecting prevailing tendencies to seek validity in structural rather than personal elements and in readers rather than writers, have become increasingly concerned with what Barthes terms the "death of the author,"[3] the emphasis of historians on biography has continued. As J. H. Hexter summarizes it, because "historiography communicates what the historian knows or thinks he knows," any significant analysis of a historian's "way of writing" must "relate it to his way of knowing."[4]

On the whole, the historical writer will probably remain somewhat more immune to the threat of extinction than the endangered (momentarily, at least) creator of fiction. In assessing works of history, historians have always taken for granted the intertextuality that in literary studies has been highlighted by the author's so-called demise. The referential constraints that in so many ways limit the historian in this instance offer him some protection. As H. Stuart Hughes points out, "By now nearly all of us have accepted Croce's dictum that the writing of history necessarily changes with the standpoint of the historian, that *all* history is contemporary in the sense that its presentation reflects the circumstances and attitudes of those who write it."[5] Because of the kinds of material on which his work is based, the literary choices made by the historian are usually more obvious and require less speculation to analyze than those of the writer of fiction; the style and structure of the historian's work more directly reflect the unique relationship he evolves with his subject. Despite the temporary and unrealistic demand in the last century that historians, like scientists, must deal with their subject with absolute objectivity, students of history have long recognized, as Theodor Mommsen succinctly noted, that "history is neither written nor made without love or hate."[6] How the historian deals with this emotional affinity, the ways in which he creates enough detachment so that he can judge and shape events as well as record them, remain central in the process of constructing a historical narrative. Separating the author from his history removes an element crucial to its proper evaluation as a text.

Like most of the first historians of the English civil wars, Clarendon was deeply involved with his subject as a partisan and a participant. What differentiates his account from the others is that his circumstances and temperament combined to give him a special kind of detachment, a professional and personal distance from his subject that was enhanced, but not entirely created, by his abilities to project this detachment linguistically. The conditions of his life, his view of himself as a public and private man, his temperament, the moral and ethical standards he upheld, and the strengths and weaknesses of his public career affected not only his credibility as a historian, but also the language, style, and thematic structure of his historical narrative.

Clarendon's unique perspective on events was the result partly of opportunity and partly of ability; his distance was both forced upon him and sought by him. Because of his background, interests, and political beliefs, Clarendon always remained to a certain extent an outsider in the various circles in which he spent his life. He lacked the noble birth or substantial wealth of most of the men who rose to Court prominence in his time. He came from a respectable Wiltshire family of landed gentry who were content with a quiet life in the country.[7] His mother during her entire life never journeyed as far as London. Although his father had traveled widely when young and had served in several Parliaments, after the death of Queen Elizabeth he retired to Wiltshire, and in over thirty years he never visited London again (*Life*, pp. 3–4). As lawyers, the Hydes had built their fortune in the sixteenth century from shrewd dealings during the dissolution of the monasteries;[8] as a lawyer and politician amid the social upheavals of the seventeenth century, Edward Hyde relied on his own abilities, along with careful cultivation of the family connections he had, to advance himself. Even as he rose, however, he never abandoned the basic attitudes and values characteristic of the country gentry. In a section of one of his essays comparing the country and the court, he argues that "a good statesman or a good courtier, must draw the principal ingredients of his wisdom from the knowledge and understanding of the country."[9] The outlook of his class always distanced Hyde from the aristocrats among whom he came to move.

77

At various times in his career, Hyde fulfilled the roles of lawyer, historian, courtier, legislator, diplomat, scholar, and judge. With his legal, theological, and political interests, he encompassed every major area of controversy in mid-seventeenth-century England. The range of his concerns contributed to the capaciousness of his historical vision. It also separated him from his associates in every period of his life, for he never found either a group or an individual who could adequately reflect the variety of his own interests and experiences.

As a young student at the Middle Temple in 1627, Hyde found London awash in what he later described as a "sea of wine, and women, and quarrels, and gaming, which almost overspread the whole kingdom" (*Life*, p. 57). After a rowdy year spent with officers from the Spanish and French wars who filled the city, having with his characteristic caution survived the dissipation "*cautè*, if not *castè*" (*CL*, 2:550), he sought other companions more suitable to his "nature and inclinations" (*Life*, p. 57). For the next decade, even in the most congenial circles he frequented, the variety of his interests set him apart. At the Middle Temple he found "polite learning and history" more absorbing than legal studies (*Life*, p. 8). In later life he was particularly proud of his connections with Ben Jonson's group, although he seems to have remained only on its fringes. When he finally began to work more diligently at the law, he maintained his ties with scholars, wits, and the larger world beyond his profession.

But if Hyde was an intellectual among lawyers, he remained a lawyer and a politician among intellectuals. As part of the circle that collected around Lucius Cary, Lord Falkland, at his home at Great Tew, Hyde found his closest friends, forming bonds that would sustain him for the rest of his life. The group included scholars, clergymen, poets, philosophers, country gentlemen, and an occasional courtier or lawyer—men as diverse as John Hales of Eton, Edmund Waller, Thomas Hobbes, Sir Francis Wenman, and Endymion Porter.[10] Oxfordshire neighbors rode over for the day; others traveled up to Tew from London or came over from Oxford, which was seventeen or eighteen miles away.[11] Hyde wrote that Falkland's house "looked like the University itself, by the company that was always found there," and explained that Falkland's guests gathered "not so much for repose as study, and to examine and refine those grosser propositions which laziness and consent made current in vulgar conversation" (*Life*, p. 36; *HR*, 3:180). Free to work in Falkland's ample library during the day, whoever happened to be in residence met each evening at supper for conversation. They discussed politics, literature, and, above all, philosophy and religion. Hyde described Falkland's "whole conversation" as "one continued *convivium philosophicum*, or *convivium theologi-cum*" (*Life*, p. 36); Kurt Weber points out that "a good half" of Falkland's guests were divines.[12]

The men at Tew were the heirs of Erasmus, Hooker, and Grotius, seeking that humanistic union of political moderation and personal Christian devotion with continuous intellectual activity. They tended to be men who lived in ideas and ideals. Typical was William Chillingworth, whose rigorous scepticism led both to his own religious peregrinations and to the ecumenical ideal of toleration brilliantly propounded in *The Religion of Protestants*, which he wrote at Great Tew. Hyde, a personally devout man whose deep faith sustained him throughout his life, shared the group's interest in religious issues. He wrote that he "had taken more pains than such men use to do, in the examination of religion" (*Life*, p. 82). George Morley, a member of the Tew group and a close friend, described Hyde as "not only a Lawyer & a States-man, but a very well grounded & a very well studyed Divine alsoe."[13] Nevertheless, Hyde's practical bent set him apart from the predominantly theoretical minds of most of the men of Great Tew.[14] Except for Gilbert Sheldon, whose adroit political manipulations after the Restoration as Bishop of London and later Archbishop of Canterbury solidly reestablished the Anglican church in England, Hyde alone among the group showed the ability and the willingness to accept political realities, to deal with circumstances and men as he found them.

It was not that others at Tew refused active roles in events. When civil war broke out, Chillingworth happily constructed siege engines for the Royalists. Sidney Godolphin, who for years had refused to make even short journeys on rainy days, and who when riding with friends would return to the house if the wind was blowing in his face, joined one of the first Royalist troops raised in the west, where he stoically endured winter marches and fought courageously (*Life*, pp. 39–40). But almost all of the men from Tew were characterized by a certain political naiveté, an inge-nuousness that Hyde never shared. In explaining Godolphin's actions, Hyde noted that his friend had become a soldier "out of the pure indigna-tion of his soul," because, being "unacquainted with contentions," he was horrified when he observed the proceedings in the House of Com-mons (*HR*, 2:457). Falkland, whom Hyde described as having "a temper and composition fitter to live in *republica Platonis* than in *faece Romuli*" (*Life*, p. 38), was the best example of such attitudes. When he served Charles I as Secretary of State, Falkland could not bring himself to deal with informers or spies or to open enemy letters for information. Both of these duties, as Hyde pointed out, were "a most necessary part of his place" (*HR*, 3:185). As the war wore on, increasingly unable to bear the daily compromises of his ideals that his service required, Falkland in effect chose not to live in a world imperfect. He sought release in the reckless and suicidal participation in battle that finally killed him at the first battle of Newbury at the age of thirty-four. Hyde recognized the costs of enduring in a fallen world where inevitable compromise taints survivors; he grimly noted in his commonplace book "the happynesse of those, who dyed in the warr, above those who lyved to indure such [?] hard calamityes, or to comply." [15] Nevertheless, he chose to try and do his best in the world as it was, and this kind of realism separated him from most of the others at Great Tew.

Hyde's position as a political outsider was particularly crucial in forming his personal and historical outlook. Throughout his career, from the time he entered Parliament in 1640 until he resigned as Lord Chancellor in 1667, [16] he maintained uneasy and anomalous relationships with his own political associates. Despite his many successes, Hyde's position remained insecure because both he and those with whom he worked recognized that his own beliefs were never entirely in accord with theirs. His whole career was devoted to establishing the rule of law, a balance of power between the monarch and Parliament, and a strong state Anglicanism. His policy as it evolved was too broad, too generous, and too vague for any single political faction to support for very long.

Hyde began his political career in 1640 as a member of the Parliamentary opposition to Charles I. After vigorously supporting early efforts to limit royal absolutism, he became alarmed as his successful colleagues, increasingly radicalized, began to undermine what he considered to be the traditional foundations of English government. In reaction, he turned to the King as the only viable protector of the English law and constitution; by 1642 he had become a Royalist and was castigated bitterly by his former allies as a turncoat. Not revolutionary enough to continue a Parliamentarian, Hyde was too much of a constitutionalist to be comfortable among the supporters of Charles I. He stayed with them because he considered monarchy necessary for a balanced constitution of government, and because no other party offered sufficient protection for what in his view were the king's essential rights. But throughout the civil wars and Interregnum Hyde found himself at odds with a bitterly divided party. As Charles I's counselor, he opposed militarists and royal absolutists, seeking a negotiated compromise with Parliament rather than victory on the battlefield. In this early period his fellow Royalists found him too moderate; in contrast, during the exile they found him too rigid. Refusing to sacrifice essential principles, Hyde held out for a restoration by English means on English terms, which would reinstate the monarchy, the constitutional balance as it had briefly existed in early 1641, and the Anglican church. He faced constant opposition in his own party, from Catholics, from the Scots and the Irish, from Queen Henrietta Maria and her group at the Louvre, from firebrands in England demanding premature rebellion, and from demoralized exiles advising compounding or capitulation. As he once told his friend Nicholas, among Charles II's followers Hyde had "the good fortune to be equally disliked by those who agree in nothing else." [17]

The tragic measure of the insecurity of Hyde's position as a state servant was the unbridgeable gap that separated him from the two kings he so faithfully served. Charles I and Charles II used him, but neither entirely liked Hyde himself or his policies. Charles I, who shared Hyde's religious principles, wanted an absolute monarchy. When he needed an effective propagandist to answer the barrage of prewar Parliamentary manifestoes, Hyde's literary abilities forged a party for him, although at the cost of enunciating a constitutional program that Charles had no intention of honoring after regaining the throne. By 1645 he was glad to dispatch Hyde to the west of England with the Prince of Wales, removing his counselor's irritating legalism and constitutionalism from his immediate presence. Charles II, a Catholic sympathizer whose political ideal was to exercise maximum power in the state with a minimum expenditure of personal effort, found Hyde's expertise as indispensable and many of his principles as tiresome as his father had. Indeed, Hyde finally assumed a central position among Charles II's counselors in exile only after the policies of everyone else had been tried and had failed dismally.

Throughout his career, Hyde was frustrated by seeing the trust both kings often withheld from him bestowed on others far less able. Charles I relied on Digby and Henrietta Maria, while Charles II showed his propensity for unsavory cabals as early as the Interregnum. After the Restoration Charles turned for advice to fellow dissipaters (Bab May, his mistresses), political opportunists (Thomas Clifford, Henry Bennet, George Downing), and bureaucrats (William Coventry). As Bacon and Strafford had discovered before Hyde, the Stuarts as a family were distinguished by their lack of appreciation for their best advisers. Because both monarchs maintained their authority by withholding complete confidence from any single person and because both neglected appointed councils to solicit advice from companions without formal positions,

Hyde usually wielded substantially less political power than the positions he held would indicate. Indeed, he develops the discrepancy between the power he actually exercised and the power others thought he had as a major theme throughout the *Continuation of the Life*.

Even early in the 1660s, when governmental authority was centered in his hands as Lord Chancellor and he seemed to be the most powerful man in England, Clarendon's triumph proved to be brief and illusory. He recognized that "the confidence the King had in him . . . proceeded more from his aversion to be troubled with the intricacies of his affairs, than from any violence of affection" (*CL*, 1:81). Ironically, Charles retained him in part because Clarendon's devotion to public business allowed the King leisure to pursue the vices his Chancellor abhorred. More crucial, the kind of moderation which Clarendon represented, which had helped to bring about the Restoration, proved impossible to sustain. Clarendon faced an increasingly divided nation. Caught between recalcitrant Puritans and furious Anglicans, Cavalier retribution and Presbyterian opposition, a burgeoning bureaucracy and a venal Court, and a King and a Parliament unable to establish a workable division of power, he successively alienated every faction in the land. Trying to balance parliamentary and monarchical privileges, Anglican and Nonconformist rights, domestic needs and foreign involvements, he sought in vain to implement the elusive compromises forged in 1640 and 1641, which were the sources of his principles of government. His political problems were exacerbated by his position as an old man in a youthful court, in many ways an Elizabethan anachronism among Restoration rakes. As traditional in his morals as he was in his politics, Clarendon found himself increasingly isolated from everyone around him. "I am in a strange country where I know nobody, and where are very few who do remember they ever knew me," he wrote to his old friend Ormonde.[18] The moderation and the sense of tradition that had so often in the past separated Clarendon from his associates left no place at all for him in the court of Charles II. His final exile from England was the climactic expression of the political alienation he had experienced throughout his career.

Thus, just as no one man or group could share all of Clarendon's varied interests, no single political faction could adequately represent the ideals he upheld. But his lifelong position as an outsider, often painful to him personally, was crucial in molding him into a historian. The careful observation of men and circumstances characteristic of the *History* derived in part from the outsider's unceasing efforts to understand nuance in order to gauge the differences that separate him from others. In the west with the Prince in 1645, on Jersey from 1646 to 1648, on the Spanish embassy from 1649 to 1651, and on the Continent directing Royalist operations in England after 1654, Hyde had gained extensive experience in evaluating events from a distance. Again and again, he had been forced to collect information for himself and reconstruct the actual status of affairs from conflicting reports. Such work was invaluable training for a historian.

Clarendon's political experiences added breadth and distance to the already wide perspective created by the range of his intellectual interests. The conventional wisdom is that history is written by the winners, but actually, in pre-nineteenth-century literary historiography, the great writers have most often been the losers. Thucydides, Commines, Machiavelli, Guicciardini, Bacon, and Raleigh all held state positions and turned to write history only when they fell from power. As H. Stuart Hughes points out, despite his temptation to apologia the failed politician possesses "a special kind of detachment, a recognition that the fault did not all lie on one side."[19] In interpreting events, such men combine the sureness of experience with the salutary hesitancy that defeat necessarily imposes on the intelligent. For Clarendon, who had begun with the Parliamentarians, moved to the Royalists, and finally suffered exile as a scapegoat hated by all sides, wholehearted endorsement of any political faction could not be an option in writing history. Moreover, the opposition he encountered had constantly forced him to view contemporary events from perspectives that were alien to his own. In order to defend himself in the midst of political turmoil, he had been required at every turn to analyze and clarify his own positions as well as to understand those of his opponents. In the process he began to evolve the distanced perspective and overview essential for writing history.

CLARENDON'S SELF-VIEW

Clarendon's remarkable ability to distance himself from the events he depicted resulted from his character and personality as well as his circumstances. But Clarendon the man has remained an elusive figure. Historians who have studied him and his age remain dissatisfied. David Ogg writes that "indistinctness still clouds the vision of posterity as it views Clarendon in the long line of English statesmen," while Sir Charles Firth concurs: "Compared to many men who achieved less, he is to-day but a vague and indistinct personality."[20] Despite the thousands of pages Clarendon wrote about his life and times, it is difficult to exhume a living, breathing "Ned Hyde" from any of his works, because both in content and in style he relentlessly submerges his private concerns in public ones. Almost everything Clarendon wrote, from his early comparison of Essex and Buckingham to the replies to Hobbes and Cressy at the end of his life, treats subjects or events directly related to his own experiences, but he strictly maintains narrative distance. For example, neither his *Life* nor his *History* directly relates what was not only one of the most interesting stories he knew but also one of the most convincing cases against the Parliament he could have made: the account of his own decision to abandon the Parliamentarians for Charles I. The commentaries on the Psalms composed during his final exile are extreme examples of his narrative impersonality; although rebellion and banishment constantly recur as themes, he always generalizes these topics and avoids any direct autobiographical references. This kind of literary detachment developed directly from his own view of himself as a public servant and a private man.

Clarendon's depictions of himself in the *History*, the *Life*, and the *Continuation of the Life* form a cumulative portrait of the ideal state servant. He establishes the broad outlines of this characterization when he portrays himself entering the Short Parliament, "wholly given . . . up to the public business" and devoted to "no other obligation than that of his own conscience and his reason" (*Life*, pp. 65, 67–68). From then on, through three decades, he remains "zealous for the preservation of the law, the religion, and true interest of the nation" (*HR*, 1:442). Only after raising vociferous objections does he reluctantly accept every official position that is offered to him. He refuses personal financial gain from his governmental posts. Because of his "natural unwariness . . . with reference to himself, when he thought his Majesty's service concerned" (*CL*, 1:394), he neglects his own political self-preservation to champion the public good. Courageous, loyal, patient, trustworthy, a principled man amid the unscrupulous, an indefatigable worker among lazy courtiers, a rigid moralist for the whores and rogues of the Restoration court—Clarendon's portrait of himself as a paragon of the conscientious minister is admirable, remarkable, tiresome, and cumulatively unbelievable.

The small amount of personal information Clarendon includes in his historical works generally translates the perfection of the state servant into the private realm. The literary artist consummately skilled in rendering the characters of others produces only a wooden sketch of himself, from which he emerges as the golden mean personified. Thus his "great infirmities"—unnamed, of course—were "seasonably restrained" from becoming habitual vices. He had ambition enough to want to rise, but not so much that he would employ unscrupulous means to do so. He enjoyed eating and drinking, but never to excess. His sharp fancy was so disciplined that not "a loose or a profane word" escaped him. His only faults were excessive generosity and absolute honesty, for his companions or Providence had corrected other dangerous tendencies very early. Firmness in religion and friendship, a good and just nature, an unblemished integrity beyond temptation, and veneration of his parents complete the character sketch (*Life*, pp. 57–59).[21] The personal equilibrium in this portrait, disturbed only by two good qualities in excess, pervades all of Clarendon's self-depictions. Under the worst conditions he remains optimistic, tolerant, and magnanimous. Even in his final exile, banished from the land he loved, disgraced after a lifetime of faithful service, a sick old man without adequate financial resources, "it pleased God in a short time, after some recollections, . . . to restore him to that serenity of mind, and resignation of himself to the disposal and good pleasure of God, that they who conversed most with him could not discover the least murmur or impatience in him, or any unevenness in his conversations" (*CL*, 2:487). His difficulties arise only because his "pride of a good conscience" (*CL*, 2:495) and his trust in his own innocence and rectitude leave him vulnerable to others' snares. Clarendon's personality remains intriguingly distant in his writings because his few remarks about it reveal mainly an impenetrable composure. The private Clarendon is presented as the perfect adjunctive personality for the public man.

Clarendon's treatment of himself was, of course, shaped by his age and its conventions for the forms in which he wrote. Studies of early autobiographers have emphasized that their lack of self-consciousness, reflecting the tendency of the era not to view the individual as central, severely limited the depth of their self-portrayals. Social inhibitions against personal revelation also generalized their focus.[22] Moreover, Roy Pascal has noted that few statesmen and politicians of any period have effectively depicted their private lives, because "the character of public political life imposes itself so relentlessly that there is often no essential relationship between the personal character of the man and his work." Pascal's general point, that "the very massiveness of political and social events makes it almost impossible to review them from an individual standpoint,"[23] is particularly relevant for those writing during and just after the English civil wars. Their works show that in those years, the national situation assumed such overwhelming significance that the private concerns of individual writers inevitably gave way to public ones. Evelyn's diary at many points becomes a history of his times. Even so massive an egotist as John Lilly, whose *History of His Life and Times* is little more than a self-obsessed astrological chronicle, forgets his own concerns long enough at the time of Marston Moor to focus entirely on the battle. From 1640 to 1660, the pressure of events became so compelling that autobiographies, diaries, journals, memoirs, and all ostensibly personal writings tended to turn into accounts of public affairs.

What makes Clarendon's self-portrayals unusual even within the impersonal context of his age and its conventions is, first, the extent to which he totally subordinates the private to the public, and second, a certain excessiveness in his depictions of his attitudes. Two examples can highlight the peculiar relentlessness characteristic of his portrayals. In Nottingham in 1642, a dispirited Charles I approached Hyde in the gallery and walked with him across the room to discuss a proposed treaty with the Parliament. When the King observed that his adviser "looked sadder than he used to do," Hyde replied that "he had not apprehended any of that trouble in his own countenance which his majesty had taken notice of, yet . . . he could not say he was without it, for he had that very morning received news of the death of a son of his, which did affect him, though it would not disturb him long." He immediately proceeded to encourage the King about the treaty with a detailed discussion of his own efforts to support it, and Charles, thoroughly reassured, described Hyde as "a very good comforter" (*HR*, 2:302–3). Twenty years later, Clarendon exhibited another unusual paternal reaction involving his private misfortunes and public responsibilities, this time when friends informed him that his daughter Anne had secretly married James, the Duke of York, and was pregnant by him. Clarendon's account records his explosion of rage at Anne's immorality and her presumptuous disobedience of both patriarchal and royal authority in marrying. He vowed to turn his daughter out of his house, ranting on that he would urge the King to commit her to the Tower and order her beheaded by an act that he himself would introduce in Parliament. No less chilling is his depiction of the calm that succeeded his fury. He informed Charles II that "he had been shortly able to recollect himself; and, upon the testimony of his own conscience, to compose his mind and spirits, and without any reluctancy to abandon any thought of his daughter, and to leave her to that misery she had deserved and brought upon herself" (*CL*, 1:48, 65–66). Neither Clarendon nor others elsewhere mention these particular reactions to his daughter, and some commentators have found his rendition of the scene so unnatural and overdrawn that they have questioned its accuracy.[24] For his son's death, a personal letter of condolence that Hyde wrote to Sir Charles Cotterell in 1654 reflects exactly the same attitudes delineated in his account: "I once lost a boy, . . . and the newes of it came to mee at Nottingham 3. dayes after the standart was sett up, wch was a most sade time, there being noe appearance of an Army, and I well remember the death of ye Child found not my heart vacant enough for any impression."[25] Even if the scene over Anne did not occur precisely as he rendered it, in terms of Clarendon's character both it and his response to his son's death are psychologically revealing. They show the kind of person Clarendon wanted to be, the thoroughly public orientation that molded his values and perspective.

Because both the history and the autobiography were written in part to vindicate Clarendon's own conduct, the temptation has been to dismiss the portrayals of the perfect public servant and the glimpses of the model private man as exaggerated self-advertisement and personal defense. Clarendon himself admitted in one of his essays that "history or experience hath transmitted the memory of very few men to us who have been notoriously prosperous in the transactions of the world, and long possessed that station, whose characters have not retained the mention of some extraordinary vice or infirmity, as well as of many notable virtues, as if those strong flights could not be made without the assistance of some iniquity."[26] Like Clarendon's enemy Cromwell, the later twentieth century demands its portraits warts and all—often viewing the warts as the most interesting part of the likeness—and thus finds Clarendon's smooth surface suspect. The validity of his self-presentation obviously has implications for his general credibility as a historian. But what is also interesting, and perhaps more important for those who find history and literature most useful when they directly illuminate the human, is the unsolved puzzle of Clarendon the man. Carlyle, considering the third of November in 1640, that historic day when the Long Parliament first convened, wrote: "Antiquarianism goes for little with me: Good Heavens, do we not know that we too shall one day be antiquities? Nevertheless, it would gratify me to understand in what manner Edward Hyde was dressed that day."[27] In addition to clarifying one aspect of his historical credibility, it is this kind of basic human curiosity that is satisfied by resuscitating as much as possible of the intriguingly distant public and private Clarendon.

Aside from his historical writings, the major record of Clarendon's life and career is the Clarendon manuscripts in the Bodleian Library, a massive collection containing thousands of letters and documents, along with the original drafts of most of his works. Many of these are the papers that Clarendon saved so carefully over the years to use in his *History*, which he had to leave behind when he fled from England. Particularly for the Royalist exile, the period most extensively documented in them, the Clarendon manuscripts provide contemporary accounts—sometimes on a daily basis—of the years covered in the *History* and the *Life*. A number of them were written at the same time that Hyde was composing the original history. They thus allow views *in medias res* of his attitudes and activities.

What Hyde wrote under the immediate pressure of events reflects the same character traits he later emphasized in his historical works. The letters show the same devotion to duty ("by the grace of God nothing shall discourage me from doing my duty"), the patience ("I can do nothing with great quietness and silence"), the tolerance of others ("we must all study to be able to live with men of all tempers"), the self-sufficiency ("ther is no trouble and vexacon [bodily health only excepted] wch it is not in our owne power to remedy and allay"), and the selflessness ("God send them both [Catholics and Presbyterians] to do their duty to the King, and send the King to enjoy what belongs to him, and it will be no matter what becomes of me").[28] Hyde is thoroughly professional, complaining to Nicholas that "it will never be well till men of business only be permitted to deal in affairs of State."[29] He never broods. "Any thinge of melancholique," he confesses to Charles II, "was nevere charged upon me. . . , hope, senselesse hope beinge my sin."[30] The occasional expressions of discouragement—"I am weary of my life," he several times admits—are mild, considering what in typical understatement he described as the "disenablenesse of our condition."[31] During the Royalists' darkest hours, his personal integrity and composure remain unshakable: "In spight of what can come, [I will] do the part of an honest man, and die by those principles I have lived."[32]

On page after page, scrawled in what Hyde himself admitted was a "vile hand,"[33] details reveal the enormous load of business he shouldered and his indefatigability in handling it. Letters were his life; Ormonde wrote teasingly that his friend loved "letters better than venison, or than I my ease."[34] For a man who could claim with some justification that he "never omitted on all occasions to write to the meanest Subject the King hath,"[35] the task of maintaining communications was unending. On Jersey in 1646, far from the centers of Royalist affairs, he still spends "one entire day" a week in writing letters: "My conscience will not suffer me to sleep after the receiving any letter before I answer it."[36] Directing operations for Charles II during the mid-1650s, he dispatches twelve letters every post day, finally lamenting that he wants to "live as other Christians do and enjoy some pleasure."[37] One letter notes that he has been too busy all day to eat; others indicate that he has scarcely been able to visit friends and has no time for himself or his family; yet another was composed in the evening when the King got him out of bed to write.[38] Hyde's problems range from minor occupational hazards—decoding one letter of Secretary Nicholas', from whom the cipher "flowed as naturally . . . as the alphabet," leaves him with a headache so bad that two nights of sleep have not cured it—to major distresses: "Some devise to get a reasonable some of money to pay our debte, and put the allmost naked servants into clothes before the cold of winter, or we are undone."[39] He deals with children sent to the Continent to be touched for the King's Evil,[40] a vivid reminder of the domestic pain continuing unabated in the midst of political upheavals. He worries when his correspondent in Rome is quarantined in his lodgings because of the plague and can send no information.[41] When he finally takes a short break, he comments ruefully that "for sure it will not be thought unreasonable to have ye minde unbent 10. dayes in 3. yeares, and to give a poore man soe much time for his owne private concernments."[42] The reader who has watched him at work can only agree.

Clarendon's contemporaries on the whole corroborate his own accounts in the Clarendon papers and in his historical writings of his diligence and integrity as a state servant. Letters from Charles I and Charles II praise his constancy to his principles and his conscientiousness.[43] In exile Sir Henry Bennet found him "the only fixed foote of yᵉ compasse"; after the Restoration Burnet concluded that he was "a good chancellor."[44] Samuel Pepys, who praised him as "a good servant to the King" and "a most able and ready man" in conducting "Tryalls," was enthralled by Clarendon's mastery of business: "I am mad in love with my Lord Chancellor, for he doth comprehend and speak as well, and with the greatest easiness and authority, that ever I saw man in my life."[45] Clarendon's industry after the Restoration was, if anything, greater than it had been during the exile. As the 1660s progressed, correspondents began to direct their queries to his son Cornbury, who assisted his father, because they knew how involved with business the Chancellor was.[46]

At the same time, the reactions to Clarendon recorded by contemporaries indicate that the very virtues which made him invaluable in state service could make life difficult for his associates. Clarendon himself described chiding as one of his "best faculties," and believed that his obligation was not only "to bear with" but also to "inform and reform those who have less understanding."[47] Such attitudes produced a stern taskmaster. Digby, by that time the Earl of Bristol, was only the most outspoken among many during the exile who fumed when Hyde pressured constantly for action. Unable to procure a signature from a Spanish official who had spent an entire afternoon playing tennis, Bristol groused: "I beleeve you will thinke it a fault . . . that I carryed it not to him myselfe to signe with his racquet." Another of Hyde's orders is "ridiculous": "to ask it of them is such a thing as I beleeve noebody ever dreamt of but yourselfe that hath ever had to doe with Princes."[48] Bristol's various testy subscripts—"God keepe you and make you lesse troublesome to your freinds [*sic*]"; "In the meane while God give you a better temper"; "God keepe you and make you if not wiser at least kinder"[49]—suggest the dictatorial peremptoriness that Hyde's conscientiousness and his confidence in his own industry and integrity could produce. Indeed, although he admitted to Bristol at one point that "I am never like to write to you, without grumbling,"[50] his demands did not let up. Unsparing of himself, he refused to accept less than total dedication from others. Nor did he mellow with age. He got worse, in part because his virtues were inherently rigid ones, and also because he suffered increasing pain from gout. After the Restoration, Pepys described Clarendon as so dominating the council table that "the King was as much afeared of saying anything there as the meanest privy-councillor." Nevertheless, by that time the years were beginning to tell; the diarist also shows Clarendon "sleeping and snoring the greater part of the time" through a meeting.[51] This combination of authority and age that made Clarendon trying was exacerbated by a temper to which his own writings sometimes fail to do full justice, although they admit its existence. Mistakenly blaming poor Pepys for ordering timber in Clarendon Park to be cut, the Chancellor raged "in the highest and most passionate manner that ever any man did speak, even to the not hearing of anything to be said to him."[52]

In addition to illuminating the less appealing sides of virtues that already appear somewhat intimidating in Clarendon's own writings, the impressions of his contemporaries indicate that several of Clarendon's best traits were extremely susceptible to misrepresentation. His general rectitude and unyielding morality could in the eyes of the less upright—who were after all the majority in the Restoration court—make him appear pompous and unnecessarily austere. The Duke of Buckingham and

Colonel Titus' famous parody of the Chancellor with bellows and coal shovel for seal and mace emphasizes the vulnerability to ridicule of Clarendon's concern for order and decorum. More dangerously for him, his unending attempts to impose economy on the court in order to stabilize the government could be attributed by his opponents to personal avarice, just as his highhandedness could be interpreted by them as an effort to hide bribery and corruption. Even among Clarendon's enemies, however, William Coventry, perhaps the least self-interested of the group who drove Clarendon from office, insisted firmly that the Chancellor's shortcomings were limited to areas of policy.[53]

In 1650, Hyde asserted to Nicholas: "I shall in the end be found to have as few private ends, and to have dedicated myself as entirely to the publick, as any poor Gentleman that suffers in this good cause."[54] Modern historians who have carefully reviewed Clarendon's career have in general substantiated this claim. The most that studies have shown against him is that he was, naturally enough, not averse to placing his actions in the best light. For example, in his financial dealings as a public official, Clarendon's opponents accused him of avarice and venality; he claimed in his works that he sought no private gain whatsoever from the public and received only the profits that were his legitimate prerogative. Although the Clarendon State Papers suggest that he did look after relatives and supporters in various ways after the Restoration, records of royal grants and details of his financial status disclosed after his flight from England indicate that his general practices were well within the range considered acceptable by seventeenth-century standards, and more scrupulous than those of many other officials.[55] Though later historians agree that Clarendon made many political mistakes, his defenses of himself in his writings are based not so much on the success of his endeavors as on the conscientiousness of his service and the disinterestedness of his motives. His treatment of Charles II's controversial marriage to Catherine of Braganza shows his characteristic approach to his own role. He structures his account to prove that "he did nothing before, in, or after that treaty, but what was necessary for a man in his condition, and what very well became a person of that trust and confidence he was in with his master" (*CL*, 1:133). Clarendon's primary concern in vindicating himself was always to show that the principles guiding his actions were proper, given his circumstances. History has tended to validate his claims for his good intentions, if not always for his judgment.

While corroborating Clarendon's self-portrait of the dedicated public servant—albeit with a few jagged edges—the Clarendon manuscripts and the comments of his contemporaries add very little to illumine the private man. Only rarely do personal concerns surface in the letters. There is, for example, his countryman's love for the cultivation of the estate. On Jersey in 1648, busy with his garden, he asks Lord Cottington to send him seeds.[56] In 1650, he writes enthusiastically of the lemons and oranges in his garden in Spain.[57] From exile in France, he instructs his son about plans for an orchard at his country house and asks him to "plant as much as you cann, and even repair those wallnutt trees in the ground which are decayed."[58] Or there are occasional minor details: an order of lace for Lady Hyde; a response to Hyde's apparent complaints about a hat and powder he received; requests for "a good provision of sherry" or "2. barrelles of Beere for us, that may be the best in the town against I come."[59] These could perhaps be read as minor reflections of the taste for ostentation and extravagance that his contemporaries noted,[60] a trait that undoubtedly encouraged the charges of financial corruption leveled by his enemies. But this tendency, like his rigidity and his temper, is acknowledged without being emphasized in Clarendon's own works. In the *Life* he admits that he had "too much a contempt of money"—although the context is his generosity to others (p. 58). He explains at length in the *Continuation* that the one thing in his life that most shamed him was the "vast expence he had made in the building of his house." (Designed to cost £20,000, it ultimately required £50,000.)[61]

Perhaps the only personal characteristic noted by Clarendon's contemporaries that would be hard to glean from his own writings is the very real charm he apparently possessed.[62] Although he mentions "the gaiety of his humour, and inoffensive and winning behavior" (*Life*, p. 50), he never presents himself as the kind of man whom John Evelyn described as having "a jolly temper, after the old English fashion."[63] This personability, which undoubtedly contributed to the genius for friendship that Clarendon and others indicated he had, does not emerge in his works, partly because of his strict avoidance of personal matters and partly because of his defensiveness. Relying on detailed arguments to explicate his political positions, he maintained literary decorum, emphasizing his earnestness and his sometimes forbidding virtues rather than trying to charm his readers into accepting his views.

Confusion over the number of children Clarendon had reflects how obscure the private man has remained. The *Dictionary of National Biography* lists only four; Clarendon's will written at Rouen in 1674 adds two more; his latest biographer credits him with nine in all, three of whom died in infancy; and the last volume of the *Calendar of the Clarendon State*

Papers mistakes one of his sons for a child of his daughter Anne.[64] Characteristically, Clarendon simply wrote in the *Life* that by his second wife he had "many children of both sexes" (p. 13); he never refers to them in the work by their Christian names. What is known of Clarendon's domestic life, especially of his family and his attitudes toward them, suggests why private concerns play so small a role in his writings. In enumerating "those Things and Blessings which God sends as the greatest Comforts of Life," Clarendon listed estates first, honors second, wives third, and children fourth.[65] His initial interest in matrimony stemmed from "no other passion . . . than an appetite to a convenient estate" (*Life*, p. 9). Later, appropriately enough for a man who believed friendship was "so much more a sacrament than marriage,"[66] his autobiography presents both of his marriages as solutions to his problems in committing himself wholeheartedly to a legal career. He explains that after his first wife died from a miscarriage brought on by an attack of smallpox less than six months after their marriage, he married again three years later because he knew that remarriage would be "the most grateful thing to his father (for whom he had always a profound reverence) he could do" (*Life*, pp. 10, 13). In the manuscript of the *Life*, he left a blank when mentioning the year of his second marriage, apparently because he did not remember the date.[67] Hyde's domestic utilitarianism led naturally to prudent and advantageous matches; both of his wives came from wealthy families with good political connections.[68]

Hyde wrote that he was devastated by his first wife's death, and he seems to have been genuinely fond of his second wife. Some of the notes he wrote to her from Spain, which are among his very few personal letters extant, are affectionate and kind; he often addresses her as "My deere little Rogue."[69] Nevertheless, they emphasize that business was his first priority. In his essay *On an active and on a contemplative Life*, Clarendon describes the man of action as seldom having "the company and conversation of his own wife," adding that only in retirement does he become "acquainted with his own children, who were before strangers to him."[70] Such was apparently his own case. During the Royalist exile his work frequently separated him from his family for long periods. In 1657 he wrote Nicholas "to chyde" his wife for "the madnesse of that fancy, that wee can be alwayes together even if we were gott to Whitehall."[71] The warning proved to be prophetic, for even after the Restoration Hyde seems to have found little time for family matters. In general, he apparently never expended on them the kind of energy he devoted to public affairs. That the numerous attacks on him during a licentious age are focused entirely on his conduct of business provides a fairly good indication that his private life was unexceptionable.[72] The records of his domestic affairs additionally suggest that it was almost nonexistent.

Thus all of the extant evidence, from the accounts of Clarendon's contemporaries and his own letters to the evaluations of later historians, supports as essentially accurate the self-view he conveys in his historical writings.[73] His voracious appetite for work and the sheer amount of it he tackled, both thoroughly documented in the Clarendon State Papers, along with the paucity of contemporary comments about him that are unconnected with business, indicate that his life was to a great extent his public service. Private concerns do not surface in his writings because in his own life they occupied comparatively little of his time and energy. In his final review of his conduct at the close of the *Continuation*, Clarendon wrote that from the time he devoted himself to the law, he had entered into "a life of too much business" (2:550); he does not depict himself at rest or at play because he so seldom was. In later years even the friendships that seem to have been his chief pleasure apart from business overlapped his work almost completely, as courtiers and politicians replaced many of the literary men and intellectuals he had known earlier. The subordination of the private to the public man emerges not simply as a habit of style, a characteristic of Clarendon's writing, but as an accurate reflection of the substance of the man and his life.

In addition, it is partly because the period of the English civil wars, Interregnum, and Restoration is marked by so many colorful and distinctive personalities—people like Strafford, Henrietta Maria, Hampden, Montrose, Cromwell, Castlemaine, Rochester, Charles II himself, and many more—that Clarendon as a man seems so bland and distant. His ability to sacrifice his private concerns to public ones meant that he never showed the picturesque individualism of a Goring, a Digby, or a Rupert. He lacked any of the lively traits required to cut a memorable figure on the pages of history. He possessed no engaging idiosyncrasies. He was not unfeeling, but he showed no trace of sentimentality; his passions were for the abstract—his principles, his work—rather than for the more immediately human. Not the man for a great deal of introspection, Clarendon approached life straightforwardly, with an optimism at times almost naive. Stout and middle-statured, he was not a dashing figure. Like his physique, his virtues were solid and unpicturesque: loyalty, industriousness, tolerance, patience, self-restraint. His adventures occurred in the bureaucracy rather than on the battlefield or in the boudoir. Content to remain in the background, he found satisfaction in solid public achievement rather than personal renown. His traits were those of the thorough professional rather than the hero; neither a man who lived in ideals, as Falkland was, nor a man of action like Cromwell, he combined both in an uneasy and indistinct synthesis. Clarendon was one of those rare individuals who possess force of character without force of personality. Indeed, his whole story emphasizes the extent to which romantic and colorful figures in history tend to eclipse men in equally important roles whose decency, industry, and personal moderation have less imaginative appeal. If by the late twentieth century social historians have begun to right the balance of parts of the general historical record, the popular view of history, centered for mnemonic reasons on personality, seems unlikely to change in a way that will render men like Clarendon their due.

What emerges from a review of the extant information about Clarendon as a public and private personality is the sense of how thoroughly suited he was to be a historian. In one of his essays he wrote that the "genius and spirit and soul of an historian . . . is contracted by the knowledge and course and method of business, and by conversation and familiarity in the inside of courts, and [with] the most active and eminent persons, in the government."[74] With such activities he had saturated himself. His position had given him immediate and extensive knowledge about the events of his time; his personality gave him the perspective to find the proper vantage point from which to write about them. He had the self-knowledge and the intellectual honesty to see himself clearly and dispassionately, a trait rare in anyone and particularly valuable for a historian. What he did in his own life he also did for his age in his *History*. Behind the distanced prose style and narrative stance is the personal equilibrium—the moderation, the reserve, the self-sufficiency—of Clarendon the man. Burnet noted that Clarendon gave advice "too much with the air of a governor or lawyer,"[75] and this manner directly reflected his character. Clarendon was a lawyer by temperament as well as by profession; judiciousness, the desire to evaluate and then act, was his essence. But his occasional outbursts of temper emphasize that his composure was imposed on rather than inherent in his temperament. The self-restraint that generally marked his personality had been hard won, and it bore fruit in his work. In his *History*, there would be partisanship and there would be anger, but, just as in his life, in his writing he would strive to control these tendencies. Clarendon could write the history of what was in effect his own ruin so effectively because of those character traits that had enabled him to face reverses throughout his career with equanimity.

The early English historians, from Raleigh and Bacon through

Hume and Gibbon, are all marked personally by a certain sanguineness, a tendency to see the favorable rather than the unfavorable. If it is true, as Hegel noted, that the great histories have tended to be dark ones, it is also true that many of the literary historiographers have been able to write their bleak histories so well because their general optimism enabled them to face and master overwhelming events. Jonathan Swift wrote to the Count de Gyllenborg that he stopped writing his history "chiefly by the indignation I conceived at the proceedings of a faction, which then prevailed," explaining that he published what he had written to encourage its completion by "those who have more youth, and leisure, and good temper than I."[76] A certain kind of "good temper," the ability to maintain personal serenity despite brutal reverses, seems to be useful if not essential in order to write history as effectively as Clarendon did.

In his *Contemplations* on the Psalms, Clarendon wrote:

The happy State and Condition of his Country is a greater Joy and Comfort to an honest Man, than his own particular State of Wealth and Prosperity can be; and he is more afflicted and cast down for any publick Misery that befals it, than for any Circumstance of it that brings Calamity to himself; he feels not his own particular Sufferings, when he sees his Country covered with Tyranny and Oppression, all its Laws violated, and its Religion contemned and profaned.[77]

All that is known of his life indicates that these sentiments accurately depict his deepest feelings. This public orientation, which was for Clarendon not only a way of writing but also a way of living, made him uniquely capable of chronicling his own times. Throughout his career, he showed the ability to look beyond himself and to see in terms larger than strictly personal ones. His tendency to repress the private meant that despite his own position at the center of events, in his work the distortions inevitable when the viewer supplants the viewed would be minimized. For almost thirty years, as his energies were devoted to public concerns at the expense of private ones, he in effect made the events of his times into the staple of his personal life. Thus for him to explain exactly what had happened during the time he had served was to explain himself. Much of the self-vindication he sought would be inherent in a review of events; because of the way he had lived his life, history itself could redeem him. The fact that with some cutting and minor verbal changes he could use his *Life* to create almost all of the last part of the *History* shows the extent to which his subsumption of private concerns into public ones allowed the form of the *History of the Rebellion* to become that of the man.

THE CONFLICTS OF THE PUBLIC MAN
AND THE HISTORIAN

Although Clarendon's partisanship and personal concerns were not entirely obliterated from the *History*, his circumstances and various elements in his character enabled him to control them for historical advantage. But if some of his personal conflicts, especially between public and private concerns, had been resolved in ways that enormously enhanced his work, one in particular remained problematical to the end. In his political career, Clarendon was both an idealist and a pragmatist. He always viewed his state service within the framework of a conception of society and government that incorporated what he considered the best of the past with the obvious needs of the present. He had the ability to articulate and hold to these principles despite all opposition. Yet at the same time he was able to accept the reality of the political world as he found it and to work with it accordingly. This combination of traits is, of course, essential in any statesman who functions as more than a timeserver or an impotent ideological symbol. However, the tumultuous period in which Clarendon lived and the ways he carried out his responsibilities left him unable ever to resolve completely the competing claims of vision and reality in his career and in his writing. The resulting political and literary costs could sometimes be considerable.

Certain expressions that Clarendon repeatedly uses in connection with his public service reveal his principled approach to his work. For example, the word "abstracted" recurs whenever he describes his motivations. A letter mentions "the most abstracted spirit of duty, loyalty, and obedience";[78] the *History of the Rebellion* notes "the most abstracted sense of loyalty to the King and duty to their country" (1:430); the *Life* emphasizes "abstractly the consideration of his duty" (p. 83). He remained a loyal follower of two sovereigns who were in many ways unworthy—"no infirmity or impiety in my prince can warrant or excuse my declension of allegiance towards him"[79]—because when problems arose he managed to look beyond the kings as individuals and focus on his duty to the institution of monarchy itself. Like Montrose and the best of the Stuarts' followers, Clarendon defended an ideal monarchy rather than the extant one. But other levels of abstraction were also involved, for his attachment to monarchy combined with his love for England and his devotion to Anglican Christianity. He considered royal service a patriotic duty: "Princes must be obeyed and served by their Subjects, who in serving them serve

97

their Countries."[80] Most important to him was the religious context of his duty. He believed that subjects submit to a king's will "because they look upon him as substituted by God to govern over them, and as his Deputy, whom they cannot resist or disobey, without being undutiful to Him whose Deputy he is."[81] When discussing Charles II's laziness in a dispirited letter to Nicholas, he admitted that "if I did not serve the King for God's sake I would not stay here a day longer."[82] The ability to think of his duty in terms of such ideals sustained Clarendon in the more unpalatable aspects of his service.

Appropriately, another of Clarendon's characteristic phrases in discussing his own and others' obligations is "the conscience of doing our duties." Although he uses "conscience" in the obsolete sense of "consciousness,"[83] his loyalty to his conscience shaped his political career. As a young lawyer, Hyde had not been afraid to assist a group of merchants who were opposing the powerful Lord Treasurer, the Earl of Portland, "when all men of name durst not appear for them" (*Life*, p. 21). For the rest of his life, he showed a marked independence of spirit in standing up for his own beliefs. As a royal counselor, he was not known for hiding his opinions. Queen Henrietta Maria told her ladies that if Clarendon thought her a whore, he would say so to her face (*HR*, 5:66–67). There remain no more vivid illustrations of his relentless insistence on his principles than his own depictions in the *Continuation of the Life* of many unfortunate conversations with Charles II. The King at one point angrily told his minister that royal opinion "was of no authority with him if it differed from his judgment, to which he would not submit against his reason" (*CL*, 2:99).

At crucial points when he saw his fundamental political beliefs imperiled, Clarendon showed his willingness to assert his principles with actions as well as words. In 1646, when Henrietta Maria and her advisers wanted the Prince to leave Jersey and join her in France, Hyde saw such a move as an unsurmountable barrier to a constitutional and Anglican restoration by English efforts alone. By broadly interpreting his mandate from Charles I as the Prince's adviser, he had already obstructed the Prince's removal from English soil several times by in effect disobeying the King's direct orders. When the Prince finally left, Hyde refused to accompany him to Paris because, as he explained in a letter to the King, "I could not in my reason and conscience . . . consent to the rules and grounds by and upon which they were to found their Counsels."[84] Similarly, two years later he again saw proceedings totally antithetical to his principles in the Royalists' negotiations with the Scottish Presbyterians.

In an agonized letter to the Queen on what his duty had to be in view of his beliefs, he wrote that others "can give themselves leave to do that which is not lawful for me."[85] Another letter to Digby explicitly outlined the way he viewed his obligations to both the King and his conscience:

I will censure nor rebel against no conclusion the King shall make; but by the grace of God I will not contribute towards, nor have any hand in any, which in my judgment promises nothing but vexation and misery to himself, and all honest men. And therefore you may easily conclude how fit a Counsellor I am like to be, when the best that is proposed, is that which I would not consent unto, to preserve the Kingdom from ashes. I can tell you worse of myself than this; which is, that there may be some reasonable expedients which possibly would in truth restore and preserve all, in which I could bear no part.[86]

Instead of going to Scotland, Hyde sought service elsewhere that he could in conscience undertake. After the Restoration, when such alternative service was no longer possible—the temporary absence of an adviser to an exiled King was hardly viable for the highest minister of the Crown—he continued to stand as firmly as he could for his principles. At the one time that he felt Anglicanism was seriously endangered, during consideration of the bill for liberty of conscience, he publicly opposed the King. When Charles II asked those who were against the bill either to be absent or to stay silent in the House of Lords, Clarendon and Southampton answered that "they should not be absent purposely, and if they were present, they hoped his Majesty would excuse them if they spake according to their conscience and judgment, which they could not forbear to do" (*CL*, 2:95). Although extremely ill with gout, Clarendon attended the session and attacked the bill.

Hyde's political principles were based on his strong sense of tradition, his belief that the best of the past should be preserved and, when necessary, reinterpreted for the future. His concern, like Burke's a century later, was always to maintain continuity. In 1642 he masterminded the Lord Keeper's escape from the Parliament so that the Great Seal of the kingdom would be in the King's custody; in exile he insisted that Charles' tattered and bedraggled little court adhere to the proper legal forms and ceremonies for such things as patents and Garter initiations.[87] He worked with churchmen to find ways to consecrate bishops during the Interregnum so that the Anglican succession would continue uninterrupted.[88] After the Restoration he kept trying to show Charles II, whom he described as "a great lover of new inventions . . . to control the superstitious dictates of our ancestors," that "the innovation and breach of all old order . . . is ever attended by many mischiefs unforeseen" (*CL*, 2:216, 207). During the constitutional turmoil of the seventeenth century, every faction in England was appealing to tradition to support its own viewpoints, studying the past for records and precedents. But Clarendon in a very real sense constructed his life around such ties with the past—"the old foundation of the established Government, and the good known laws"; "the old rock of established law." [89] His whole career was an attempt to transform past constitutional and Anglican traditions into present political reality.

Hyde stood for moral as well as political tradition. During the exile he had been dismayed by the misbehavior of Charles II and some of his followers, once going so far as to urge the writer of a dedicatory epistle to the King: "Above all, I beseech you review and allay those two hyperbolical expressions of the modesty and severity of our Court, where, God knows, the Fabricii nor the Camilli can be found." [90] His tendency throughout his life was to see the world in moral terms. But it was as an old-fashioned relic adrift in the unending revels that passed for Charles' court after the Restoration that Clarendon made his most determined stand for moral rectitude. He chided the King for his excesses and endlessly nagged at him to stop neglecting government for pleasure. While other courtiers and politicians rushed to Lady Castlemaine's lodgings— where Charles himself often in effect held court—to pay their respects and make application to the powerful mistress, Clarendon, in what Burnet described as "the maintaining the decencies of virtue in a very solemn manner," [91] refused even to pay her a visit. Nor would he allow his wife to do so. (Ironically, once his daughter Anne was finally recognized as Duchess of York after bearing the Duke's child, she also refused to admit Charles' mistresses into her presence.) [92] When the King in one interview questioned Clarendon's behavior toward Castlemaine, the Chancellor bluntly informed him that personal integrity demanded such treatment of "persons infamous for any vice, for which by the laws of God and man they ought to be odious, and to be exposed to the judgment of the Church and State" (*CL*, 2:288). He was also concerned, however, with the political ramifications of the situation. Because he considered "honour and reputation" to be "the life itself of princes" (*HR*, 1:260), he believed that the conduct of the King and his associates played a vital role in molding subjects' attitudes toward the government. As Clarendon noted in the *Contemplations* on the Psalms, "the Integrity of their [Princes'] Courts makes a strong Impression upon the Affection of their Subjects, and disposes them to a Respect and Reverence for the great Master of so illustrious a Family."[93] In his conversation with the King, he emphasized that royal ministers must behave with a dignity befitting their offices, for scandals about the court directly endangered the monarchy by undermining popular respect and support.

Henry Bennet, later the Earl of Arlington, who was also present during the interview, deftly turned Clarendon's sermonizing into a joke, much to the King's delight. The whole vignette provides a vivid explanation of precisely why Bennet steadily rose in Charles' favor as Clarendon declined. The conversation is also a good example of the ways in which moral and political issues tended to merge in Clarendon's thought. Just as in dealing with Castlemaine he found political implications in moral behavior, at his best throughout his career he placed practical politics within a larger moral matrix. This merging of political concerns with moral ones is one of Clarendon's strongest links with the past. As the seventeenth century progressed, the tendency in the state (as well as in historical writing) was to separate the political from the moral, following the tenets of Machiavelli and his followers and interpreters. In this context, certain movements during the civil wars and the Interregnum can be seen as attempts on the part of various individuals and factions (most notably, of course, the Independents) to return the nation to their own versions of older concepts of moral political behavior. For Clarendon too the effort to fuse politics and morals underlay his stands for his own ideals.

In explaining to Digby the adherence to principles that had led him to remain on Jersey in 1646, Hyde concluded that he was "fitter for a Monastery, than a Court."[94] But despite such principles and the courage to uphold them, realism was an equally prominent trait in Hyde's character. He could accept the fact that discrepancies between the moral and the political worlds were inevitable; as he once explained rather bitterly to Nicholas, "the truth is, there is naturally that absence of the chief Elements of Christian religion, charity, humility, justice, and brotherly compassion, in the very policy and institution of Princes and Sovereign States."[95] Nevertheless, he always believed that the world's imperfections in no way absolved men from the responsibility for playing their part in it: "Let the World be as vayne and as bad as it can be, good Men will be able to doe some good in it"; "Men of Virtue and Wisdome . . . though they cannot doe as much good as they desire to doe, they will prevent some hurt."[96] Accordingly, he operated as an eminently practical man. Over and over again in his letters to Nicholas, Hyde stresses the necessity of adapting themselves to prevailing conditions. In the process, he provides his friend with a sort of primer for responsible political attitudes and behavior—and peace of mind—under the most adverse circumstances. Without abandoning their own ideals, they must work within the parameters of the possible: "I confess it were to be wished that we could be always joined with men who proceed upon our principles, at least who proceed upon any; but if that happiness cannot be, we must not be discouraged and give over doing that which is our duty."[97] When their efforts fail, they must still proceed positively: "It is our parts to use our utmost endeavour to prevent the King's doing any thing that is amiss, but when it is done to make the best of it."[98] Above all, they must acquiesce in the inevitable: "It is to no purpose to censure any thing that cannot be mended"; "for what is here otherwise then it should be, you must when all is done be contented to bear the infirmities of nature which you cannot cure."[99]

Because of Clarendon's realism, after he had strongly urged his own ideas, he would usually fall into line with royal policies. He not only executed orders that he considered wrong, but he went about his assigned tasks with a somewhat distasteful thoroughness and energy. Although he was horrified at Charles II's insistence that his wife accept his mistress as one of her ladies of the bedchamber, he wrote that "by all the ways he could devise," he urged the Queen "to submit to that cheerfully, that she could not resist" (*CL*, 1:301, 304). Significantly, in asserting his principles, he at no time refused to serve at all; he simply rejected certain assignments. Clarendon's realism marked his personal as well as his professional life. His reaction to his final banishment from England reflects a lifetime's practice of adjusting his expectations to his circumstances; he wrote that "by all possible administrations" he subdued his feelings and did everything necessary "to make his mind conformable to his present fortune" (*CL*, 2:567).

Clarendon's pragmatism was nowhere better shown than in his dislike of the theoretical and the speculative. In his essays he pointed out that Christ in the Sermon on the Mount, "which comprehends all Christianity," avoided "speculative doctrine . . . to resolve all into practice"; similarly, in the *Contemplations* on the Psalms he opposed wasting time in debating "what we should Think" while never considering "what we are to Do."[100] In an age of theoretical politicians like Lilburne and political theorists like Harrington and Hobbes, he refused to systematize his political beliefs. His outrage at Hobbes' approach, which was compounded by his old friend's apostasy from the Great Tew circle and all that it represented, is vented in the answer to *Leviathan* that was composed in his final exile. In Clarendon's view, Hobbes' judgment was "fix'd under Philosophical and Metaphysical notions," and as a result he "doth despise all Precedents, and will not observe any Rules of practice." Clarendon showers contempt on Hobbes' "imaginary Government" erected by "Rules of Arithmetic and Geometry."[101] Like Burke, Clarendon found speculative and abstract political doctrine reductive because it failed to take adequate account of past experience and especially of human nature. Throughout his life, he saw the world in terms of the individual men in it, with their infinitely variable idiosyncrasies and frailties. This kind of individually oriented vision made theoretical rigidity impossible. The operations of the kind of government he desired, composed of a monarch and a parliament working together with a strong privy council mediating, were too heavily dependent on personal factors to be codified. Although Clarendon's refusal to be systematic about these beliefs created some difficulties for him, it did allow him a breadth and flexibility unusual for his time. His was an era of political extremes, from the Levellers and the sects that were pushing toward democracy to diehard monarchists, supported by theoreticians such as Filmer, who were seeking absolutism. From the 1640s on, a succession of parties with single, narrow aims found temporary success, only to be displaced because their power bases proved too limited. Because Clarendon was content to forgo the stability along with the rigidity offered by theory, he at times managed to unify disparate elements by holding the broad middle ground.

Hyde's realistic attitudes reflect that peculiarly British strain of political empiricism that stretches in the seventeenth and eighteenth centuries from Hooker to Burke. In a larger sense, his kind of pragmatism is characteristic of most of the early literary historiographers. These men as a whole showed a considerable capacity to adjust themselves to whatever circumstances demanded; when they could no longer participate in making history, they wrote it. Such pragmatism accounts in part for their general sanguineness, but it also accounts for certain other traits they shared. For example, with the exception of More, their commitment to the actual dictated that they would never be heroes. This acquiescence, exemplified at its most extreme and unsavory by Josephus and to a lesser degree by Bacon, encouraged neither the resistance to nor the redemption of contemporary forces that molds the heroic temper. Accepting and working with life as they found it, these men naturally turned to history instead of to imaginative literature when they became authors. They preferred to stay as close as possible to the actual worlds they had known, recreating them in the most direct form they could. Insofar as the fictional is at some level an escape, no matter how oblique, they had no need or desire for it.

For the task of writing a history that had literary qualities, Clarendon's combination of idealism and principles along with pragmatism was enormously useful. The ability he showed throughout his career to maintain in the midst of present chaos a vision of the past for future use reflects an imaginative capacity that, in its historical perspective, was crucial in constructing a credible and meaningful narrative of events. To actively seek continuity in human actions and to discover the significant relationships among them requires the ability to illumine the general through the particular that separates the literary historiographer from the chronicler and the ordinary historian. The same sense of a living tradition, which Clarendon had too often been unable to translate into direct political action, was essential in giving meaning to his history. Similarly, his characteristic fusion of the political and the moral proved extremely useful in literary terms for translating raw events into a larger structural overview. Thus, while Clarendon's presentation of his wider perspectives provided artistic unity, his lifelong commitment to the actual meant that factual evidence would remain the bedrock of his history. He had confined himself for too long within the limits of the possible to allow himself to impose his own vision where circumstances would not warrant it.

Unfortunately, the balance between idealism and pragmatism necessary for effective public service as well as for good literary historiography can be difficult to maintain. Clarendon knew his principles and he knew the necessity of working with what was possible in any given situation. But in his career, circumstances, along with his own methods of operating, seldom allowed him to realize his ideas in practice.

Like Cromwell and so many others in mid-seventeenth-century England, Clarendon could see his political ends clearly, but he faltered on the intermediate steps that were necessary for achieving them. His pragmatism occasionally led him to lose sight of his long-term goals; he would end up working at cross purposes with himself by making compromises as temporary expedients that undercut his basic principles. Trevor-Roper has traced the process through which Clarendon's tolerant, rational, and ecumenical religious ideals, formed among Falkland's circle at Great Tew, became obscured in practice as he followed Sheldon's party in reestablishing Anglican power after the Restoration.[102] A basic problem was the kings he served; given their characters, he could never reconcile the loyalty and obedience he believed he owed to them with his own principles. All too often he found his possibilities for action limited to improvising frantically among various undesirable courses. Thus, despite John Evelyn's remark that Clarendon above all others "kept up the forme & substance of things in the nation," [103] in dealing with the Stuarts he sometimes allowed form to take precedence over substance. Clarendon knew, although he fought his own recognition of the truth, that Charles I's political principles and Charles II's lack of any ascertainable principles at all were almost insurmountable obstacles to the kind of nation he wanted England to be. He labored ceaselessly to instill his own political and moral ideals into both kings, but whenever he failed—which was, of course, much of the time—his pragmatism led him to do his utmost to hide their shortcomings from others. This constant practice in the thankless task of trying to cover for them made presentable exteriors sometimes become ends rather than means.

Because he was one of the few conscientious Royalists in state service, Clarendon was throughout his career burdened with too many responsibilities. The sheer weight of work that he carried sometimes made it difficult for him to see ends clearly. After the Restoration, for example, he was too busy with daily operations to develop the long-term colonial policy then needed. [104] His methods of conducting business exacerbated his tendency to fall back on temporary expedients. Although he was a tireless worker, in administrative tasks his industry exceeded his ability. He lacked the efficiency—and the ruthlessness—of a Strafford. Except in legal affairs, Clarendon had little actual administrative experience before the Restoration. He made his mistakes accordingly. He disliked delegating authority, and his desire to oversee everything himself, along with his belief that state business should be conducted by privy councilors of noble rank rather than middle-level bureaucrats, left him with inadequate control of increasingly complex administrative operations. When faced with many alternatives for action, he became immersed in detail; the more he had to do, the more compromises he made, and the more mistakes. This tendency to focus on daily details rather than general policy is epitomized by his error in accepting the office of Lord Chancellor at the Restoration. As J. R. Jones points out, the position involved a heavy burden of routine administrative chores without accompanying political importance. [105]

Because of his pragmatic strain, Clarendon's vision of his own ideals was truest in times of extremity. He was at his best during the period of the Royalist exile, when the limited power the King had was concentrated in his hands, and when there was little to do except to hold firmly to the principle of a Restoration by English and Anglican elements, to take the few steps possible for realizing these goals, and to wait. The static quality in his perspective, his ability to maintain the best of the past in the present, made him unmatched in his stubborn support of essential ideals in adverse circumstances. It also limited his ability in the innovative political construction England needed after 1660 to bridge the present and the future. Central to Clarendon's conception of government was a pivotal role for the privy council, but because he tended to think mainly in terms of the way such a body could have functioned during the Elizabethan era, he could seldom exploit the resources that made it the forerunner of modern cabinet government. His ability for constructive foresight in action was also limited because his viewpoint was tempered by his years of operating in the opposition. S. R. Gardiner and others have criticized Clarendon's "policy of negation,"[106] but circumstances as much as defective ideology dictated this stance. A moderate in an age of fanatics, his fate was to spend his career trying to curb other people: Parliamentary extremists and a despot manqué in the early 1640s; Royalist militarists and absolutists from the mid-1640s until 1660; vindictive Cavaliers, angry Nonconformists, and a dissolute court after the Restoration. As a vital link between an older England and the new one emerging after the middle of the century, Clarendon was at every point a major restraining influence. Some of the most dangerous political experiments in the century were conducted by former associates of his after he left them. But this long experience in opposition accustomed him to react to others rather than to initiate action himself.

Clarendon's shortcomings did not prevent him from making substantial contributions to English political life. Indeed, English history might well have followed a markedly different course had he not been Charles II's chief adviser in the mid-1650s and especially in the crucial year of 1660. As the major negotiator of the Restoration on the Royalist side, he helped to insure that England would remain a monarchy. At the same time, his terms recognized the rights of Parliament and protected its role in government. Above all, he reestablished the primacy of law, which events from 1640 to 1660 had so seriously undermined. After the Restoration, his insistence on a wide general indemnity for past acts laid a firm foundation for the long process of healing and reuniting the nation. But Clarendon could do no more to realize his own goals for England, because they proved to be unworkable in practice. English history from 1640 to 1688 is basically a series of adjustments, ongoing violent and nonviolent experiments seeking the necessary balance between legislative and executive powers for the government, along with the proper role for religion in the state. The compromises between King and Parliament made in 1640 and 1641, on which Clarendon based his political principles, required too tenuous and delicate a balance between the executive and the legislative and too selfless an effort from too many individuals to be a viable form of government.

Only at the Restoration, when all parties were momentarily willing to operate with the political generosity that Clarendon himself had always shown, was he able to make a beginning toward the kind of government he wanted. Even then he could not settle its operations securely in accordance with his own principles. To protect the monarchy, Clarendon managed to return Charles II to the throne with virtually no restrictions on royal power. Simultaneously, because of his belief in the importance of Parliamentary prerogatives—and probably also because of his knowledge of Charles' character—he left the King totally dependent on Parliament financially, thereby curbing his ability to exercise the power he had. (Typically, in the rush he failed to assure adequate support for the King; D. T. Witcombe has shown that from the beginning, the failure to assess existing debts, the miscalculation of the excise, and delays in developing efficient methods of collecting revenues left insufficient funds for the Court to function.) [107] The measures Clarendon had expected to safeguard the balance between monarchical and Parliamentary privileges produced instead a growing impasse, a stalemate between warring factions that led to government inefficiency and paralysis. Given his circumstances, Clarendon's tendency to work with the moment and his lack of theoretical rigor left him unable to see the insurmountable difficulties inherent in his principles.

Clarendon was not a man to give up. Unable satisfactorily to reconcile his ideals with circumstances throughout his career, he was also unwilling to admit that the two were irreconcilable. He had failed to move the nation very far toward the kind of society he desired, but with words he could make a final effort to keep his beliefs alive. He turned to history to try once more to create and to serve. Although he was more successful in historical writing than he had been in politics, he was nevertheless at times unable to control with words the events he had failed to control in life.

What happened to Clarendon the state servant recurred to a lesser extent with Clarendon the literary historiographer: his large vision on occasion faltered among details. For example, there is his famous digression on the Privy Council, in which his description of the kind of man who should serve ends with "and integrity above all." These last four words, the best-known part of the passage, were written into the original history at a later period (*HR*, 1:261). In the rush of writing, just as in the rush of business, Clarendon might occasionally neglect some of the most important things that he knew, believed in, and ultimately lived by. If the initial omission is characteristic, the later insertion is equally so; in writing, as in politics, he might momentarily forget, but he never lost his perspective for long. Alternatively, in certain sections the *History* becomes a mass of undigested detail as he crams too much information into unwieldy sentences. Such prolixity also leads his perspective to falter. Like Gibbon, who never synthesizes the various reasons he offers for Rome's decline into a consistent explanation of the empire's collapse, Clarendon in the final *History* describes each of at least half a dozen actions as the single source of England's calamities.[108] In his state service, Clarendon had sometimes focused on details rather than larger issues to avoid facing unpleasant truths about the men around him or about the serious flaws in his political ideas. (Another reason that he functioned most effectively in opposition and tended toward passivity was that a certain proportion of his energies was devoted to battling his own recognition of such truths.) Similarly, in his writing he occasionally amasses individual facts indiscriminately to escape facing the conclusions that effective marshaling of evidence would have produced, and the coherency of his narrative suffers accordingly.

At another level, however, the detail that creates literary difficulties in the *History* was necessary to fulfill one of Clarendon's major purposes in writing it. Clarendon wrote the *History of the Rebellion* for vindication, for instruction, and for memorialization. He wanted posterity to understand the past, to remember it, and to learn from it. But above all, he personally wanted to come to terms with what had happened to him and to all England. Even when he entertained hopes of posthumous publication, Clarendon was accustomed to view his writing as a private method of learning and of assimilating personal experience. He described the purpose of his essays as "the informing and exercising my own understanding," while the *Continuation of the Life* was "to serve only for a memorial to cast my own eyes upon, when I cannot but reflect upon those proceedings."[109] He had begun the original history in part for himself and his friends, "to comfort us in what we have done" (*HR*, 1:3). In his final exile, confronted with the ruins of a lifetime's devoted efforts, the only possible solace left for him was the acceptance which could come from the kind of comprehensive explanation of his experiences that would put his mind at ease—an explanation which, because of his own character and beliefs, would involve the history of the entire nation.

From the beginning, the readers that his history might eventually find were of secondary concern to Clarendon. Less than a year after he began the original history, he informed Bristol that "I have no hope of bringing this wild story within any reasonable bounds, to invite Readers by the smallness of the bulk." [110] The way in which the *History of the Rebellion* was written reflects the fact that Clarendon's primary audience was always in a real sense himself. Thus the periodic style that distances and controls experience collapsed into loose structures that reproduce experience as Clarendon tried to confront the past directly in order to understand it. Details were often piled on in his long sentences because in the process of personally coming to terms with events, he could not afford to neglect any piece of information he had as irrelevant. He wanted to consider all the possibilities for action and all their potential consequences. His emphasis on discourse as an element almost as important as story also reflected his needs as well as his interests; he could not describe events until he had thoroughly analyzed them for himself. His abbreviated dialectic allowed him to rethink events as he depicted them, clarifying problems in his own view about what actually happened. The act of writing was the process through which Clarendon struggled to come to terms fully and honestly with his past, and he employed the only prose style and narrative structure that were appropriate for his effort. He required any interested reader to assume no less of a burden than he had himself.

Ultimately, despite the stylistic and structural difficulties created by Clarendon's detailed quest for personal understanding, the *History of the Rebellion* is a greater literary work because he never entirely comprehended what had happened to him. *Religion and Policy*, his study of papal jurisdiction, shows what occurs when Clarendon is absolutely sure of his ground. His conclusion is that the popes lack a legitimate claim to temporal power and are therefore wrong to try to exercise any; he relentlessly illustrates it over and over again. As doctrinaire explanation takes over, he narrows his focus and argues by rote in uninteresting prose. In contrast, because of his own uncertainties, his *History* could not become formulaic. Instead Clarendon was forced to rely more heavily on literary means to come to terms with his experiences. He needed the abbreviated dialectic and the variable internal focalization to reconstruct the past in a form through which he personally could confront and comprehend it. Despite his controlled impersonality as a writer, the urgency of his own need to understand, rendered through the sense of struggle in the language and the structures he employs, gives the *History* an enormous authenticity. Moreover, the tragic implications of his experience, which Clarendon with his sanguineness, composure, and detachment always refused to acknowledge directly in his work or in his life, can clearly emerge in his text. The story he wants to tell, and tries to tell, is one of noble ideals doomed by ignoble circumstances. In the end, what he actually shows is that defeat was inevitable not only because of circumstances, but also because of basic flaws in the ideals themselves. The literary reconciliation that he attempted between the actual and his own principles is only partially successful. But in the process of trying to make it, he constructed another story of mythic validity about the tragic conflicts of public man.

Many of the literary tensions in the *History of the Rebellion* derive from tensions in Clarendon the man. And the fragmentation of his own sensibility paralleled the fragmentation of the times. His self-divisions—the loyalties to both King and Parliament, the adherence to Anglicanism and to the ecumenism of Great Tew, the idealism and the pragmatism—were in many ways those of his age as a whole, particularly of its best minds. Thus the *History* is the story of England's tragedy, and of Clarendon's own tragedy. Irrational forces overwhelmed the commonwealth. It was a time for visionaries or fanatics—for men like John Lilburne, Charles I, Cromwell, the Diggers and the Ranters, all the individuals and groups who would impose their own truth, their one way, on the nation. In such chaos, the rational man of good intentions found himself powerless. He could only wait, and hope, and do the best that he could with inadequate choices until the Furies subsided in a world that had gone out of control. With the distanced perspective produced by his experiences as an outsider and his subsumption of the private into the public, Clarendon rendered his personal struggles, which reflected microcosmically the agonies of a nation in transition, in a way that illumined the timeless within time.

4

Clarendon's Literary Background

He is the poorest type of historian who without experience or knowledge of good literature undertakes (with insufficient preparation) the writing of history. This is the most important criterion in the selection of historians.

> Jean Bodin, *Method for the Easy Comprehension of History*, 1565

Thus you see I please myself with the talk of books, and indeed desire nothing so much as to have leisure and leave in any corner to read them.

> Letter from Hyde to Nicholas, 1653

Yes, he [Clarendon] was a greate lover at least of books, & furnish'd a very ample library, writ himselfe an elegant style.

> Letter from John Evelyn to Samuel Pepys, 1689

The distinctions were only beginning to be made which for later ages shut off poetry from science, metaphor from fact, fancy from judgment. The point about these different worlds was not that they were divided, but that they were simultaneously available. The major interests of life had not as yet been mechanically apportioned to specialists, so that one must dedicate oneself wholly to fact, or wholly to value.

> Basil Willey, *The Seventeenth Century Background*

EARLY LITERARY ENDEAVORS AND FRIENDS

Clarendon's literary development reflected in miniature the general tendencies of his era. As Maurice Ashley notes, even in the first half of the seventeenth century, "religion and politics had been the topics dearest to prose writers and gradually submerged pure literature."[1] In his youth Clarendon was involved with poetry, drama, and belles-lettres generally—with those fields of aesthetic and intellectual endeavor that later centuries, with narrower concepts of what pursuits should be considered literary, called "literature," and that Clarendon himself usually described as "polite learning." These early experiences were formative in crucial ways, for throughout his life Clarendon continued to be associated with general literary and scholarly concerns. Literature ultimately became for him not an end in itself but a means to other ends, an integrating force among his disparate interests. The nature of Clarendon's relationship to literature, both in its evolution from his youth until his maturity and in its later manifestations, explains to a large extent the kind of role that literary art would assume in his *History*.

In Clarendon's dialogue on education, he wrote that time spent at the Inns of Court provides "a Breeding, that sure contributes as much to the making [of] wise Men, as any different Education that can be assigned."[2] It was there that his own connections with literature first emerge clearly, when he was a student at the Middle Temple in the late 1620s. Anthony Wood recorded that Hyde "in his younger years . . . was noted by some persons in the university for his polite learning, good language and poetry,"[3] but the reference is probably to reactions at Oxford to Hyde's achievements after he left. Although he had been at Magdalen College and received his bachelor's degree, Hyde himself viewed his years at Oxford as contributing little to any part of his intellectual development. In retrospect he wrote that at college he had been more noted for his potential than for any improvement of it there; he admitted that he had lacked "discipline," mentioning that his older brother gave him "some example" toward the "custome of drinking" then prevalent (*Life*, p. 6).[4]

The Inns of Court did not confine their residents exclusively to legal studies. They offered instruction in the liberal arts, urging students to view such studies as "an indispensable basis and complement to legal learning."[5] In dedicating *Every Man Out of his Humor* to the Inns, Ben Jonson called them the "Noblest Nourceries of Humanity"; Alfred Harbage has described them as furnishing "the nearest approach to a liberal education obtainable in England at the time."[6] The kind of loose and flexible course of study offered by the Inns and the diversity of their intellectual life often stimulated writing, while their convenient locations and quiet and pleasant settings made them ideal gathering spots for literary men in London. As a result, with only slight exaggeration, A. Wigfall Green has described the Inns of Court during the sixteenth and seventeenth centuries as "the center of literary activity in the nation."[7] By Hyde's time the student with literary inclinations (or pretensions) had become a stereotypical figure. A poem in 1628 depicted residents of Gray's Inn as "stuffed with Ballades, Masques and Rymes." Frances Lenton's character sketch of the typical student at the Inns included a strong preference for "Shakespeare's plaies instead of my Lord Coke";[8] such tastes were encouraged by theaters nearby on both sides of the river. Green observes that "many of the young lawyers thought, with Disraeli, that the law depresses but that literature exalts."[9] Hyde eventually became one of these young men, although it took a while for him to settle down.

In 1625 Hyde's uncle entered him into the Middle Temple, where his father had studied, but an outbreak of plague in London, followed by the long complications of an ague, prevented his establishment there until 1626. He spent his first year gaining "some experience" in "the license of those times" and confessed that he was "without great application to the study of the law for some years." When he studied at all, his efforts were expended on "polite learning and history" (*Life*, pp. 3, 7–8). His literary studies were enhanced by his associations. Hyde wrote in the *Life* that as a law student, his "chief acquaintance" were Ben Jonson and his circle (p. 25). Aside from John Selden and Charles Cotton (the father of the poet), the group he enumerates was of course predominantly literary: Sir Kenelm Digby, the courtier and man of letters who would edit Jonson's works; Thomas May, translator of Lucan and the *Georgics* and also a poet and dramatist in his own right; the lyric poet Thomas Carew; and John Vaughan, a law student who, like Hyde, "at that time indulged more to the politer learning" (*Life*, p. 28). As a young man in his late teens, Hyde was thus on the fringes of the group that collected around Jonson at the Devil Tavern at Temple Bar. In 1628, after about two years in London, Hyde indicated that he was beginning to devote more time to his legal studies, although "without declining the politer learning, to which his humour and his conversation kept him always very indulgent" (*Life*, p. 9). During that year his budding literary interests were undoubtedly stimulated when he shared his chambers at the Temple—complete with study, kitchen, and woodshed—with William Davenant.[10]

Because of Davenant, Hyde made his first excursion into poetry. He joined with seven others to produce commendatory verses to be printed before Davenant's play *The Tragedy of Albovine, King of the Lombards*. This lurid revenge drama, described by a sympathetic biographer of Davenant's as an "appalling performance,"[11] was an early effort that the theaters had wisely refused to produce. In 1629, after three of his other plays that had reached the stage had been either ignored or damned, Davenant decided that publishing *Albovine* with "such a battery of congratulatory verses as London had seldom seen" might brighten his prospects.[12] For one of the contributors, his chamber-mate was not only a natural choice, but potentially a profitable one; Davenant had already used Hyde's name, along with that of his uncle Nicholas Hyde, Chief Justice of the King's Bench, in a letter seeking preferment.[13] Most of the rest of the putative poets were also garnered from Davenant's friends at the Inns of Court. The results suggest that Roger Lorte was not the only one who was

> . . . but newly for thy sake
> A fierce Poet, and doubtlesse had been one
> Ne'r but for thee, or else had been unknowne.[14]

None of them subsequently attained poetic eminence, although Lorte produced a slim volume of Latin epigrams, William Habington praised his wife Lucy Herbert in his "Castara" poems, and Richard Clerke managed some vicarious poetic fame via a very early poem of Cowley's commemorating his death. Prose better served more than one member of the group, for Henry Blount later garnered some renown by recounting his travels to the Levant.[15]

Hyde's verses ask, "Can ought of mine / Inrich thy Volume?,"[16] and despite the shortcomings of Davenant's play, the question is a valid one. However, unlike some of his peers, he manages to minimize the embarrassing overwriting endemic among neophytes and writers of dedications; Hyde's effort is not the worst of the group. His reference to his "industrious accents" (l. 2) succinctly sums up both the strengths and the weaknesses of the poem. It is competent and workmanlike, but uninspired and somewhat laborious. References to Davenant's achievement in *Albovine* outlasting pyramids and marble reflect Horace and perhaps Shakespeare, albeit somewhat awkwardly when Hyde predicts that marble pillars will receive a funeral before Davenant's "great Muse" (ll. 4–6). Hyde's real talent, his natural political instinct, is suggested by his care to compliment not only the author but the dedicatee, the Earl of Somerset. How many people actually read Hyde's maiden foray into poetry is unclear, but copies of the edition are not common.[17] Coincidentally, both *Albovine* and Hyde were fated to end in prose. For the 1673 folio collection, the play's blank verse was rewritten in prose, an ironic conversion in view of one commendatory poet's assertion that *Albovine* had made him laugh at writers "that are so dull, to melt their thoughts in Prose."[18]

It is almost certain that Hyde made a final public appearance as a poet, this time in more distinguished company to praise a greater writer. In 1632, two unsigned elegies on John Donne appeared in the first edition of *Deaths Duell*, his last sermon. When with a few changes the two were reprinted along with other elegies at the end of Donne's 1633 *Poems*, the second had acquired the title "On the death of Dr Donne" and the signature of "Edw. Hyde."[19] Although early editors attributed the poem to Edward Hyde, D.D., a Cambridge divine who was a cousin of Clarendon's, more recent commentators have reclaimed the poem for Clarendon himself. In making the case, John Sampson cited earlier attributions and Clarendon's other literary activities, arguing that the divine, who usually spelled his name "Hide," was in 1632 an obscure frequenter of Cambridge academic circles.[20] In addition, it is significant that Hide's other known poems are all in Latin. Sir Geoffrey Keynes also noted a manuscript collection of the poems of Donne and Strode that included several signatures of the young Hyde, along with doodling that suggested his authorship of the poem. On the basis of the handwriting, Keynes concluded that Hyde first owned the manuscript when he was under twenty years old,[21] a pre-1629 dating that accords well with what is known of Hyde's literary interests at the time.

There is no indication that Hyde knew Donne personally. Indeed, the opening line of the poem may well imply that the writer is not among Donne's close friends. However, a portrait of Donne was included in Clarendon's collection, and he also knew Donne's religious writings.[22] In 1641 Donne's son wrote to Hyde asking for advice on a petition to the Commons concerning legal problems with one of his livings, a move that might suggest some prior acquaintance.[23] Among the elegists in the 1633 *Poems* were Falkland and several poets associated with his group: Carew, Godolphin, Jasper Mayne, and Endymion Porter. But why verses by Hyde would have appeared earlier in *Deaths Duell* along with those of Henry King, Donne's executor and intimate friend who was involved in the publication of the sermon, remains puzzling. King's friends included some of the men Hyde knew: Ben Jonson, George Sandys from the Tew group, and Henry Blount from the *Albovine* poets.[24] Nevertheless, no evidence exists that he and Hyde were acquainted.

Hyde's poem shows a marked improvement over the verses to Davenant three years before. It is a longer and more sophisticated effort, less straightforward in language and structure, and, appropriately for the subject, more metaphysical than the *Albovine* poem. In it Hyde manages some felicitous expressions, such as the "busie gathering friend" in line nine, as well as an effective concluding couplet. He shows some cleverness, although the major themes of the poem—Donne's exhaustion of the language of wit, his dual excellence as poet and divine, and the inadequacy of any poet except Donne himself to write in his praise—appear in almost all of the elegies.[25] Among poets far more able than the *Albovine* group, Hyde does not disgrace himself, although the elegy does not prompt great regret that henceforth he would confine himself to prose.

Despite such literary endeavors, during the early 1630s Hyde had become more involved with legal concerns, although his vacations were still devoted entirely to general study and conversation. Even as he prospered in the law, he emphasized that "he would never suffer himself to be deprived of some hours (which commonly he borrowed from the night) to refresh himself with polite learning, in which he still made some progress" (*Life*, p. 24). However, as time passed he found less time for such pursuits. From working at law "with no more passion than was necessary to keep up the reputation of a man that had no purpose to be idle," he grew "more retired to his more serious [legal] studies" and "more intent on business and more engaged in practice, so that he could not assign so much time as he had used to do to his beloved conversation" (*Life*, pp. 49–50, 31, 51). One consequence was the loosening of his ties with the Jonson circle. Although he continued his friendships with members of the group, he spent less time with them. In doing so, he alienated Jonson himself, who, Hyde explained, "had for many years an extraordinary kindness for Mr. Hyde, till he found he betook himself to business, which he believed ought never to be preferred before his company" (*Life*, p. 26). The gradual shifting of Hyde's interests is clear when he notes that the only one among Jonson's group to whom he continued to devote substantial amounts of time was John Selden. The great scholar's moderation, constitutionalism, and massive historical sense were vital influences on Hyde's development into a politician and a historian.

One of Hyde's activities in 1634 illustrates the merging of literary concerns into legal and political ones that was characteristic of these years of transition for him. Like his predecessor Bacon,[26] he became involved with a masque that the four Inns of Court joined together to produce for Charles I and Henrietta Maria. It had long been the custom for the Inns to entertain monarchs with various performances; ever since *Gorboduc*, they had been an influential force in English drama, particularly in the masque. On this occasion, the recent birth of the Duke of York furnished an additional incentive.[27] However, the most immediate stimulus for the masque was *Histriomastix*, the violent attack on plays written by William Prynne, who happened to be a barrister at Lincoln's Inn. Problems had arisen because Prynne in opposing female performers had associated them with whores. When the Queen appeared in a pastoral at Somerset House, Laud and various enemies who were eager to punish Prynne for other reasons convinced the authorities that Prynne had slurred the Crown, even though his work had been published six weeks before Henrietta Maria's foray onto the stage.[28]

Shorn of his ears, set in the pillory, fined £5,000, deprived of his university degree, disbarred from the legal profession, expelled from Lincoln's Inn, and imprisoned for life, the hapless Prynne still remained an embarrassment to his fellow members of the Inns of Court. Bulstrode Whitelocke's *Memorials* contain a detailed account of the Inns' decision to make amends to the Crown for their errant ex-associate by presenting James Shirley's *The Triumph of Peace* "as an expression of their love and duty to their majesties." According to Whitelocke, the plan particularly appealed to the younger members of the Inns, men who, like Hyde, were already involved in literary endeavors. In order "to have this solemnity performed in the noblest and most stately manner that could be invented," Whitelocke explained that each Inn picked two of its members who were judged "fittest for such a business" as a committee to plan and direct the masque.[29] Hyde was chosen from the Middle Temple. His associations with dramatists were perhaps a factor in his selection; he may well have already known Shirley, for Davenant and some of the *Albovine* poets had many connections with residents of Gray's Inn, where Shirley was living at the time.[30] But that in this instance politics was as important as drama was shown by the presence on the planning committee of Attorney General Noy, notorious for his connection with ship money, and Sir John Finch, who as Speaker of the House a few years earlier had been held down in his chair by Holles and others to prevent his adjourning the session at the King's command. In fact, four of the eight members of the committee subsequently became Keepers of the Great Seal.[31]

The committee had heavy responsibilities. Shirley's first and best masque required more than three months of preparation, including weeks of rehearsals when a contemporary described the Inns as "all turned into dancing schools." [32] *The Triumph of Peace* has been described as "the most spectacular masque presented by the Inns of Court, and perhaps the most luxurious ever produced in England." [33] Estimates of its cost range from £21,000 to £24,000, an astronomical sum if Green is correct in estimating that £24,000 was about the equivalent of a million American dollars in 1931. [34] Even at the time, one of the Earl of Strafford's correspondents bemoaned the expense: "Oh that they would once give over these Things, or lay them aside for a Time, and bend all their Endeavours to make the King Rich!" [35] Whitelocke wrote that the committee "took great pains, and neglected no meetings for the management of this great business." Unfortunately, there is no record that indicates on which of the four subcommittees—script, dancing, properties, and music—Hyde served. When the production was almost ready, he and Whitelocke were chosen to meet with the Lord Chamberlain and the Comptroller of the King's Household to coordinate all the arrangements. The two also supervised final preparations in the Banqueting House, where the masque was staged. [36]

The evening began with a magnificent procession of members of the Inns from Ely House in Holborn down Chancery Lane to Whitehall. A contemporary poet wrote that when he first saw "all the glitteringe of this comely traine," he believed "the silver age was now returned againe." [37] *The Triumph of Peace* seems to have been a great success, apparently unmarred by a scuffle in which the Earl of Pembroke cracked his staff over the shoulders of Hyde's friend Tom May. [38] With music by William Lawes and Simon Ives, and scenery by Inigo Jones, the masque was judged by Whitelocke as "incomparably performed." He also felt that the music "excelled any . . . that ever before that time had been heard in England"—a not surprising reaction, since he himself had chaired that particular subcommittee. [39] Strafford's correspondent wrote that the production "far exceeded in Bravery any Masque that had formerly been presented by those Societies." [40] The Queen, who claimed she had never seen a nobler masque, was so delighted that she requested another performance of it. [41] Even the audience contributed to the sumptuous effects; in his preface to the first edition of his work, Shirley recalled with pride that they "gave a great grace to this spectacle, especially being all richly attired." [42] A few weeks after the production, Hyde was among those from the planning committee sent to thank the King and Queen on behalf of the Inns of Court for their kindness in accepting and attending the masque. [43] He must have been proud of the successful merger of art and politics in which he had played an important role.

For the sake of professional advancement, Hyde had been willing to let his friendships with Jonson's circle lapse. In contrast, no matter how busy he became, he maintained and strengthened his ties with Falkland's group at Great Tew. These connections began a few years after those with the Jonson circle; Hyde himself dated his "most entire friendship without reserve" with Falkland from 1630 (*Life*, p. 31). Most of the men around Jonson had been older than Hyde, guides and mentors rather than equals. Falkland and his group were closer to Hyde's own age, and many of them more compatibly reflected his changing interests.

Falkland had a number of literary associations.[44] A poet himself, he had been "sealed of the tribe of Ben," and kept in close contact with Jonson.[45] He also loved the theater and dramatic works.[46] Among his friends were some of the same writers Hyde had known in the Jonson group: Carew and Digby, along with Selden and Vaughan; the connections between Great Tew and the Jonson circle reflect how closely knit English literary society of the time tended to be. Falkland knew Henry Killigrew, the dramatist and poet. Another friend was Sir John Suckling, whom Hyde probably also knew, since Suckling and Davenant were very close. In addition, Falkland was acquainted with John Donne; in Drury Lane Donne had occupied lodgings very near the house leased by Falkland's grandfather, with whom the young Falkland had spent much time.[47] The poets Edmund Waller, Sidney Godolphin, and George Sandys (who was also the translator of Ovid's *Metamorphoses*) were frequent guests at Tew. Falkland may have met Abraham Cowley during the late 1630s; in any case, he came to know the poet well when both were at Royalist headquarters, along with Hyde, at Oxford in 1643/4. Not all of these literary men actually journeyed to Tew, for Falkland saw some of them on visits to London. His longest sojourn in the city during this period occurred in the winter of 1633/4, when he was settling affairs after his father's death.[48] Hyde was by this time a close friend, and it is not unreasonable to expect that he met the literary men Falkland knew in London as well as in Oxfordshire, particularly in view of the overlaps between the Jonson and Tew circles.

Significantly, in all that he wrote about Falkland, Hyde never mentions his poems. In the *Life* he assesses in detail the scholarly accomplishments and intellectual abilities of the Tew group; in contrast, literature arises only three times in his character sketches of them. (He briefly praises Waller's poetry, Earle's poems and prose, and Morley's abilities in "all polite learning" [*Life*, pp. 40, 43, 42].) He entirely omits Sandys and other literary men who are known to have spent time at Tew, and he never indicates that Godolphin was a poet. In delineating the circle, he includes Waller and Godolphin, but focuses mainly on the scholars and the divines: Gilbert Sheldon, John Hales of Eton, William Chillingworth, George Morley, and John Earle, along with Sir Francis Wenman, the country gentleman who was Falkland's neighbor (*Life*, pp. 31, 36). Even into this more saintly group, however, the Muses had made inroads. Thus Hales, Wenman, Chillingworth, and Selden are among those assembled for "the trial for the bays" in Suckling's "The Wits" ("A Sessions [*sic*] of the Poets"),[49] although presumably because of their literary associations or critical abilities rather than for any poetry of their own.

Hyde's list is incomplete in part because he was focusing only on the men he knew and liked best at Tew. He omits several divines known to have visited there, and—undoubtedly because Hyde disapproved of his later activities—he also leaves out Thomas Hobbes, who "made himself a trying guest" by doing geometry problems in bed, with figures drawn on his thighs and the sheets.[50] However, Hyde's account depicts not only the men who were the most congenial to him, but also those for whose activities Tew is most famous. Despite Falkland's many literary ties, it is not primarily for belles-lettres that he and Great Tew are remembered.

More gradually than Hyde, but just as surely, Falkland during the middle years of the 1630s had begun to turn away from poetry and other strictly literary concerns. He became increasingly immersed in theological issues, particularly questions of religious authority, tolerance, and the role of reason in religion. By 1637, Suckling remarked the change in Falkland:

> He was of late so gone with Divinity
> That he had almost forgot his Poetry;
> Though to say the truth (and *Apollo* did know it)
> He might have been both his Priest and his Poet.[51]

In 1638 Falkland himself referred to his "dying Muse,"[52] although he still occasionally wrote poems. Others in the Tew group with early literary connections followed a similar path. Robert Cresswell thanked Falkland in 1638 for encouraging him to study divinity rather than poetry and indicated that the change had been a profitable one.[53] Wood recorded that Earle's "younger years were adorned with oratory, poetry, and witty fancies; and his elder with quaint preaching and subtile disputes."[54] Morley, an ascetic in his old age, had when young been a capable poet who enjoyed the reputation of being a son of Ben; Jasper Mayne had been a poet and dramatist. Like Falkland's London friend Henry Killigrew, all these men left literary activities for theology and became distinguished divines.[55] Even Hobbes had enjoyed some early literary fame as a translator of Thucydides, although his divergence from literature took other directions than the religious ones of most at Tew.

Many in the early seventeenth century considered literature, and more particularly poetry, as a natural and even laudable pursuit for the young that should be abandoned at maturity. Archbishop Ussher explained that as a boy he had been "extremely addicted to poetry," but that "he shook it off" when he was older for "more resolved, serious and profitable studies."[56] Clarendon also felt that poetry was most appropriate for younger men. He wrote of Waller that "at the age when other men used to give over writing verses, (for he was near thirty years of age when he first engaged himself in that exercise, at least that he was known to do so,) he surprised the town with two or three pieces of that kind; as if a tenth muse had been newly born, to cherish drooping poetry" (*Life*, p. 40). Waller would have been about thirty during the period from 1635 to 1637, exactly the time when Hyde's own waning interest in poetry might lead him to describe it as "drooping." Poetic endeavors were seen as lacking the dignity necessary for those of stature in the world. Hyde's mentor Selden was outspoken on the subject:

'Tis ridiculous for a Lord to Print Verses, 'tis well enough to make them to please himself, but to make them publick, is foolish. If a man in his private Chamber twirls his Bandstrings, or plays with a Rush to please himself, 'tis well enough, but if he should go into *Fleet street*, and sit upon a Stall, and twirl a Bandstring, or play with a Rush, then all the Boys in the Street would laugh at him.[57]

Various members of the Tew group discovered, as Donne had earlier, that youthful poetry could later become a professional liability. Jasper Mayne by 1653 was refusing to write prefatory verses, in part because his published poems had been criticized as unbefitting a divine;[58] Hyde noted that Earle suppressed many of his "incomparably good" poems "out of an austerity to those sallies of his youth" (*Life*, p. 43).

Hyde's view of poetry and "polite learning" as youthful pursuits that were incongruous with serious business could only have been strengthened over the years by his experiences with literary men in politics. Many of those he knew became involved in state affairs during the civil wars and the Interregnum. Charles I himself had advised Sir John Denham "to abstain from versifying while engaged in politics,"[59] although in general, the record suggests that the poets might more profitably have stayed with their versifying. Hyde's opinion of the role of the literati and their contributions could hardly have been a positive one. His former friend Tom May opposed the King during the civil wars, ultimately writing his history for the Parliament. Within the Royalist camp, many literary men were associated with Henrietta Maria and her group at the Louvre, who bitterly opposed Hyde. Davenant, who at the Queen's request had received the laureateship after Jonson's death, was one of the group sent to remove Charles II from Jersey; Cowley served as secretary to Henry Jermyn and Henrietta Maria; Sir Kenelm Digby was appointed her Chancellor.[60] Several of the literati vacillated in their allegiances. In 1656 Digby's connections with Cromwell were noted by Hyde in a political pamphlet,[61] and after Cowley's return to England in the same year, the Royalists questioned his loyalty. Waller proved the worst, with his ineptness in the 1643 plot that bears his name exceeded only by his pusillanimity in informing on his associates to save himself. In the original history, Hyde confined himself to noting Waller's "unhappy demeanour in this time of his affliction" (*HR*, 3:51). But when he came to write the *Life*, probably influenced by his former friend's role in his impeachment, he more strongly denounced the poet's "miserable behavior," describing Waller's submissive speech to the Parliament as showing "such a meanness and lowness of spirit that life itself was no recompense for it" (p. 65).

Even among the literary men who remained faithful to the Royalists, attachments to belles-lettres often directly hampered their political effectiveness. Lord Norwich's jesting postscript in a letter to Hyde about having "already read : 7 : of ten vollumes" of romances in order to make him "valliant enough to releive ye seege of Exceter"[62] reflects the prevailing opinion that literature was not the best preparation for dealing with political realities. Describing the Marquis of Newcastle as "amorous in poetry and music, to which he indulged the greatest part of his time," Hyde commented that "many inconveniences fell out" for the Royalists because of their general's refusal to interrupt his artistic activities for pressing military business (*HR*, 3:381, 383). (Sir Philip Warwick more bluntly explained that Newcastle "had the misfortune to have somewhat of the poet in him.")[63] Ballads joked about Suckling's cowardliness as a soldier against the Scots,[64] and as a plotter he showed no more prowess, although substantially more integrity, than Waller. Davenant, appropriately enough chosen by the poetic Newcastle as his Lieutenant General of the Ordnance, began his political career as a participant in Suckling's plot and earned a reputation for inefficiency both as a munitions transporter and as a diplomatic envoy. Hyde's depiction of Davenant's numerous blunderings through a disastrous interview with Charles I as the Queen's emissary has been judged as overstated by the poet's biographers,[65] but it reflects Hyde's general attitude toward literary men in politics: Davenant was "an honest man and a witty, but in all respects inferior to such a trust" (*HR*, 4:205). Hyde's experiences during the 1640s and 1650s offered him no incentive to return to belles-lettres as a useful adjunct to political endeavors.

Even had the literati proved to be more politically adept, the dubious morals of many of them would have deeply disturbed Hyde as he matured. The behavior of Jonson's circle fell far short of both their leader's lofty moral ideals and Hyde's later personal standards. Digby had his notorious relationship with Venetia Stanley; May was a rake; Davenant's nose had been sacrificed to venereal disease; Suckling admitted that he "loved not the Muses as well as his sport."[66] Hyde's verdict on Carew's life and talents reveals his priorities:

He . . . made many poems, (especially in the amorous way,) which for the sharpness of the fancy, and the elegancy of the language in which that fancy was spread, were at least equal, if not superior to any of that time: but his glory was, that after fifty years of his life, spent with less severity or exactness than it ought to have been, he died with the greatest remorse for that license, and with the greatest manifestation of Christianity, that his best friends could desire. (*Life*, pp. 30–31)

Given such attitudes, one can only regret that Clarendon missed Rochester's deathbed conversion. Indeed, if the morals and characters of many of the literati offended Hyde before the Restoration, they could only have provided nightmares for him after 1660. With Buckingham and Rochester leading the pack, the debauchery of the literary men in Charles II's court has become legend. Moreover, their tendency to congregate around Lady Castlemaine added political ramifications to moral chaos. Little in Hyde's life after the Tew years could have encouraged him to view literature in itself as a safe, dignified, moral, or useful pursuit for upright men of business.

The major shift of Hyde's interests and efforts away from strictly literary concerns seems to have come in 1634. In July of that year he married, an event he later emphasized as crucial in his turn toward the law:

"From the time of his marriage he laid aside all other thoughts but of his profession" (*Life*, p. 14). In December he was appointed Keeper of the Writs and Rolls of the Common Pleas. His new priorities were apparent by 1637, when he did not join Falkland, other friends from Tew (Waller, Godolphin, Mayne), and earlier acquaintances (Habington, May) in contributing elegies in memory of Ben Jonson.[67] His account of his early years in the *Life* ends when he "grew so much in love with [legal] business and practice, that he gave up his whole heart to it; resolving, by a course of severe study, to recover the time he had lost upon less profitable learning" (p. 56). Thematically, the move from literary to professional concerns provides a convenient line of narrative development in the *Life* for his early experiences. The pattern is neatly Pauline: as a young man he loves poetry and polite learning, and when he becomes a man, he puts away childish things. At the most basic level, the account is accurate; Hyde would never again be concerned with pure literature, with literature for its own sake or for ornamental and aesthetic use. But although the break with poetic dabbling and other such pursuits was complete, the break with attitudes and endeavors that were literary in a more general sense was not, just as the move from the Jonson to the Tew circle was not as much of an abandonment of literature as Hyde's account might imply. After the mid-1630s Hyde would have a different kind of relationship to literature, more distant and less specifically belletristic, but concomitantly more fruitful for his historical work than the conventional relationship of his youth could have been.

THE LITERARY PROGRESSION: FROM POETRY TO HISTORY

Literature remained a part of Hyde's life in his later years. Indeed, its importance in his own view of himself is shown by the emphasis he placed on his early literary studies and friendships in the *Life*. For a man who reveals so very little in his writing about his personal activities and interests, his lengthy and detailed treatment suggests the significant role that literature played in his own self-concept. Moreover, although he might view poetry and "polite learning" as young men's pursuits, he recognized their formative value for the individual. Thus in accounting for Sir John Colepeper's personal shortcomings, he attributed them in part to

Colepeper's "having never sacrificed to the Muses" (*Life*, p. 80). In Hyde's view, literary experience was important for molding men with the character and attributes necessary for effective participation in national life; his description of Puritan reforms at Oxford as endeavors "to extinguish all good literature and allegiance" (*HR*, 4:259) is no mere syllepsis. He listed literature along with education, industry, and a love of virtue among the qualifications that were vital for a minister of state (*HR*, 3:227).

Clarendon's collection of portraits also reflects his later stance toward literature. Although courtiers and state servants make up the bulk of what Evelyn described as an "Assembly of the Learned and Heroic persons of England," the collection also included some literary figures.[68] Significantly, the portraits Evelyn noted as "most agreeable to his Lᵖˢ general humor" were those of the literary men. Evelyn's list begins with "old Chaucer," whom Clarendon mentions parenthetically in the *History* when the Royalists garrisoned Donnington Castle, "a house of John Packer's, but more famous for having been the seat of Geoffrey Chaucer" (3:176). There were also portraits of Shakespeare, Beaumont and Fletcher, and Spenser.[69] Among contemporary poets, the inclusion of Waller despite his early apostacies suggests that only his participation in the impeachment finally turned Clarendon away from his old friend. "Hudibras," whom Clarendon quotes in his answer to *Leviathan*,[70] and the inevitable Cowley, whom Clarendon, with the age, believed had "made a flight beyond all men" (*Life*, p. 26), complete Evelyn's list. Butler, whose merging of literature and politics would have been particularly congenial to Clarendon, was placed, according to Evelyn, "in the roome where he us'd to eate & dine in publiq." Sidney, Raleigh, Donne, Bacon, Hooker, and More were also in the collection, although Evelyn enumerates them in nonliterary categories. Lady Theresa Lewis adds portraits of Ben Jonson and Sir Kenelm Digby to the group.[71] Clarendon's collection, and particularly the attitude toward the literary portraits that Evelyn recorded, indicate that literature retained a small but secure place in his world view.

Moreover, a pattern of association with literature and general literary activities runs through the rest of Hyde's life. He always maintained the reputation of an excellent writer, an avid reader, and a lover of books. "No man borrows Bookes so sildome as I doe, nor doe I in truth ever borrow any yᵗ I can buy," Hyde wrote to one of his correspondents in 1659.[72] He was not overstating. From at least 1637, when he was considering buying books from Bishop Williams' library,[73] and undoubtedly earlier, Clarendon was a dedicated book collector. The orders from Westminster in 1644 assigning his chambers in the Middle Temple to a Parliamentary loyalist mention "his printed books and manuscripts."[74] The *History* includes a glimpse of Cottington conferring with the Spanish President while Hyde peruses the books in the President's library, the finest private collection in Madrid (*HR*, 5:154). He also amassed a good collection of Spanish books of his own.

After the Restoration a petitioner wrote to Clarendon that it was reported around town that he was so great a lover of learning that he had "beene seene byond seas to have beene oftentimes buisy in buying of Books, when t'was coniectur'd by many that yor L^{d}s^{ipp} did in a manner want monie to buy Bread."[75] His letters during the Royalist exile are filled with requests for books: friends, relatives, spies, ambassadors, and merchants were enlisted to locate and ship the volumes he wanted. The scramble was unending. In Livorno, the King's Resident in Italy procured a book prohibited in Venice, which Secretary Nicholas had told him that Hyde wanted, and shipped it to a Scottish merchant in Amsterdam.[76] Nicholas' son John was asked to supply catalogues of all of Vossius' and Salmasius' works.[77] From Brussels Bristol snapped characteristically that the usual custom when requesting anything was to write its name legibly, and that he would make every effort to find what Hyde wanted as soon as he could read the title of the book.[78] Hyde's demands reflected his varied interests, and also his turn from strictly literary concerns to political, religious, and historical ones: "twelve tomes of Baronius," de la Vega's *History of Peru*, "the Italian dictionary just printed at London," Sextus Empiricus, the lives of Cardinal Richelieu and Philip III, *Assertor Gallicus Contra Chiffletium*, Stowe's *Chronicle*, "the Acts of Parliament" in 1658, Latin histories of Denmark and the German principalities and emperors.[79] About a month before the Restoration he tried to get a bookbinder to return with the Royalists to England in order to "teach our countrymen his art, which they have not yet arrived to."[80] Later, the sole gift he took from Louis XIV was copies of all the books printed at the Louvre.[81] Only in his final exile is there no record of Clarendon's buying books for himself, probably because of financial difficulties. Even then he bought vicariously, negotiating the purchase of an annotated Josephus for the Delegates of the Oxford University Press.[82]

Clarendon was also known as a friend to literary and intellectual endeavors. P. H. Hardacre points out that during the Royalist exile, Hyde encouraged others in their writing.[83] When he became Chancellor of Oxford after the Restoration, Robert Whitehall's verses saluted him as one "by whose beams Our Muses thrive."[84] However far politics had taken him from his early poetic proclivities, literary men had no intention of allowing either Clarendon or others to forget them. In dedicating *The Siege of Rhodes* to him, Davenant referred to the Chancellor's employment of his abilities years before "to vindicate authors,"[85] undoubtedly a reference to *Albovine*. Davenant's prologue for a special performance of Sir Samuel Tuke's *The Adventures of Five Hours*, at which Clarendon was the guest of honor, depicted him in his "early youth" as "Patron and as Censor too of Wit."[86] Similarly, Dryden's New Year's poem to Clarendon in 1662 discussed the Chancellor's "early courtship" of the Muses.[87] Not without some indulgence in wish fulfillment, Dryden portrays Clarendon's former "Mistresses" (l. 8) sharing in the Chancellor's exaltation, as cardinals do in the Pope's:

> For still they look on you with such kind eyes
> As those that see the Churches Soveraign rise
> From their own Order chose, in whose high State
> They think themselves the second choice of Fate.
> When our Great Monarch into Exile went
> Wit and Religion suffer'd banishment:
> . . .
> At length the Muses stand restor'd again
> To that great charge which Nature did ordain;
> And their lov'd Druyds seem reviv'd by Fate,
> While you dispence the Laws and guide the State.
>
> (ll. 13–18, 23–26)

After Clarendon's death, a monumental inscription and an elegy commemorated him as "*Musarum Comes, Idemq Candidatus*" and "*Musarum Parens / Bonis, et Litteratis venerandus.*"[88]

Of course, some of the panegyrics were merely self-interested attempts to flatter a powerful potential patron. But accolades to Clarendon's participation in literary and learned endeavors did not rest solely on his youthful forays at the Inns. At other times Hyde had turned to books, study, and writing. In his years on Jersey, alone except for the friendship of Sir George Carteret, able to afford only one good meal a day, Hyde spent three hours daily writing the original history and devoted his remaining hours to "other study and books."[89] With time on his hands during the fruitless embassy to Spain, "the less of business he had, he was the more vacant to study the language and the manners and the government of that nation" (*CL*, 2:565). On that mission he began writing his meditations on the Psalms. In his final exile he completed that work, and in addition to the *Life* and the final *History*, composed *Religion and Polity*, his answers to Hobbes and Cressy, most of his essays, and probably his dialogues. He also learned Italian and French for reading. After Clarendon's death, Dr. Stephen Gough wrote that during his last years the former Chancellor "was pleased to entertaine a particular and kind commerce with me by ample letters in literary matters."[90]

Clarendon's priority was always action rather than contemplation. In a letter to the Prince of Wales, he wrote that the solitude on Jersey was necessary for work on his history, "since a head no better composed than mine, would have been hardly vacant to it, in a greater noise and diversity of thoughts."[91] Self-denigration aside, the record shows that books inevitably gave way to business whenever the opportunity arose for Hyde. At the same time, his letters from the periods when he was engaged in reading and writing leave no doubt of the substantial pleasure and contentment he derived from literary and scholarly pursuits. During the Royalist exile Hyde constantly expressed his desire to retreat into a life of study: "God of Heaven send . . . me into any quiet corner of the world with bread and books"; "I wish I were quiet at my book in any part of the world, for I am not for these conflicts."[92] Study was in part a consoling prospect in the midst of continual troubles: "I am persuaded, if I might be quiet and left to my books I should outlive this storm."[93] More centrally, however, it was for Hyde a personally sustaining activity: "While I have Bread and Bookes, I shall thinke my selfe very rich."[94] The genuine intellectual interest and commitment motivating him are clear in an ironically phrased aside in one letter to Nicholas: "And do you not think me a very foolish fellow, now there are so many ordinances against justice and learning, that I spend my time in studying Law and Greek, neglecting to get so much French as may serve to beg with when I am driven into that Country? but I will grow wiser."[95] Although it is true that throughout Hyde's career scholarship and literary pursuits were always an alternative, a substitute for political activity more than an adjunct to it, it is equally true that they were an alternative he genuinely loved, one which was extremely important to him personally.

Tracing precisely the role of literature in Hyde's endeavors is more complicated after his turn away from belles-lettres in the mid-1630s, because literature became subsumed as one element within the context of his broadening general concerns. A few years after the Restoration, Samuel Sorbière in his *Relation d'un Voyage en Angleterre* admitted Clarendon's legal ability and eloquence but wrote that he was "ignorant of the *Belles Lettres*." Accusing Sorbière of disliking "*our Statesmen for not being Gram-*

marians and Criticks," Thomas Sprat's reply strongly defended Clarendon: "Whence did he fetch this Idea of Eloquence? Let him produce his Notes out of *Aristotle, Tully, Quintilian, Seneca,* or any of the Rhetoricians of Antiquity, and then let him tell me whether they do not all with one Voice consent that an Orator must of necessity be acquainted with all Sorts of useful Knowledge?" Of all the English statesmen, Sprat continued, "there was never any Man that has so much resembled Sir *Thomas More,* and the Lord *Bacon,* in their several Excellencies, as the Earl of *Clarendon.*"[96] Sprat correctly defends Clarendon's literary knowledge in the context of his general intellectual attainments rather than as an isolated achievement. Clarendon's versatility came from his ability to integrate his disparate experiences and interests. He managed to unite both scholarly and literary elements in his *History* because he maintained an interest in literature even while changing his major focus to legal, religious, and political concerns.

The extended treatment of the theater in Clarendon's dialogue on education is a good illustration of his characteristic approaches. Moral and quasi-theological issues surface almost immediately in a debate about the propriety of women appearing on the stage and possible theatrical violations of Biblical sanctions against one sex wearing the clothing of the other (Deuteronomy 22:5). The dialogue strongly defends the theater and playgoing, but on practical rather than literary grounds. Clarendon's belief in the need for a balanced life emerges as one speaker insists that plays can supply the relaxation and diversion that the mind as well as the body requires: "the Noise of the Stage . . . [gives] great Life to the Silence of the Study."[97] In addition to the benefits the theater offers to individuals, the dialogue elaborates on its vital role in the state. To Clarendon, men's "natural Inclinations to Gazing and Spectacles" are a political concern: "It is amongst the greatest and most difficult Mysteries of Government to bring the People together to Recreations and Spectacles, which may delight and inform, and cannot hurt them." For such appetites, he considers plays an ideal outlet. Years of civil war turmoil echo in the background as he writes of the theater: "No Man ever plotted against the State there, or contrived how to ruin the Church in those Assemblies; and I much doubt whether so many People meet so innocently together in any other Place."[98]

Not surprisingly, this dialogue shows that the aesthetic element most important to Clarendon is dramatic realism. The London theaters are praised because there "Action and Representation, Words and Perspectives appear with the most Life and Vivacity, and with the least Violence offer'd to Nature, that have been ever yet offer'd to the World in any Part of it."[99] Clarendon's primary concern is the relationship of drama and the theater to everyday life. He constantly assimilates literary issues into wider personal and national contexts. Similarly, when one speaker recommends that students in grammar schools and universities present more plays both in Latin and in English, he emphasizes the value of such productions for developing talents in public speaking.[100] Clarendon always viewed any learning that was merely academic, that had no direct connection with human affairs, as potentially dangerous to its possessor and to others. Remarks in all his writings denigrate mere "drudgery in Books," emphasizing the limitations of those whose knowledge has been gained solely through study.[101] He disliked isolating learning of any kind from life, and literature was no exception.

Clarendon's reading suggests the nature of his literary concerns after the mid-1630s and the ways in which they merged with his other interests. From Clarendon's correspondence, Hardacre concluded that "closest to his heart were the 16th- and 17th-century historians and religio-political controversialists."[102] However, these were hardly the writers to help him in evolving an effective literary style for history. Clarendon bought these authors and he read them, but the extant records of his reading—two commonplace books and the published catalogue of manuscripts he wrote during his final exile—indicate that more recent historians and religious and political polemicists were not all that he read. The earliest commonplace book (MS. Clarendon 127) was probably written mainly during the middle or late 1630s.[103] The second commonplace book (MS. Clarendon 126, most of which was compiled on Jersey from 1646 to 1648)[104] and the 1764 sale catalogue of his manuscripts are particularly valuable because they cover the periods when he was writing the original history and the final *History of the Rebellion*. These records obviously do not cover all of Hyde's reading, particularly the occasional contemporary pieces that he perused as a matter of course whenever he could get them. (In 1647, for example, he told Nicholas that he had been reading Lilburne, Prynne, and Milton's divorce tracts: "In earnest I find a great benefit by reading ill books, for though they want judgment and logick to prove what they promise, yet they bring good materials to prove somewhat else they do not think of.")[105] What the commonplace books and the list of manuscripts reveal are the works Hyde considered important enough to spend time and effort excerpting in detail.

The strong historical and political overtones of Barclay's *Argenis*, the Latin romance that opens the earliest commonplace book,[106] reflect the subsumption of literary interests into other concerns that was characteristic of Hyde from the mid-1630s onward. His steadily increasing interest in religious matters and theological controversy emerges clearly. No such writings appear in the first commonplace book. In the second, four out of the eleven writers he read on Jersey are religious controversialists or historians, although extracts from them occupy only about a quarter of the pages he wrote.[107] By the time of his final exile, works concerning religion predominate in the manuscripts, both because of his own interests and particularly because of the research required for his work on the papacy.

In the three records of Clarendon's reading and writing, the authors who have the clearest claims to be considered primarily literary are Cicero and Seneca, both of whom are quoted several times in the *History of the Rebellion*.[108] From Seneca, the third writer he excerpted during his final exile, Clarendon wrote seventy-five pages of extracts, complete with an index.[109] As early as 1646 he had praised Seneca's "excellent morality,"[110] but in 1668 Clarendon was also using him for literary purposes. At the time he was writing his own essays; he often quotes Seneca in them, and the structure of certain ones suggests that he was using Seneca as a model.[111] Seven months before he died, Clarendon interrupted his excerpting from Henry Spelman and his work on *Religion and Policy* to make extracts from Cicero. Aside from the *De Natura Deorum*, the works he read were chiefly concerned with rhetoric—the *Brutus*, "*De Orator*" (probably *De Oratore*, though perhaps the *Orator*), and the *Ad Herennium*, then generally attributed to Cicero.[112] Significantly, his letters indicate that while he was on Jersey, Hyde also read almost all of Cicero's works.[113] Along with Seneca, Cicero strongly influenced his essays and also his dialogues. Cicero and Seneca were, of course, the two major classical literary influences on early seventeenth-century English prose style, with Seneca dominant and Cicero considered the more old-fashioned. Although Hyde occasionally employed Senecan point, particularly in his character sketches, he seems to have preferred Cicero.[114] The periodic elements in his style that add so much weight and dignity were undoubtedly influenced strongly by his reading of Cicero.

Most significant in terms of literary influence and models are the historians Clarendon read. Discussions of Clarendon often associate him with more contemporary historians, in part because his own most extended analysis of historical writing is of four historians of the late sixteenth and early seventeenth centuries[115]—Hugo Grotius and Famianus Strada (both of whom wrote in Latin), and the Italians, Cardinal Guido Bentivoglio and Enrico Davila (a Royalist favorite, translated by Clarendon's brother-in-law).[116] In addition, he described Mézeray in one of his essays as "the best modern historian."[117] There is no question that Clarendon was well acquainted with the major Continental and English historians of the period. The *Bibliotheca Clarendoniana* includes a remarkably complete collection of both early and contemporary historians; even without it, among the English, his correspondence shows his knowledge of Holinshed, Bacon, Stowe, Daniel, Baker, and also the obscure Robert Johnston, while the *Life* reveals that he was reading to his father from Camden's *Annals* (in Latin) when they learned of Buckingham's assassination.[118] In general, however, the moderns seem to have influenced the content of Hyde's *History* more than its form.

For most of the nations of Europe, the period from 1550 to 1650 was marked by deeply divisive civil strife, occasional revolution, and ideological warfare. Thus any historian would naturally find many affinities between the situations he had to depict and events recently chronicled by historians of neighboring nations. Clarendon was no exception. For example, Davila's analysis of the French civil wars has obvious parallels in the *History of the Rebellion*. Hyde appreciated Davila's approach, lauding him for recognizing the substantial difference "between troubling the series of grave and weighty actions and counsels with tedious relations of formal despatches (though of notable moment), and the relating solemn acts and consultations, from which all the matter of action is raised and continued."[119] His translation of this distinction into literary terms, however, was unfortunate for the *History*. Hyde's praise occurs when he cites Davila as a precedent for his own decision to insert many long Parliamentary and Royalist manifestoes verbatim into the original history. These declarations, at best unexciting reading, seriously disrupt the narrative, particularly in Book 5 of the *History*.[120] Hyde picked the four modern historians to analyze at length as much for the many bases of comparison among them—he noted that they all wrote accounts of "the same or near the same times"—as for their intrinsic worth as historians. Moreover, he turns to them only after mentioning Livy, Polybius, and Tacitus, citing his standard for judging them in terms of which ones "may worthily stand by the sides of the best of the ancients."[121] In another essay, he rather vehemently attacked, on the grounds of both content and style, "the histories which have been written, and the relations which have been made, of the transactions [of] the last hundred years within the compass of Europe."[122] Significantly, the only modern secular historians from whom he excerpted were his greatest Elizabethan predecessor Camden (the *Britannia*) and the chronicler Speed in his first exile, and Mariana, along with the chronologer Calvisius, in his final one.[123] Grotius was represented by his *De Juro Belli et Pacis* rather than his history.[124] It was not so much the moderns but the great literary historiographers who received Hyde's extended study and consideration.

From his earliest youth, Hyde wrote that he "had been always conversant" in history, "especially in the Roman" (*Life*, p. 8). He had also studied history during the years at the Temple devoted to polite learning, and this interest did not diminish over the years. As he moved away from belles-lettres, one of the key links between his early literary experiences and his later literary achievements in historical writing was the influence of the literary historiographers. The commonplace books and the manuscript list show his continual recourse to them. In the first commonplace book Hyde excerpted from Plutarch and Thucydides, and also from Commines (who would become another Royalist favorite).[125] On Jersey, as he wrote the original history, he again turned to Plutarch, and also read Livy. While working with Camden, he took time out to make excerpts from Josephus.[126] A letter to Sheldon indicates that by the end of August 1647 he had also "read over" Tacitus, although excerpts from his works do not appear in the commonplace book.[127] The primarily theological reading of his last exile was interrupted during the period that he was composing the final *History of the Rebellion*, when he returned to Tacitus. (Although his quotations in the *History* are all from the *Agricola* and the *Histories*, he also made excerpts from the *Annals*.)[128] In addition, Clarendon read the *Augustan Histories*, which he attributed to Suetonius.[129] At some point, most probably in 1670 as he was completing the *Life*, he read Velleius Paterculus, that minor antidote to Tacitus and the real Suetonius.[130]

Reading the classical literary historiographers influenced Clarendon artistically in two major ways. His most obvious use of them was for quotations for his own history; over half the writers whom he quotes are ancient historians. Such quotations generally appear in those sections of the history—the character of Falkland, for example—on which it is known that he expended the greatest literary effort. However, in contrast to other historians of his time, Hyde does not employ a great many individual quotations. (Thomas May is perhaps the best example of the tendency to embellish histories liberally with classical allusions, thereby showing off the historian's own knowledge for decorative effects.) One of Hyde's minor contributions to literary historiography was to improve narrative development by removing such obtrusive incumbrances. His references are succinct and always functional. They add depth and scope by placing the events and men of the period in larger historical contexts. Charles I addressing his army is compared to Trajan in Tacitus; rebellious clergymen are judged by the standard of Plutarch's "Athenian nun" in the *Life of Alcibiades*; in connection with the Earl of Holland's defections and returns, Fabius' counsel in Livy is invoked in discussing the treatment of traitors (*HR*, 2:312, 321–22; 3:247–49). Clarendon generally places his quotations judiciously for maximum narrative effect. He obviously wanted a powerful ending for Book 11, which covers 1648/9, that "year of reproach and infamy above all years which had passed before it" (*HR*, 4:511), when the trial and execution of Charles I had been followed by similar proceedings against leading supporters. In his commonplace book, Clarendon's extracts from Tacitus are dated 13 November 1671; Book 11, which he completed a week later on November 21,[131] ends with two quotations from the *Agricola* and the *Histories*. Similarly, in the opening of Book 15 he uses Velleius Paterculus to make a striking comparison of Charles II in exile at Cologne to Marius banished among the ruins of Carthage. Moving immediately to survey the general situation, Clarendon includes in his opening clause one of his rare indirect aspersions on Charles: "If the king's nature could have been delighted with such reflections . . ." (6:1). In this instance, as in so many others, what Charles II lacked, Clarendon possessed in abundance; his ability to employ to good literary effect what his reading had shown of the past immeasurably enriched his history.

Indirectly the classical historians seem to have done a great deal more for Clarendon's literary art than simply provide occasional quotations, for the extracts in his commonplace books indicate that his records were not simply inert repositories. The case of Josephus is illustrative. In 1647 Hyde interrupted his excerpting from Camden's *Britannia* to spend two and a half weeks on Josephus. The choice was appropriate; he began Josephus on the day before he started to write Book 6 of the original history,[132] which covers the year when actual fighting began, and most of his extracts come from sections describing events after the Jewish revolt broke out. Yet Hyde never quotes from Josephus in the *History of the Rebellion*, nor do the parts of Book 6 that he was writing at the time contain indirect verbal reflections of his reading. Indeed, aside from passages that reflect his own personal interests (descriptions of the Jewish sects, for example), many of his extracts focus on the kind of material he never includes in his own history: atrocities, geographical descriptions, grotesque or picturesque occurrences. It is as if making the extracts became in a sense a compensatory critical exercise for him. In reading, studying, and excerpting the literary historiographers, Hyde was clearly using their works to think about what good history should be, what it should include, and how it should be written.

One of his letters shows that he was consciously reading these authors as models of form as well as content.[133] In writing to Earle in 1647, he worried that in his portrait of Falkland, he might have "insisted longer upon the argument than may be agreeable to the rules to be observed in such a work; though it be not much longer than Livy is in recollecting the virtues of one of the Scipio's [*sic*] after his death." He wrote that if Earle felt the piece was "unproportionable for the place where it is," it could be enlarged and published separately, as Tacitus had done with the *Agricola* before the *Annals* and the *Histories*. This letter would not be required as proof that Hyde had the *Agricola* in mind when writing of Falkland, for he quotes from it four times in the twelve-page character. However, other comments in the letter are useful because they make overt the formative literary role that Hyde's historiographical reading played. He proceeds to tell Earle:

I am contented you should laugh at me for a fop in talking of Livy and Tacitus; when all I can hope for is to side Hollingshead, and Stow, or (because he is a poor Knight too, and worse than either of them) Sir Richard Baker. But if I had not hooked them in this way, how should I have been able to tell you, that I have this year read over Livy and Tacitus; which will never be found by the language and less by the Latin.

Hyde's self-deprecatory jesting conceals neither his clear sense of the available levels of historical style nor his own ambitions. Significantly, it was Earle, the one in the Tew group whose abilities in both poetry and prose he particularly extolled in the *Life*, to whom he confided his concern. When he later wrote to Sheldon, he confined himself to briefly noting the authors he had read and the "near 300 large sheets of paper" he had written on the history.[134]

Clarendon's reading reflects his own priorities in writing history. During the seventeenth century, interest generally shifted from those historians whose emphases were moral and literary to those who focused primarily on analyses of statecraft.[135] But Clarendon was concerned with both political and moral instruction as well as literary art; in historiogra-

135

phy, just as in politics, he represents an attempt to retain the best of the past in the present. He chose his historians accordingly. He followed his age in reading and using Tacitus, whom he quotes twice as often as any other historian in the *History of the Rebellion*. However, he employs Tacitus' observations on characters more often than his political insights. He seems to have been more interested in Tacitus the moralist and stylist, in attributes of the Roman that, although recognized by some in the seventeenth century, were much more controversial than his political acumen. Clarendon's own career had given him ample experience in *realpolitik*; it was the historians with heavily literary or moral emphases whom he apparently found especially useful. Thus he was comparatively uninterested in Polybius and Thucydides, historians often associated with Tacitus whose popularity rose substantially during the seventeenth century. Clarendon uses an example from Polybius in the second commonplace book,[136] but there is no record of his studying this disdainer of historical eloquence in detail. Although he excerpted from Thucydides in his first commonplace book and quoted him early in the *History*,[137] the Greek undoubtedly came to suffer in Clarendon's mind partly for the sins of his translator. In the answer to *Leviathan* he would assail Thucydides as one who "contains more of the Science of Mutiny and Sedition, and teaches more of that Oratory that contributes thereunto, then [*sic*] all that *Aristotle* and *Cicero* have publish'd in all their Writings."[138] Sallust, whom he described in one of his polemical tracts as an "excellent Historian,"[139] seems to have interested him no more than Polybius. Instead, he turned to Plutarch and Livy, both of whom had been greatly admired during the sixteenth century but whose popularity declined precipitously in the seventeenth. Plutarch's reputation was based primarily on his moralism, which Hyde himself praised.[140] Livy, also appreciated as a moralist, was famed for his eloquence and his narrative ability. Even Speed, the lone chronicler he excerpts, follows similar patterns. Although Speed used some antiquarian scholarship, he focused on moral rather than political instruction, and in style he followed Livy rather than Tacitus.[141] Aside from Tacitus, the only historical favorite of his age to whom Clarendon devoted significant attention was that strange minor figure Velleius Paterculus, whom the seventeenth century resuscitated briefly from oblivion[142] and whom he termed in the *History* a "good Roman historian" (6:82). The literary and moral dimensions Clarendon sought for his own historical writing required other models.

CLARENDON'S LITERARY EXPERIENCES AND HIS WRITING

Clarendon's experiences with literature thus began with a conventional youthful interest in belles-lettres and ended in reading and writing that were literary in a more broadly general sense. What remains to be assessed are the specific contributions to his development and achievements that were made by this evolving relationship with literature. First of all, the sensitivity to language and to literary style that was a prominent characteristic of Clarendon developed in part from his experiences with literature. Comments scattered throughout his letters and other writings show his sensitivity to the prose styles of other writers; he was concerned with all levels of style. While writing his contemplations on the Psalms, he noted that he "could not be without Reflexion upon the vulgar *Latin*" in them.[143] At the other extreme, he advised his secretary to read Ossalt's letters and those of Cardinal Perron as models of style in conducting business.[144] He corresponded with the Duke of York's tutor about problems he saw in the Prince's prose style, and he even commented on the prose styles of various agents and friends who wrote to him.[145] His differentiation of the Apocrypha and the canonical Scriptures is based partly on style: "For sure the gravity, style, matter, and expression in those books are very different from the books of Scripture; as the vulgarity of matter and language of Tobit, the high and rhetorical dialect of Esdras, the Romance of Maccabees . . . I believe are not agreeable to the books of the Prophets, and the history of Kings."[146] The quality of English translations of Latin and Greek authors also concerned him; he felt that French versions were better because, although the English translators knew the classical languages, they were "very far from understanding their own mother-tongue, and being versed in the fruitful productions of the English language."[147] He was not concerned only with written style; in his character sketches he carefully evaluated his subjects' abilities in speaking.

Along with his remarks about others' writing and speaking, Clarendon's practices as an author show his sensitivity to language and style. The major written sources he had for the *History* were by men like Walker and Hopton, whose prose was undistinguished. In following their accounts closely for certain sections of the history, Clarendon consistently raised the level of their language to create a more dignified style appropriate for historical narrative. However, when he found isolated felicitous expressions in their reports, he carefully preserved them in his own account. His stylistic range shows his recognition of the subtle features that differentiate individual styles. Not only was he himself a good prose stylist, but he was a master at imitating the styles of others. His literary agility confused his friends and created havoc among his enemies. Cromwell angrily blamed Denzil Holles for a pamphlet that Clarendon produced, while Charles I lost a bet with Falkland for failing to recognize Hyde's authorship of two speeches supposedly by Lord Brooke and the Earl of Pembroke.[148] Pseudonymous letters among the Clarendon State Papers offer further evidence of his talents.[149] Whether reproducing Pembroke's inept speaking or the dignity of address necessary for royal proclamations, Clarendon showed considerable adeptness at adjusting his prose style to different *personae*. The detached and objective tone of a historian was only one of many narrative voices he mastered.

Clarendon's sensitivity to specifically literary elements in style is nowhere better shown than in his sense of stylistic variations among genres. Parts of his dialogues, for example, are written with an informality and a dramatic immediacy found nowhere else in his writings. His essays too are composed in a style different from that of the *History*. They are in general more polished, with many more metaphors, classical allusions, and examples than his historical prose. His style alters in the essays not because Clarendon put more effort into them—it was the *History* that he described as "the work which his heart was most set upon" (*CL*, 2:566)—but because by his time the essay, unlike history, was a form with established stylistic conventions, among which were the use of metaphors, classical allusions, and examples.[150] Similarly, Clarendon's character sketches are so artistically effective in part because his language in them is marked by the compactness and concreteness characteristic of the genre. Clarendon's deployment of quotations in the *History* demonstrates his literary awareness of genres. Most of these references occur either in his character sketches or in the digressions that are in effect short essays inserted into the text—in sections, that is, where he was especially sensitive to specifically literary concerns. The majority of his quotations come in the portions of the *History of the Rebellion* originally written as history, rather than in sections taken from the *Life*. This distribution occurs partly because almost all his digressions on political instruction, where quotations are heavily used, occur in the original history. But more important, although in Clarendon's age the literary requirements for history as a genre were minimal, autobiography, barely emerging as a separate form, had none at all.

Complementing Clarendon's stylistic range was his sense of stylistic decorum. His experiences with literature had developed the understanding of genre that enabled him to recognize which literary forms he could appropriate for historical use and which would be unsuitable. His skill in deploying these varied stylistic conventions appropriately is shown by his use of the Bible and biblical style in the *History*. The Bible was one of the most pervasive literary influences on Hyde's writings as a whole. He knew it well, particularly the Old Testament and the Apocrypha, and he constantly collected excerpts from it. In Madrid he wrote meditations on the Scriptures; during his final exile he produced similar reflections. He also wrote separate remarks on the book of Proverbs, probably for use in his contemplations on the Psalms, in which he constantly quotes from Proverbs.[151] His writing on the Psalms shows his ability to reproduce the biblical cadences and metaphors characteristic of the King James version. He used this kind of language and biblical quotations frequently in such sections of the *Continuation of the Life* as the almost apocalyptic description of the disintegration of English communal life during the Interregnum (1:37–40). His speeches also filled with the biblical allusions so popular in contemporary oratory.[152] But in the *History* he is extremely careful with biblical language and references. Biblical influence is clear. About a quarter of his direct quotations are taken from the Bible, along with many indirect references in similes, deployed as judiciously for literary effect as his classical quotations. Clarendon also prefaces three books of the *History* (11, 12, and 13) with appropriate verses from the Scriptures.[153] But the biblical language and cadences he could employ so adeptly seldom appear in the text of the *History*. Very rarely he will insert a short sentence that is indirectly biblical in its phrasing or simplicity to vary his prose. But he seems to have recognized that the poetic and emotive overtones inevitable in biblical style would be out of place in the kind of history he wanted to write. Just as with the literary historiographers, Clarendon is extremely careful that the Bible is used in an artistically effective way in his *History*.

Hyde's early experiences with literature cannot be viewed as the sole, or even the major, impetus to his lasting concern with language. Although these experiences were an origin of his concern and were central in its early development, his later legal, theological, and political endeavors also proved vital. His belletristic period provided a broad and general background from which his more specifically professional interests in language could evolve. Law, of course, rests on the effectiveness of language as a precise medium of definition. Language is equally crucial in theological inquiry, the whole history of which amply documents, as Gibbon pointed out, that "the sense, or rather the sound, of a syllable was sufficient to disturb the peace of an empire."[154] Hyde's concern with stylistic exactness is heavily attributable to his legal and theological studies. But it was politics that played the largest role in shaping his concern with language.

Hyde's experiences with literature provided excellent training and background for his political career. Firth points out that in Parliament Hyde's speeches pleased because his "combination of literary gifts and legal training" was a rare one. More crucially, Firth continues, Hyde's "literary skill . . . laid the foundation" for his political advancement,[155] because Charles needed a skilled writer on his side during the many months of "paper skirmishes" (*HR*, 2:206) that preceded the actual fighting. Historians agree that the immediate result of Hyde's penmanship was to sway public opinion so that Charles I could garner enough support to field an army.[156] The long-term result of these experiences was that Hyde in his *History* was able to offer penetrating analyses of the role of language in political life. On the psychological level he shows how public attitudes were shaped by the language employed by each side. In tracing how the expressions used by both Parliamentarians and Royalists altered over the course of the conflict, he illustrates how language became an important index of political developments. The *History* is a sophisticated study of the political consequences of language, an examination in detail of the relationship between words and deeds in the state. Strafford after all died for the glosses that other men made on words he may or may not have spoken. As even the King's supporters became too terrified to "speak that plain English the state of affairs required" (*HR*, 2:251), the breakdown of language mirrors the destruction of the political process itself. Sprat and other writers after the Restoration would decry the deleterious effects of the civil wars on the English tongue;[157] the *History of the Rebellion* is the most detailed record from the Royalist point of view of precisely what happened to language during those years.

While Hyde's legal, theological, and political interests enormously increased his understanding of the power of language, on the whole they taught him more about its misuse than its literary dimensions. A major theme in the consideration of political language in the *History* is Parliament's manipulation of language to distort reality. "License of language," a favorite charge against Hyde's opponents, echoes throughout the work. As the Parliamentarians increasingly separate expression from meaning, their debasement of language becomes in the *History* a symbol of their political debasement. Hyde hated language deliberately employed to confuse or conceal. One of his polemical pieces sounds a typical note when he attacks his opponent's "wonderful delight to make easy things hard, and to perplex the common people with difficult words."[158] Similarly, in theology he castigates the schoolmen for "the wilderness of their affected words," created by "canting terms, which are not capable of being translated into any language": ▶

> They have corrupted and spoiled the noblest and most significant language of the world; a language of the greatest eloquence and greatest clearness, . . . and have left Latin without a monosyllable, or one soft or grateful word; and instead thereof, have filled the mouth so full of large and unwieldy words, that it can hardly utter in a dialect that is intelligible, and hath made the whole mass of the language fitter to be used in the Bear-Garden than in places of civil conversation.[159]

His answer to *Leviathan* is a blistering attack on Hobbes' abilities to use style to mislead readers by making them "intoxicated with terms and Allegorical expressions, which puzzel [*sic*] their understandings, and lead them into perplexities, from whence they cannot disentangle themselves."[160] Because Clarendon respected and to a certain extent feared the power of language, he himself used it with extreme care. As he wrote in a letter about an argument with Arlington over a declaration, "I told him, by that time he had writ as many declarations as I had done, hee would find they are a very ticklish commodity; and that the first care is to bee that it shall do no hurt."[161] Clarendon's recognition of language's potential for misuse was an important influence in shaping the precision of his style.

Ultimately, however, in Clarendon's writing, the lawyer, the theological disputant, and the political controversialist too often hindered rather than helped the literary historiographer. His experiences in all three areas encouraged an authoritative formality and an exactness in expression that were useful. But in other ways, the interests of his later years inculcated some unfortunate stylistic habits. The overly long sentences, loose grammatical constructions, and repetitiousness that can create difficulties in Clarendon's prose are all characteristic of legal writing.[162] The style of religious debate in the seventeenth century was similar. Falkland's *Discourse of Infallibility*, a typical specimen, shows the verbosity, syntactical involutions, and interminable sentences characteristic of Clarendon at his worst in the *History*. (Significantly, he commends Falkland's "sharpness of style" in his discourses [*HR*, 3:181].) Clarendon's political writing encouraged eloquence more than his legal and theological work did, but the minute and exhaustive analysis that was a standard feature of seventeenth-century polemic also encouraged verbosity. For example, the printed declaration supporting Parliament's 1648 vote of no more addresses to the King runs to 32 pages; Hyde's answer to it required 211.[163] The point-by-point replies to another work characteristic of seventeenth-century propaganda—which Hyde employed even in his letters[164]—accustomed him to a straightforward sequential organization that lacked literary impact. Most of all, law, theology, and politics encouraged the tendency to become embroiled in involved arguments that could wreak havoc on his style. In his writings an argument was to Clarendon what Samuel Johnson claimed a quibble was to Shakespeare: "He follows it at all adventures, it is sure to lead him out of his way, and sure to engulf him in the mire."[165] Problems arose because Clarendon's syntactical control was too often inversely proportional to his involvement in the argument at hand. His dialogue on the respect due to old age opens with sentences that are smooth and well modulated, but as he becomes engrossed in the exchanges, his syntax increasingly breaks down. Even in his essays, when he discusses controversial subjects he abandons stylistic efforts as his argument progresses, and the same thing sometimes occurs in the *History*. Clarendon's experiences with politics, law, and theology were invaluable to him as a historian of mid-seventeenth-century England. The evidence clearly indicates, however, that without the leavening of his early experiences with literature, his later interests would have produced a history notable for its content rather than for its form.

Above all, Clarendon's experiences with literature insured that he would recognize that literary art had a place in the writing of history. Although style was never his primary concern, it was an element he never ignored. He cared nothing for merely decorative effects; he wrote too rapidly and his concerns were too encompassing to lavish attention on small stylistic details for their own sake. But from his early belletristic pursuits and the literary associations that continued throughout his life had evolved an appreciation for literary style and an understanding of its importance. Direct imitation of other writers, such as the echoes of Hooker in the opening sentence of the *History*,[166] are extremely rare in Clarendon. He seems to have sought the spirit rather than the letter in those he studied, and so his literary debts tend to be general rather than allusively specific. Through years of studying, reading, and writing, he had imbibed and assimilated literary standards until they had become instinctive. Indeed, it is in part because literature was so integral a part of

him that he never discussed it in detail; the essential role of literary concerns was so firmly established in his mind, so much a given, that he took
it for granted. Clarendon's relationship to literature is a telling argument
for the formative powers of literary study, for the ways in which early
experiences can merge with later practical and professional concerns to
produce substantive artistic achievement.

In answering critics of Clarendon's political analyses, Trevor-Roper
wrote that Clarendon's strength was precisely that he was a practical rather
than an academic politician.[167] The same distinction holds true for him as
a literary artist. Just as certain art historians are bothered by the fact that
Clarendon chose the portraits in his collection primarily for their subjects
rather than for their artistic excellence,[168] some literary critics find his
mixture of aesthetic and practical concerns disturbing. But within his
own seventeenth-century context, and in the general context of the development of literary historiography in England, what is significant is that
Clarendon showed as much concern as he did about literary art. This kind
of attitude was enormously important for historical writing at that time.
Had Clarendon been a man who prized belletristic literature above history—a Milton, for example—he would have expended his best efforts
elsewhere and penned the kind of history Milton did, a lackluster production more truly written with his left hand than any of his controversial
tracts. Although Clarendon clearly valued history more than he did belles-
lettres, he nevertheless believed that literature was important enough to
insure that his history would not lack literary art. The great eighteenth-
century English literary historiographers were skilled writers who were
seriously interested in literary questions; both Gibbon and Hume, for example, wrote literary criticism. But before such men would employ the
full range of their talents in historical writing, history had to be reestablished as an area in which literature had an important role. Daniel, Milton, and earlier literary men who turned to history had believed that their
artistic abilities would be inappropriately applied there. In England, the
History of the Rebellion was the milestone. Clarendon's achievement insured that after its publication, his admirers, his critics, and the general
public who read history would recognize in his performance the potential
power of literary art in historiography.

5

Clarendon's Achievement in Perspective:
The Character Sketches

Vandyke little thought, when he drew Sir Edward Hyde, that a greater master than himself was sitting to him.

> Walpole, *A Catalogue of the Royal and Noble Authors of England*, 1796

The period of the Stuarts is the only portion of our history interesting to the heart of man. . . . From the moment that the grand contest excited under the Stuarts was quieted by the Revolution, our history assumes its most insipid and insufferable form. It is the history of negotiation and trick, it is the history of revenues and debts; it is the history of corruption and political profligacy; but it is not the history of genuine, independent men.

> William Godwin, in a MS. essay

And so, too, with Charles and his Cavaliers, we want to know what they were like and what they did, for neither will they ever come again.

> George M. Trevelyan, *Clio, A Muse*

Behind the features of landscape, behind tools or machinery, behind what appear to be the most formalized written documents, and behind institutions, which seem almost entirely detached from their founders, there are men, and it is men that history seeks to grasp. Failing that, it will be at best but an exercise in erudition. The good historian is like the giant of the fairy tale. He knows that wherever he catches the scent of human flesh, there his quarry lies.

> Marc Bloch, *The Historian's Craft*

THE LITERARY AND PERSONAL GENESIS OF CLARENDON'S CHARACTER SKETCHES

Shortly after the *History of the Rebellion* was published, the unique quality of Clarendon's character sketches was universally recognized. In 1710 Jean Le Clerc wrote that Clarendon "indulges more to it [character drawing] than any known Historian," and claimed that "*Salust* [*sic*] has not much better succeeded in the Characters so cry'd up."[1] A defender of the *History* in 1732 pointed out that the characters "are allowed to be the most distinguished and beautiful Part of the Work, and to have something of Original in them that is not to be imitated."[2] Within a decade after the *History* appeared, Ned Ward had released a collection of portraits excerpted from it,[3] inaugurating the tradition of publishing Clarendon's individual characters separately. Vivid and succinct, the character sketches have long provided convenient fodder for anthologists. But the result of this divorce of the sketches from the historical narrative has been widespread misunderstanding of where Clarendon's literary success lies, both in the individual characters themselves and in the *History* as a whole. More than any other, this particular historical convention played to Clarendon's personal and literary strengths, to what he was as a man and to what he knew of literary tradition. Thus he enormously expanded the literary role of the character in history, through the range of his sketches, their verisimilitude, and particularly their varied narrative functions. Effective as discrete pieces, the character sketches also function as an integral part of Clarendon's larger structural and thematic literary achievement in the *History of the Rebellion*.

As the generic variations in his style show, Clarendon was a writer sensitive to literary traditions. Conventions for portraying character would have particularly interested him, for as an author he tended to be biographically oriented. *The Difference and Disparity Between the Estates and Conditions of George Duke of Buckingham, and Robert Earl of Essex* was his first work, which supposedly so impressed Charles I that he wanted Clarendon to compose a life of Buckingham.[4] Similarly, the last work he wrote, *Religion and Policy*, was a review of papal claims to temporal power through an "examination and survey of the lives of the successive Popes."[5] Neither can approach the literary quality of Clarendon's characters in the *History*, but both reveal his fascination with personality. Just as English art of the seventeenth century focused most successfully on portraits and miniatures, the literature of the period presents an array of experiments in

146

depicting human nature. Humor characters in drama, homiletic characters, Theophrastan characters, and later characters drawn in terms of the "ruling passion" used an individual to represent a type or class of men. Such portrayals are at the end of a long literary tradition of generalizing the individual, which had developed from Roman comedy, from the works of Theophrastus, and from certain religious writings, dating as far back as the character of the good woman in the last chapter of Proverbs and extending through medieval hagiography and the characters in many sermons. A quite different approach was to be found in the short and realistic sketches of particular individuals inserted into seventeenth-century histories and in the longer summary characters that often concluded biographies and histories of single reigns. The frequency of such portraits in the later seventeenth century reflects the growing interest in men as individuals that would shape the eighteenth century's development of biography as a genre. Clarendon has associations with both approaches, although the historical tradition of drawing individual men was for him by far the more important.

Commentators on historical writing had traditionally considered lives as one branch of history. John Hayward early in the seventeenth century was the first to differentiate biography from history,[6] and the two diverged very slowly. As English historians began to organize their works in terms of individual reigns, the common practice was to follow a chronological account of events with a set piece summarizing the monarch's character. Bacon, Habington, Richard Knolles, and Lord Herbert of Cherbury used this kind of structure, which was ultimately more influential in English biography than in historical writing.[7] More fruitful for the literary development of history itself were the short character sketches of individuals that increasingly marked the works of seventeenth-century historians. These had appeared in England as early as Polydore Vergil, and were used by Hall, Speed, and also by Camden, who ended his account of each year in the *Annals* with a set of characters of those who had died during the period.[8] Clarendon knew Bacon, Camden, and probably most if not all of his English predecessors, but his own sketches are so much more finely drawn than theirs that specific influences seem unlikely. His excerpts from Camden in his second commonplace book, for example, are not from the *Annals*, which contains characters, but from the *Britannia*.[9] With the Continental historians he knew, such as Commines and particularly Davila,[10] Clarendon had more affinities. Davila introduced characters into his history with a line of personal description and included longer character sketches when they died; like Clarendon, he weighed men's capabilities in terms of the demands of their times. Nevertheless, because Davila, like Bacon and others, tended to focus too exclusively on political considerations in delineating his characters,[11] his sketches lack the scope of Clarendon's.

Whatever their format, for all these early historians who wrote character sketches, the great models were classical: Suetonius, Plutarch, and Tacitus. Clarendon wrote excerpts during his final exile from the *Augustan Histories*, which he attributed to Suetonius and which employs Suetonian methods.[12] But his characters show neither the lack of internal connection and chronology nor the tendency to split personality from deeds that generally indicates Suetonian influence.[13] The records of his reading indicate that Plutarch and Tacitus, both of whom appear twice, were the character writers most important to him. In drawing their characters, both Plutarch and Tacitus strove for realism through the use of particulars, usually by including anecdotes and detailed personal information. Thus they provided Clarendon with methods of creating vividness and a sense of immediacy in his own sketches. In addition, Plutarch's moral aims would also have appealed to him. He excerpted from Plutarch in 1636 in his first commonplace book, and turned to consider him again in early February of 1645/6, just before beginning the original history on 18 March.[14] While writing it he also read Tacitus.[15] Significantly, however, in the midst of composing the final *History of the Rebellion* in 1671, he returned to Tacitus, but Plutarch nowhere appears in the account of his later reading.[16] The great Roman, whose realism was exceeded only by his art and whose moralism was less overt than Plutarch's, ultimately proved of more lasting interest to Clarendon.

In the character sketches, as in all of the *History*, Clarendon's debts to Plutarch, Tacitus, and others are general rather than specific. Comments in a letter to Earle and several quotations within his character of Falkland, for example, indicate that he had the *Agricola* in mind while composing it.[17] The parallel between two good men in times unworthy of their nobility is obvious, and Clarendon's allusions add richness and depth to his depiction of his best friend. But in structure, in expression, or in any literary area except general conception and allusion, specific resemblances between the *Agricola* and Clarendon's Falkland are impossible to establish. Clarendon does not model individual characters on specific portraits in other historians, although he sometimes picks up salient traits. He was alert to possible resemblances; in his commonplace book, for example, he noted affinities between Otho and the Earl of Essex.[18] Similarly, when he found one aspect of Velleius Paterculus' Cinna that was characteristic of

Cromwell, he quoted it, but he did not use the whole portrait (*HR*, 6:91). Such specific borrowings are relatively rare. Insofar as Clarendon's achievement in his character sketches derives from the examples of other historians, it does so because he gained from assimilating their methods and approaches into his own understanding of human beings and his own skill in depicting them.

In the second major category of seventeenth-century characters, the depiction of a type, Clarendon's theological interests would have insured his knowledge of various homiletic characters. He knew Thomas Fuller, who had been Hopton's chaplain, although the excerpts from Fuller in his second commonplace book are from the *Holy Warre*.[19] From his association with Ben Jonson and his group, Clarendon would obviously have known the humor characters in drama. Indeed, because of these and because of Jonson's connections with Sir Thomas Overbury, Wendell Clausen claims that "in its development and popularity, the English [Theophrastan] Character is traceable to the literary temper of the Jonsonian Circle."[20] Among type characters, however, the Theophrastan is the form most often mentioned as an influence on Clarendon's sketches. English books of Theophrastan characters appeared most frequently in the years from 1628 to 1632,[21] precisely the period when Hyde was especially involved with belletristic pursuits. More important, John Earle, a member of the Tew group and the best of the English Theophrastan writers, was a close friend. But Clarendon mentions Earle's characters only indirectly, as "some very witty and sharp discourses" (*Life*, p. 43), and specific influences from Earle on Clarendon are minimal and unimportant. Clarendon's sketch of William Chillingworth has been connected with Earle's "A Skeptic in Religion,"[22] but it is difficult to imagine how an effective depiction of Chillingworth could possibly fail to resemble the general type in obvious ways. In addition, although his ties with Earle undoubtedly stimulated his interest in the character sketch as a form, his comparison of Buckingham and Essex may already have been writen before his close friendship with Earle developed.[23]

Clarendon's case is only one example of the general tendency of commentators to overestimate the literary influence of the Theophrastan character. It almost inevitably surfaces whenever depictions of character in any genre from the Renaissance to the nineteenth century are discussed, and such critical obeisance has obscured the considerable difficulties in establishing any influence that the Theophrastan form alone exerted. Its extremely rapid rise and development—the first collection in English, Joseph Hall's, appeared in 1608, and Benjamin Boyce calls the Theophrastan character "perfectly developed by 1632"[24]—suggest both the self-contained quality and the lack of flexibility that limited its further applications. The Theophrastan form does have many affinities with other characters of the time, such as the homiletic characters, the humor characters, characters in the earlier "Literature of the Estates,"[25] and later characters drawn in terms of the "ruling passion." But the humor characters actually developed independently, while the homiletic characters show similarities to certain depictions in Plutarch's *Moralia*, which in turn suggests ties to his work in the *Lives*. Because of these kinds of overlaps, specific traditions when traced carefully become increasingly indistinguishable.

This merging of the Theophrastan character with other forms suggests the larger problems in ascertaining the precise relationships between the various branches of the character sketch during the seventeenth century. For example, although the biographical character sketches and those in histories share common roots in the classical writers, their differing purposes led to different kinds of development in each, and their later effects on each other tend to be general rather than specific. The polemical and satirical characters of John Cleveland and others at midcentury have strong ties to the historical sketches, with some lesser reflections of the Theophrastan. In addition, rhetorical conventions of praise and blame and of decorum exerted continuing influence on all character portrayals. Rhetoric included formulas for depictions of character—*effictio, notatio, ethopoeia, prosopopoeia, descriptio*, and at least ten others, varying according to the commentator—and writing a character had long been a common rhetorical exercise.[26] Finally, the characters in midcentury French romances and memoirs, which were probably unimportant for Clarendon but influential on others,[27] further compound the muddle.

The constant qualifications necessary in dealing with specific influences from the different kinds of seventeenth-century characters lead mainly to literary dead ends. Fortunately, what is more clear and much more important are certain general influences that the various branches of the character sketch exerted collectively during the period. For Clarendon, these are particularly useful, because of the general rather than specific ways in which he assimilated and used literary traditions. Certain conventions common to all of the sketches exerted literary pressure on any treatment of character at the time. For example, there was a tendency to show a moral bias, an approach particularly congenial to Clarendon's own outlook and purposes in the *History*. Although modern classicists see Theophrastus as a natural scientist recording his observations of human beings as descriptive data, the older critical view of him was as a moralist, the follower of Aristotle who illustrated his master's doctrine of the golden mean.[28] Isaac Casaubon, whose late-sixteenth-century editions made Theophrastus widely available, claimed that Theophrastus' sole motivation for writing characters was the improvement of morals.[29] In England Joseph Hall's and John Earle's religious and spiritual emphases strengthened the moral connections, and the association of history and biography with ethical instruction also encouraged such approaches. Here Clarendon's rereadings of Plutarch and his observations of Earle's ability to combine psychological analysis with a moral overview undoubtedly offered useful examples to him.

Casaubon considered the character sketch "a Medium between Moral Philosophy and Poetry."[30] As such, an artificial and self-consciously literary style was particularly associated with it; by the eighteenth century, Hugh Blair pointed out that "characters are generally considered, as professed exhibitions of fine writing."[31] The English Theophrastans wrote in the Senecan style, with antithesis, aphorism, and point. Sallust's and especially Tacitus' similar styles influenced historical and biographical sketches. Both the style and the content of characters encouraged irony. Theophrastus and his various imitators generally favored drawing vices over virtues,[32] and Tacitus, with Sallust, again provided reinforcement. One of Clarendon's most important literary debts to the character tradition was stylistic. He was especially conscious of literary style in the characters; for example, he employed substantially more metaphors in them than is usual in his writing. The conventions of the character also encouraged exercise of his considerable talents in irony, particularly in the understatement and sarcasm to which he was inclined and which were often associated with the character. Above all, the brevity characteristic of the genre tightened Clarendon's writing in his sketches. Their compactness enhanced his own precision in expression to produce a clarity found few other places in his work, and the diffuseness that sometimes weakens his sentences elsewhere seldom appears in them.

However, other qualities common to the various forms of the character sketch as it had developed until Clarendon's time were less useful to him. All of the major forms involved a certain level of abstraction, because of the deductive method writers usually employed. An author's concept of a character was imposed and illustrated rather than exposed inductively. Most character sketches became reductive, as each of the early forms, for differing reasons, oversimplified the human beings they depicted. The longer characters appended to biographies or histories usually rendered models, not recognizable individuals. Bacon's character sketch at the end of his history presented Henry VII as an ideal politician rather than a human being. In depicting Sir Matthew Hale's character, Gilbert Burnet found "so much here to be commended, and proposed for the imitation of others, that I am afraid some may imagine I am rather making a picture of him, from an abstracted idea of great virtues and perfections, than setting him out as he truly was."[33] The effect Burnet feared was precisely what most seventeenth-century biographers and historians produced in their sketches of character. Roger North wrote that "one may walk in a Gallery, and extract as fair an account from the air of their Countenances or the cut of their whiskers" as from "the many Scetches [sic] or profiles of great mens [sic] lives."[34]

Although the short sketches inserted in histories tended to be more realistic, even these were limited because historians considered fully rounded depictions unnecessary for establishing the roles that individuals played in events. Throughout the seventeenth century, historical and moral purposes combined with the highly wrought prose demanded for the character sketch to sacrifice life to art. Too often characters became detachable ornaments, set pieces insufficiently integrated into the narrative. The Theophrastan character, of course, never developed narrative connections. Of the characters that did, the status of the longer biographical ones as awkward appendages to *res gestae* epitomizes the difficulties. The tendency for these sketches to function autonomously was shown by some early English histories and biographies in which the summary of events in a life and the character sketch were written by two different authors.[35] Camden's obituaries and Speed's series of portraits of British leaders against the Saxons also function almost as independent galleries.[36] The character sketch, whether it portrayed the type or the individual, was in its essence a static form. To make it an integral part of a narrative rather than a disruptive intrusion required a fusion of synchronic and diachronic elements that few early historians were able to achieve.

The lack of realism and of narrative connections in depictions of character particularly concerned Clarendon. In his sketches in the *History*, he actively sought the verisimilitude and the immediacy that he usually shaped his prose style and narrative to avoid. The character apparently originated as a rhetorical device for adding vividness in prose, and Clarendon clearly viewed this as a primary purpose; "lively" is a word he uses to commend the characters of others.[37] What he wanted is shown by his criticism of Grotius' history, which he felt lacked "a lively representation of persons and actors, which makes the reader present at all they say or do."[38] The reference to making the reader "present" is a commonplace among early writers on historical style.[39] Significantly, however, while other commentators connect this kind of reader response with the events a historian portrays, Clarendon limits it solely to the characters. He also recognized that creating a sense of immediacy in character sketches could disrupt the larger perspective of the ongoing narrative. He was concerned, for instance, that his character of Falkland might be "unproportionable for the place where it is."[40] He was well aware that unless the sketch could be integrated into the text in ways that appropriately supported the narrative, the narrative itself would not be enriched. He criticized Strada for writing "the life and character of Alexander Farnesius . . . [rather] than the history of that time which he pretends to do."[41] Clarendon's purpose was to write history, and he intended to subordinate his effects and devices accordingly. The literary traditions of character writing offered him no entirely satisfactory models of realistic sketches that were fully integrated into a narrative. Tacitus was the best, but even he was not averse to serving literature rather than life by sacrificing essence to aphorism. Moreover, as G. B. Townend points out, "even in Tacitus history continually threatened to become little more than the history of the emperor rather than the empire."[42] Clarendon's knowledge of the literary traditions of the character shaped his moral overview and particularly his style in his sketches, but his achievement in them is only partly stylistic and thematic. The uniqueness of the characters in the *History of the Rebellion* derives equally from Clarendon's own personality and experiences.

In order to portray a character effectively, Clarendon usually had to be drawing from life. His long series of sketches of the popes in *Religion and Policy* is a wooden and lifeless collection, even though he had thoroughly researched them[43] and showed considerable imaginative insight in reconstructing their historical contexts. Julian the Apostate, whom he had discussed in two letters in 1656 that reflect the stance he would take years later in *Religion and Policy*, is a good example. "Concerning Julian," he wrote, "I confesse I have a good mind to have a better opinion of him, then [*sic*] the Fathers have," and he then explained why he preferred Ammianus Marcellinus' account over those of St. Gregory, St. Cyril, and Baronius. He exhibits considerable independence of judgment and sympathy with Julian as he praises "the manner of his death and his wordes" and likens him to "Trajan, & the best of the Heathen Emperours."[44] Nevertheless, even discounting the shadow that Gibbon's subsequent portrayal has cast over other historians' Julians, Clarendon's sketch of the emperor in *Religion and Policy* has no vitality. The failure of his characters in

Religion and Policy is partially attributable to the nature of the work as a whole, which remained antiquarian and polemical rather than creative because it lacked an imaginative referent like that of the *History*. But, with a few exceptions, Clarendon recreated men well only from personal acquaintance and not from books. Even among those he knew, the extent of his own experience with them directly influenced his literary effectiveness. His portrayal of Laud, whom he knew well, is drawn much more skillfully than that of Strafford, to whom he had no personal ties.

Because the character sketch evolved as a limited form that was arbitrary in certain ways, its effectiveness depends heavily upon the perceptiveness of the individual writer. The ability to understand others is, of course, grounded in an ability to understand the self, and the general accuracy of Clarendon's self-portrayals shows his unusually unillusioned view of his own strengths and weaknesses. His three exiles from active political involvement, on Jersey, in Spain, and in France, had provided special opportunities for him to review his own behavior and to understand his motivations and feelings. As he wrote to Sheldon in 1647 from Jersey, "I have been now above a twelvemonth more conversant with myself, because less with other men, than in all my life before."[45] Having come to terms with what he was at crucial points throughout his career, he was freer and better able to look candidly and sensitively at others. His concern with solid achievement rather than personal recognition also meant that he lacked the kind of ego that distorts a person's perceptions of his associates.

Clarendon's character sketches, like his portrait collection, reflect a genuine fascination with people, for like all good biographers he was endlessly curious about his fellow men. He watched them with eagerness and zest, and he could seldom resist the urge to draw them. In a long independent sketch of Digby produced early in his final exile, he inserted a brief depiction of the Irish nuncio Rinuccini, creating in effect a character within a character.[46] But despite this kind of interest in and attraction to character for its own sake, for Clarendon the study of human beings was not an idle pastime, but an essential intellectual pursuit. He described "the knowing our selves, and the knowing other Men" as "the principal Ingredients into Wisdom."[47] Moreover, learning about the characters of others was also in his view a moral and religious duty. In his commentaries on the *Psalms* he wrote that "Men cannot propose a better or more easy Way to themselves to attain to a Perfection in any commendable Course of Life, or in pleasing and becoming acceptable to God Almighty, than by treading in the Steps, and following the Example of Persons eminent in Skill and Virtue."[48] To find such examples, he noted in one of his essays that "we cannot do better than recollect as many of those as our own experience, or histories of uncontroverted veracity, or the observation of other men, can suggest to us."[49] For Clarendon, understanding the characters of others was a means of helping—indeed, saving—himself.

Clarendon's personal experiences gave him the kind of insight into men that was required in order to produce effective character sketches. The circumstances of his life demanded considerable abilities in reading human character. As a young lawyer he managed to advance himself by cultivating the connections he had and by picking up powerful supporters such as Laud. His political experiences in the Short and Long Parliaments, in Charles I's fractious councils, and in the thankless position of Chancellor of the Exchequer fostered his abilities. Above all, the years of exile, torn by Royalist intrigue against usurpers in England and against each other, required him constantly to make judgments of character. The Royalists abroad were geographically scattered, financially strapped, and psychologically demoralized; those in England found the exiles at best a burden and an embarrassment and at worst a danger. Hyde recognized "how much we depend on others for the performance of any thing we can promise,"[50] and such dependence demanded a thorough knowledge of people. During the exile he was at the center of operations, coordinating espionage, collecting information, monitoring the incessant intrigue, and deciding whom to trust. "But it is most necessary," he wrote to one of his agents, "for you there and us here, to help each other in the knowledge of men, without which we shall both be too often deceived."[51] Hyde developed a sharp eye for the essential traits of individuals. His letters are filled with descriptions of people, including many of the briefly incisive summaries of character that mark his sketches. Glengary, though "very honest, is not able to conduct a great design"; Sir Marmaduke Langdale is "a man hard to please, and of a very weak understanding, yet proud and much in love with his own judgment"; Dr. Fraizer is "good at his business, otherwise the maddest fool alive"; Edward Massey is "a wonderful vain, weak man, but very busy and undertaking, and really I think means exceeding well and faithfully to the King, and would serve him without limitations, which few of the rest will do."[52] Like his best analyses of statecraft, Clarendon's characters are literary successes that evolved from practical political necessity.

From its beginnings in England, the character sketch as a genre had Anglican and then Royalist associations,[53] and Hyde was able to turn these to practical use as polemical characters became propaganda tools during the civil wars and the Interregnum. Certain letters reveal that he was composing characters for political purposes during the late 1650s. John Mordaunt wrote to Hyde that "the characters of particular men from your Lordship will be of great advantage, for we have many wolves in sheep's clothing."[54] Another correspondent wrote: "S^r, I am desired by some persons of quality to moove you, as every way the fittest for it, to write a character of 364. [Written above the number in a different hand is "ye King of England."] You are the best knowen to him of any man, & the best able for such a necessary work, which they are persuaded at this season would advance him much." He added that although he knew Hyde had "little leasure for such an imployment, yet things of such a nature are as easy to yr penn, as this scrible" was for him.[55] In the early eighteenth century one writer noted that Hyde immeasurably advanced the Restoration by "the fine Picture he drew of the King in his Letters to his Friends"—an achievement for which the Earl of Southampton, disillusioned by Charles II after the Restoration, had bitterly reproached him.[56]

Clarendon was able to learn so much about human character because his moderation and pragmatism led him to do his best to accept men as they were and to work with them accordingly. He exerted great efforts during the exile and throughout his career to remain tolerant of other people. Over and over again in his letters he urged Nicholas to recognize that "there cannot be a greater error than to expect all men to be of one mind, or not to live very frankly with those who we know are not altogether so perfect as we wish them, and should endeavour to make ourselves."[57] His description of his treatment of Wilmot shows his characteristic subordination of private feelings to public concerns:

The King well knows my opinion of Lord Wilmot, how improper I take him for that employment and how much I dissuaded it, but when it cannot be altered I do assist him by giving the best advice, preparing the most particular instructions and making all dispatches as if he were my brother, because I know the King's business depends upon it, and I think all honest men ought to be of that temper, and he who endeavours to cross the service or render it unsuccessful because it is undertaken by such a man whom he loves not, is no less a Rebel than Cromwell.[58]

From the time he entered public life, Hyde worked with some of the most difficult personalities in mid-seventeenth-century England—with the irascible Colepeper and the volatile Digby in the beginning of the conflicts; with Sir John Berkeley, George Goring, and Sir Richard Gren-ville in the west; with the wily Cottington in Spain; with Jermyn and the Louvre group abroad; with the Restoration court; and, above all, with Charles I and Charles II. He was able to deal with such people because he sought to maintain the distanced perspective on individuals that is re-flected in a comment to Nicholas: "You will not be much misled if you remember often that few good men are as good as they are conceived to be, and they who are ill spoken of are not half so bad as they are reported to be, and few are so bad as to be good for nothing." [59] From such a view-point evolved the tolerance, moderation, and balance of the character sketches in the *History*.

Clarendon's imaginative grasp of the effects of the unusually difficult circumstances of his era also contributed to his understanding of the characters of his contemporaries. As early as his comparison of Buck-ingham and Essex, he had written that knowing "somewhat of the disposition and spirit of this time" was necessary to understand the differ-ences between the two courtiers. [60] Amid the shifting allegiances of the 1650s, he had been forced to keep an open mind about individuals and their loyalties and capabilities. As he explained to one of his agents, "we cannot be sure never to be used ill again by the same persons, . . . when the corruption, or the defects are so universal." [61] He had watched men like the Earls of Holland and Hamilton and Generals Goring and Monck serve one side, switch over to the other, and then turn again, in some cases more than once, and he recognized their behavior as that of many nameless Englishmen writ large. He believed that such actions were only partly attributable to the personal characters of individuals, and that the times themselves were in important ways responsible.

In 1655 Hyde wrote a pamphlet using as his *persona* an early sup-porter of the rebellion who had by then become thoroughly disillusioned by the course of events and particularly by Cromwell. Despite his rhe-torical disguise, one passage carries a great deal of conviction as an ex-pression of his own personal beliefs:

Yet I may tell you, that whosoever hath not been deceived in the Current of these last fifteen years, hath been preserved from being so, by such an absence of friendship, confidence and Charity in and to Mankinde, by such a measure of distrust, jealousie and villany in his Nature, that I had rather be a Dog than that man: For my self I am not ashamed to confesse before God and the world, that I have been much deceived, miserably, and wretchedly deceived. [62]

157

After all, in the early days of the Long Parliament, Hyde himself had ridden for exercise with Nat Fiennes, "lived very familiarly" with (of all people) Henry Marten, and dined at John Pym's lodging, where John Hampden, Arthur Hesilrige, and others of their group had "transacted much business" (*Life*, pp. 67–68). In 1660 the Restoration had effected countless metamorphoses; Sir William Hastings' letter, recalling himself to Hyde "after a silence of 14 years," was typical of many he received.[63] As Lord Chancellor, Clarendon had watched some of his closest associates turn against him personally and politically. The Earl of Bristol, who as Lord Digby had been instrumental in introducing him into Charles I's service, and who led an abortive attempt to impeach him in 1663, is only the most glaring example. He had learned from bitter experience how little the closest ties availed individuals in adverse situations. When Clarendon faced impeachment, Lord Sandwich told Pepys that he would "not actually joyne in anything against the Chancellor, whom he doth own to be his most sure friend and to have been his greatest—& therefore [he] will . . . passively carry himself even."[64] As Clarendon watched men change with their circumstances, he evolved a more fluid concept of human nature to explain what he had seen. In contrast, early historians almost without exception worked in terms of static conceptions of character. Although Clarendon shared their emphasis on certain key traits that determine general behavior, he also recognized ways in which circumstances alter what men do. Such relativity bore fruit in his character sketches, for he shows the most developed sense of diachronic elements in character of any English historian before Gibbon.

To the distanced perspective on character fostered by his circumstances, his own personality, and the attitudes he cultivated, Clarendon added an enormous capacity to exercise a sympathetic imagination. "It is very difficult to persuade me to think ill of a man, of whom I have ever thought well; for I do not only stay till I hear what he can say for himself, but I consider what I could say for myself if I were in his place," he wrote to Earle.[65] He might be pragmatic about his fellow human beings, but he was also generous to them. Despite many painful experiences, he was a man with strong personal attachments who maintained extremely high ideals of friendship. He was the most faithful of friends. Only he and one other wrote regularly to the lonely Cottington, forgotten in Valladolid at the end of his life; in 1665, in the midst of war and plague, at a time when secretaries took care of most of his correspondence, he still found time to send a handwritten letter to his old friend Nicholas, who had been ignored after being replaced as Secretary of State by Sir Henry Bennet.[66] In his character sketches he was able to draw on his deepest feelings for his friends to create some of his most unforgettable portraits. He was equally able to use a man's relationships to evaluate his character negatively, as when he noted of Sir John Berkeley that "he that loved him best was very willing to be without him" (*HR*, 4:232).

Clarendon's experiences had shown him the importance of friendships not only to the individual but to the state. Close relationships had been crucial in forming his own character; he wrote in the *Life* that "he was often heard to say, that '. . . he owed all the little he knew, and the little good was that in him'" to the friendships he had made (pp. 24–25). Clarendon recognized that such ties, which molded the individual, also carried larger potential political consequences. Pym, for example, who alone seemed to rule the House of Commons, was actually in private "much governed by Mr. Hambden and Mr. St. John" (*HR*, 3:322). Just as loyal counselors were essential to the government as Clarendon envisioned it, friendships were vital for the individual politician. In the *History*, he uses the experiences of Sir Thomas Coventry, Strafford, and the old Earl of Bristol, among many others, to prove that total self-reliance is dangerous (*HR*, 1:58–59, 342; 2:532). He emphasizes that both Laud and Buckingham were hampered by lacking close friends who could advise them with complete frankness (*Life*, p. 52; *HR*, 1:42–43). Throughout the *History* Clarendon develops his characters both as individuals and in terms of the personal and political ramifications of their relationships.

Finally, Clarendon's personal experiences and attitudes gave him not only the ability to write character sketches, but a deep need to do so. Like Richard Baxter, on no subject was he more vehement than on the damages wrought by slander.[67] He noted in a letter to Lady Morton that "if we did enough consider the difficulty of repayring the wrong wch every sharpe word does to the reputacon, we would not thinke the peace to be only broken by the hands."[68] Throughout his career, from the time he abandoned the Parliamentarians until well after he left England for his final exile, Clarendon was smeared with the most vicious calumnies. He was constantly blamed during the Royalist exile and after the Restoration by those who failed to obtain preferments or rewards from Charles II. In the 1660s he bore the brunt of popular displeasure with government policies that in many cases he had strongly opposed. The bulk of his problems came from others' views of him, from the power they thought he wielded rather than the actual influence he possessed. Clarendon's reaction was to defend himself in writing with extremely detailed justifications of his conduct. His sense of urgency in a letter to Sheldon is typical: "Though

I have writ twice to you this week; yet having not satisfied myself, I cannot believe I have satisfied you. . . . For not to clear any misapprehension or misrepresentation that may be made of me would be a fault in me."[69]

Clarendon's almost obsessive concern for his reputation stemmed in part from practical considerations. He wrote to Lord Percy that "whoever does so much despise what all men say or thinke of him, will by degrees too much contemn that reputation & good name, wthout w^{ch}, let our innocency & wisdome be what it will, we shall not be able to doe halfe the good to ourselves or our Country, wch we cannot but wish to doe."[70] He had recognized Laud's and Strafford's active disdain for public opinion (*HR*, 1:196, 341–42) as major faults and had seen the consequences of it in both cases; he was understandably not eager to repeat their experiences. More important, he believed that careful justification of one's actions was a spiritual responsibility as well as a historical one. In a will composed in 1647 when he expected Jersey to be captured by Parliamentary forces, his extended explanation of why he wrote "somewhat more of myself, than is usual, or hath been convenient to be said in wills" reveals his attitude. Such justification was required by "the strange times in which we live, so full of scandal and calumny," and also by "the part which I have acted in those times, to which more than an ordinary share hath been applied of those scandals and calumnies." His main point is that "next [to] the provision and care for our souls in the next world, and in order to that, the preserving our consciences entire and blameless in this, a good Christian is to take care that he leaves his fame and memory as unspotted as may be: which is a duty he owes to justice and truth."[71] Such care was imperative because Clarendon viewed posthumous reputation as second in importance only to salvation itself. One of his letters to Lady Dalkeith indicates that men's being "fairly mentioned after their deaths" in this world is "the most glorious and desirable blessing" after their "being saved in the next world."[72] Thus, in an unusual extension of the emulative and memorial traditions of history that date back to Plutarch, Clarendon felt that men's fame and merit had to be transmitted not only so that posterity could benefit from remembering and imitating them, but also for the sake of the individuals themselves. "The dead suffer when their memory and reputation is objected to question and reproach," he wrote to Earle.[73] Clarendon was determined to leave a clear record of his own conduct, and what he sought for himself, he did his best to provide for others. As a historian and a Christian, he felt the deepest personal obligation to be fair. His concern for accurately rendering the characters of others grew directly from his concern for his own.

Clarendon's life gave him rich and varied exposure to human character. He wrote in his commentaries on the Psalms that "Affliction and Distress" were the "best Expedient[s]" for teaching an individual about himself and other men, and of such experiences he had a full measure.[74] He believed that the "genius and spirit and soul of an historian" developed in part from "conversation and familiarity" with "the most active and eminent persons in the government,"[75] and he knew all of these men. From his extensive knowledge came the realism in his character sketches and also his reluctance to be reductive. If his political work had given him practice in making succinct judgments of character, it had also revealed the dangers that the complexity of every individual posed to such judgments. Clarendon's own interest in character was of the broadest kind, and the attitudes he had cultivated in order to deal with his contemporaries had allowed him to gain a wide knowledge of human nature. His personal experiences and the capacious view of man that he had developed in his own life demanded the depiction of rounded human beings in his *History*, so that the work could accurately reflect the reality he had known.

CLARENDON'S ART OF PORTRAITURE AND THE NARRATIVE FUNCTIONS OF THE CHARACTERS

Clarendon believed that he understood his contemporaries. He was not always correct in his judgments, but he was sure, and his prose reflects his confidence. He viewed each man's character as a whole, and in depicting it, he could therefore simplify in the convincing way that an artist does when he sees most profoundly. In his sketches he does not present every aspect of a man, but only his essential qualities. For example, the portrait of Cromwell never mentions him as a warrior, but because the information Clarendon does include produces so coherent and credible a character, the omission is insignificant. His characters are created in terms of a realism that is selective and limited, but nevertheless convincing. He succinctly conveys enough to stimulate the reader's imagination to provide the rest.

Clarendon varies the arrangement and the content of his characters to accommodate each individual. In structure, he follows no fixed internal order and employs no formula or single descriptive category (family, fortune, education, friends, moral or political principles, for example) in all of the sketches. Yet unlike his contemporary Burnet, whose lack of selectivity produced a rudimentary realism in his characters at the expense of artistic presentation, Clarendon never offers simply a haphazard collection of traits. Secure in the fullness of his imaginative apprehension of his subjects, he had no problems in marshaling detail and felt no need to deviate into the arguments usually characteristic of his writing. He often focuses on one prominent feature of a man—the Earl of Southampton's melancholy, Archbishop Williams' "fiery temper," the Earl of Salisbury's muteness "except in hunting and hawking, in which he only knew how to behave himself" (*HR*, 2:529–31; 1:464; 2:543). With such a trait as his matrix, Clarendon develops the rest of the character by analyzing other facets of the life and personality, modifying or amplifying rather than simply illustrating the dominant trait. He also juxtaposes characters to clarify individual traits or to develop whole personalities: Montrose and Argyle, Mazarin and Richelieu, Lanark and Lauderdale, and, above all, Goring and Wilmot, a comic masterpiece (5:121–22, 4:160–61, 320–21; 3:444–45). The detachment characteristic of Clarendon as a man and a historian marks his character sketches. Unlike other contemporaries who wrote characters, particularly Burnet and Sir Philip Warwick, he never draws characters overtly in terms of their relationships to him.[76] The liveliness and immediacy that Clarendon sought in his characters was achieved through his tighter and clearer prose style and through his deployment of vivid detail; his own narrative perspective remained distant.

Like Plutarch, Clarendon was interested in inner qualities rather than physical appearance. He seldom describes how his characters looked. Nevertheless, he avoids abstraction and generality by the adept use of small details about men. Clarendon excels most of his predecessors and all of his contemporaries in his ability to incorporate minor details that enhance both the immediate reality of the character and the historical quality of his work. Early historians seldom included such information, because they considered it too trivial and personal for history. Thus when Camden indicates in his character of Roger Ascham that he "lived and died a poor man" because he was "too-too much given to Dicing and Cock fighting," the historian has already apologized for the entire sketch as "my short Digression";[77] such information seldom enters his characters of public figures. In contrast, the character sketches of Clarendon's contemporaries teem with trivial details. Burnet wholesales gossip, while Warwick is mesmerized by men's manners and their dress. His portrait of Charles I opens by detailing the King's diet. He devotes so much of his attention to Cromwell's clothes—"a plain cloth-suit, which seemed to have been made by an ill country tailor; his linen . . . plain, and not very clean; . . . a speck or two of blood upon his little band, which was not much larger than his collar; his hat . . . without a hatband"—that when Cromwell rises to rule, the impression is that "having had a better tailor"[78] was the key to his success. Like John Aubrey, Burnet and Warwick often lose the historical personage and certainly the essence of his character amid a mass of extraneous information. Clarendon knew how to choose those details that could add interest and immediacy to his characters without sacrificing either their dignity or his tone. Even in descriptions of his closest friends, his minor details are never overly familiar.

Clarendon's character sketches differ from those of his predecessors and contemporaries not only in their individual excellence, but also in their frequency and variety. He developed his sketches in terms of the same principles that governed his concepts of history. Two of his most important purposes in including the characters were emulative and memorial; like earlier historians, he believed that "celebrating the memory of eminent and extraordinary persons, and transmitting their great virtues for the imitation of posterity" was "one of the principal ends and duties of history."[79] Similarly, those of weak character and little virtue would serve to warn of the consequences of men's frailties. The third of Clarendon's primary purposes in drawing characters was causal. The complexities of human personalities form the basis of many of his most acute historical explanations. In practice these three purposes tended to overlap and combine. Many causal characters in the *History* simultaneously celebrate the memory of historical personages, while both causal and memorial characters often transmit examples of virtue for imitation or frailty to be shunned.

The emulative traditions of historical writing were particularly important to Clarendon. He considered history one of the best forms for inculcating examples: "The short History of one Man's Deliverance hath always more Reputation, than the most exact Prescription of general Rules and Directions for our Comportment."[80] Thus he was deeply concerned over what he saw as the decline of classical traditions of emulative historiography over the centuries. He lamented in one of his essays that "there hath been so great a negligence since Christianity hath been received, in transmitting the particular lives of great and meritorious men in that manner, as to inflame others to follow and imitate their examples."[81] Clarendon saw these traditions as particularly crucial for his own era, when, as he notes in the long opening sentence of the *History*, good men dedicated to "duty and conscience" too often seemed to have been lost and forgotten amid the chaos and wreckage of the times. He insisted that his age "abounds as plentifully" in virtuous and pious men "as any age that hath been before it."[82] In his own *History* he intended to do these men justice, and to allow their virtues to live on for posterity.

Despite all his moral concerns, Clarendon knew human beings too well to draw models rather than men. He had some genuine heroes to depict—men like Montrose, for example—as well as many other fascinating contemporaries who seemed in a sense larger than life. But the *History of the Rebellion* presents no unalloyed heroes or villains. "Yet his memory must not be so flattered that his virtues and good inclinations may be believed without some allay of vice," he wrote in his character sketch of the Earl of Pembroke (*HR*, 1:72). Clarendon emphasized his own "love of truth, which ought, in common honesty, to be preserved in history as the soul of it, towards all persons who come to be mentioned in it" (*HR*, 4:184). This commitment to the historical truth, along with the deep obligations he felt for the sake of the individuals themselves, led him to do his best to portray characters accurately and fairly. In letters written while he was composing the original history and also in remarks within the work itself, he was adamant about his impartiality toward individuals. "Upon my word there shall not be any untruth, nor partiallity toward Persons or Sydes," he assured Berkeley.[83] Several times he referred to his honest and impartial renderings of his contemporaries as one of the major barriers to any contemporary publication of the original history,[84] and of course he had even less reason to be reticent in the *Life*. The result was a series of impressively balanced portrayals of both his friends and his enemies in the final *History*. He wrote to Earle that "I am careful to do justice to every man who hath fallen in the quarrel, on which side soever, as you will find by what I have said of Mr. Hambden [*sic*] himself."[85]

Clarendon's portraits of Hampden and Cromwell, who politically were his archenemies, illustrate how he achieved the fairness he sought. Even though he blames Hampden for fomenting the war and describes his death as "a great deliverance to the nation," Clarendon still does full justice to Hampden's wisdom, courage, industry, and political abilities: "He was an enemy not to be wished wherever he might have been made a friend, and as much to be apprehended where he was so as any man could deserve to be" (*HR*, 3:64). There is probably some wistfulness in the comment, along with the obvious respect. As one of the reformers in the early days of the Long Parliament, Hyde had been closely associated with Hampden and had liked him. In contrast, Oliver Cromwell was a man whom he knew very slightly and whom he could never have understood—a military genius, a religious fanatic, a regicide. Clarendon's major explanations of Cromwell's conduct throughout the *History* portray him only as a master hypocrite and dissembler. Yet when he sums up Cromwell in the portrait after his death, he opens by emphasizing that Cromwell's accomplishments required great virtues as well as great wickedness, and he reiterates the point once more in the sketch before closing with it: "In a word, as he had all the wickednesses against which damnation is denounced and for which hell-fire is prepared, so he had some virtues which have caused the memory of some men in all ages to be celebrated" (*HR*, 6:91, 97). Few of Cromwell's supporters could have more accurately—even, perhaps, generously—assessed his strengths: his "wonderful understanding in the natures and humours of men," his "great spirit," his "very prodigious address," his "admirable circumspection and sagacity," and his "most magnanimous resolution" (*HR*, 6:91, 94).

Lucian, Plutarch, and also Josephus, in a passage Clarendon excerpted in his commonplace book as a "rule for History," had warned against excessive condemnation of wicked characters.[86] But the balance clear in Clarendon's presentations of his enemies also appears in those of his friends, for his feelings for them seldom blinded him to their shortcomings in historical terms. His sketches of Falkland, Lord Capel, Sir Henry Killigrew, and others are in many ways prose equivalents of the celebrations of friendship in Cavalier poetry. Yet even his deeply moving depiction of Falkland, whom Hyde was determined "yᵉ next age shall be taught to valew more than yᵉ present did,"[87] shows how his friend was "too much a contemner of those arts, which must be indulged in the transactions of human affairs" (*HR*, 3:181). Similarly, just after Hopton's death, Hyde wrote in a letter that his friend was "as faultless a person, as full of courage, industry, integrity and religion as I ever knew man."[88] He pays tribute to these virtues in his portrait in the *History*, but ends it by explaining why, despite all his good qualities, Hopton was "rather fit for the second than for the supreme command in any army" (*HR*, 3:346).

Clarendon's portrait of Charles I in many ways parallels that of Cromwell in its moderation and balance. When Charles I was alive, Hyde wrote that he "would never consent that the King should acknowledge himself to be in the wrong, to save his three Kingdoms"; after Charles' death, he wrote that he felt an "obligation, which, if all others could, can never be dissolved . . . that is, the reverence I pay to the precious memory of my dear Master."[89] Twenty years later, in the *Life*, he still described himself as one "who had the greatest love for his person and the greatest reverence for his memory that any faithful servant could express" (*HR*, 4:489). In the *History*, Clarendon definitely presents the strongest defense of the King that he can, by stressing "his private qualifications as a man" (*HR*, 4:489). However, unlike Warwick, whose sketch is positive because he focuses only on Charles' personal virtues and on a few inarguable public ones (the dignity of his court and his support for religion, for example), Clarendon measures Charles' "kingly virtues" and concludes, reluctantly but accurately, that "he was not the best King" (*HR*, 4:490, 492). The sketch has been criticized for its lack of color and focus,[90] but Charles' basically weak character and his regal rigidity would have made such literary efforts inappropriate and, in Clarendon's view, dishonest. Indeed, recognizing the literary effect of the ambiguity necessary in his sketch of Charles, he ends the eleventh book of the *History* not with the King, but with the character of Lord Capel, a Royalist in whom even "the malice of his enemies could discover very few faults" (*HR*, 4:510), and whose courageous fidelity makes a much more satisfactory conclusion. Clarendon's balance in treating Charles remains apparent even in comparison with David Hume almost a century later. Hume is inexplicably emphatic about Charles' good faith—"probity and honor ought justly to be numbered among his most shining qualities"—and insists that "scarce any of his faults rose to that pitch as to merit the appellation of vices."[91] Even Clarendon's devotion as one of Charles I's most faithful servants would never have extended so far.

Despite his efforts to be fair, Clarendon's record in portraying the men in his *History* is by no means perfect. In some instances he simply had not known individuals well enough; in others, his prejudices obtruded. Clarendon never liked the Scots. Even Montrose, whom Hyde described in a letter a few months after his death as "y[e] worthyest and y[e] noblest person y[e] Nation ever bred,"[92] fails to emerge from the pages of the *History* as effectively as comparable English characters. Although he ranks Montrose "amongst the most illustrious persons of the age" (*HR*, 5:122), he never quite manages to convey either the nobility or the passion of one of the most colorful figures in the civil wars. The slightly romantic shading obligatory for even the most straightforward and accurate account of Montrose was, of course, alien to Clarendon's personal outlook and literary style, and in addition, he himself had some problems while abroad in dealing with Montrose (*HR*, 5:15–16, 36). Moreover, he had little understanding of war operations and even less appreciation for military ability—shortcomings that the behavior of the military advisers in Charles I's councils had done nothing to encourage him to remedy. Thus Prince Rupert appears more often in the *History* as a disruptive element in Council than as a brilliant cavalry commander (albeit with some limitations). Similarly, Fairfax is portrayed most effectively as a dull-witted tool of Cromwell's. Clarendon had little respect for either man personally, and he apparently did not appreciate many of the political ramifications of their military prowess. Even with these two, however, Clarendon makes a rudimentary attempt to remain fair. He negatively depicts the characters of both throughout his narrative, but he never draws a full character sketch of either of them, an omission too unusual to be unintentional. While Clarendon does occasionally err in describing individual men, his general knowledge of human nature and his determination to be just contribute a great deal to compensate for his mistakes.

Although the emulative traditions of historiography that were proving so pernicious in seventeenth-century biographies did not mar Clarendon's characters, memorial traditions created some difficulties in one set of sketches. Usually historians were concerned to preserve only the lives and deeds of the most important personages in their works. Cicero mentions "such as are outstanding in renown and dignity,"[93] while Clarendon himself refers to "celebrating the memory of eminent and extraordinary persons" (*HR*, 3:178). But to one group, some of whose statures would not normally have been sufficient to give them places in a history, Clarendon felt a special obligation. These were the men killed in the civil wars. In a letter to Hopton requesting information about his campaigns, Hyde particularly desired "the full losse, and names of gallant persons lost, for to their memories I am bound to sacrifice: though I flatter not the lyvinge."[94] The reiteration of "lost" after "loss" shows Hyde's special concern, and the word "flatter" is both revealing and uncharacteristic. In the character sketches of the dead that follow his accounts of battles in the *History*, Clarendon covers both sides. But here the political status of the Parliamentarians insured a certain amount of balance in their characters. No similar restraint existed for the Royalists, whom Hyde had described in 1648 as "those glorious persons, who have payed the full debt they owed to His Majesty and their Country, by loosing [*sic*] their lives in His righteous cause, and whose memories must be kept fresh and pretious to succeeding ages."[95] As a group, the sketches memorializing the Royalist dead are among the least satisfactory in the *History*. Here what Clarendon saw as an obligation became at the literary level an almost automatic response, and in the *History* he produced what amounts to an ongoing Royalist martyrology. These sketches do contribute to the somber aspect of the times that Clarendon intended to render in his work. But too often the characters are vague and general, types of perfect loyalty rather than individuals. In some cases, one could be substituted for another. This kind of obituary character is, of course, never easy to write; even some of Tacitus' posthumous summaries can be vague. But with certain notable exceptions, the great character sketch of Falkland being the most obvious, Clarendon's memorial characters of the Royalists lack the realism and the balance characteristic of the rest of his sketches.

In terms of the development of his historical narrative, the most important characters Clarendon draws are causal. Convinced by his own experiences in public affairs that conduct and character were inextricably joined, he considered it the historian's obligation to present this relationship in recounting matters of fact. He constantly ties the evolution of events in the *History* to the behavior and personalities of individual men.[96] The western army's "prodigious" difficulties arose in part because "the money that was raised for the maintenance and payment of that army was entirely upon the reputation, credit, and interest of particular men" (*HR*, 2:458). He discusses jealousies among courtiers in detail because "these distempers and indispositions and infirmities of particular men had a great influence upon the public affairs, and disturbed and weakened the whole frame and fabric of the King's designs" (*HR*, 3:228). As the *History* opens, Clarendon locates the origin of the disturbances in the beginning of Charles I's reign and reveals the point of view he will develop throughout the work. He writes that by surveying the country and the court at that time,

we may discern the minds of men prepared, of some to do, and of others to suffer, all that hath since happened: the pride of this man, and the popularity of that; the levity of one, and the morosity of another; . . . the spirit of craft and subtlety in some, and the rude and unpolished integrity of others, too much despising craft or art; like so many atoms contributing jointly to this mass of confusion before us. (*HR*, 1:4)

To deal with these "atoms," the attributes of individuals that he considered basic components of events, the character sketch became Clarendon's most important literary method for historical explanation.

Just as Clarendon believed that the quality of a history depended on the caliber of the man who wrote it, he felt that the course of events was determined in part by the quality of the men who participated in them. Thus to explain why the fiasco of Charles I's escape to the Isle of Wight occurred, and to adjudicate the responsibility for it, he analyzes the characters of both Berkeley and Ashburnham, the King's companions on the flight (*HR*, 4:263–73). He surveys "the constitution of the Court" after Buckingham's death in a set of character sketches that reveal "how equal their faculties and qualifications were for those high transactions." The series in itself serves as a preparatory explanation for what was to come, as Clarendon concludes from his "lively reflections upon the qualities and qualifications of the several persons in authority in Court and Council" that "no man could expect the vigorous designs and enterprises undertaken by the duke would be pursued with equal resolution and courage" (*HR*, 1:56, 83). Other historians had, of course, commented on the characters of individuals in interpreting historical events, but their treatments were usually brief and superficial. Tom May's introduction of Sir William Waller before discussing his campaigns is typical of the practice of Clarendon's English predecessors and contemporaries: "He was a Gentleman of faire experience in Military affaires by former travels, and services abroad; of good judgement, and great industry; of which he gave many testimonies to the Kingdome."[97] Descriptions of this kind were of mild interest but served no important function, causal or otherwise, in the narrative of events. In contrast, Clarendon enormously expanded the scope of the causal character in historical writing.

Assessments of the *History* inevitably charge Clarendon with overestimating the importance of personality in determining events and overemphasizing personal causation in his text. Modern historians, suspicious of *histoire événementielle*, and proud of what Fernand Braudel describes as the transcendance of "the individual and the particular event . . . fully accomplished only in our time,"[98] have criticized Clarendon's focus on individuals as a serious flaw in the *History*. There is no question that Clarendon tended to see events in terms of personalities, and that in his political career and in his writing he sometimes made mistakes in interpretation because of this focus. For these errors, however, he has perhaps overpaid. The difficulties resulting in the *History* have sometimes been overemphasized because commentators, misled by the literary excellence of individual character sketches, have focused only on them and have usually ignored the larger narrative contexts within which the characters function. Clarendon's general narrative perspective considerably modifies his emphasis on personal causation in important ways.

First of all, Clarendon is quite emphatic throughout the *History* that

individual character was only one cause of events. His own private conflicts made him unable to come to grips fully with some events, but at
another level he recognized that in many cases rational explanation was
entirely insufficient to account for what had happened. He presents the
period of the civil wars as a time of chaos, when events assumed a momentum of their own and seemed in the end larger than the men par-
ticipating in them. The Parliamentary leaders, the Scots, and the Army
found themselves ultimately unable to control the forces they had un-
leashed; not even Cromwell himself seemed able to mold history to his
will like an Alexander or a Caesar. What Clarendon develops as the
nature of the times themselves, "when neither religion, or loyalty, or law,
or wisdom, could have provided for any man's security" (*HR*, 1:69), necessarily limited the impact of any single individual on the outcome of
events. Consequently, in the *History* Clarendon highlights the dichotomy
between men's intentions and the results they achieved. Intending to be
"the preserver, and not the destroyer, of the King and kingdom," Essex
"launched out into that sea where he met with nothing but rocks and
shelves, and from whence he could never discover any safe port to har-
bour in" (*HR*, 2:542). When the "poor earl of Pembroke" was offered the
governorship of the Isle of Wight by the Parliament, he "kindly accepted
it, as a testimony of their favour, and so got into actual rebellion, which
he never intended to do" (*HR*, 2:541). Even in the case of Pym, who
receives heavy blame for contriving "the miseries of the kingdom," Clarendon insists, "and yet I believe they grew much higher even in his life
than he designed" (*HR*, 3:321). Despite his concern with individuals,
throughout the *History* Clarendon shows that men are the prisoners of
circumstances as much as the creators of events.

In his text Clarendon constantly makes reference to certain irrational
matrices out of which the events of the civil wars had evolved. Sometimes
he accounts for this causal level in Providential terms. More often, when
rational explanation is elusive or events seem to combine in an inexplic-
able way, he refers to "accidents," a word that reverberates through the
History as it recurs: "the wonderful concurrence of many fatal accidents to
disfigure the government of two excellent kings"; "an accident that gave
them much trouble"; "the most prodigious accidents"; "new accidents
and alterations of a very extraordinary nature"; "wonderful and unex-
pected accidents" (*HR*, 1:55; 2:106; 4:2; 5:273; 6:88–89). Clarendon
constantly links chance and character in the *History* for causal purposes.
In attributing problems in the early years of Charles I's reign to Buck-

ingham, he writes: "These calamities originally sprung from the inordinate appetite and passion of this young man, under the too much easiness of two indulgent masters, and the concurrence of a thousand other accidents" (*HR*, 1:51). Similarly, he describes the passing of the bill of attainder against Strafford so "that it may be observed from how little accidents and small circumstances, by the art and industry of those men, the greatest matters have flowed towards the confusion we now labour under" (*HR*, 1:322). Clarendon could only acknowledge the existence of the "little accidents and small circumstances"; he could do little to enable himself or others to understand this kind of cause. In contrast, human character—the "art and industry" of men—was an area of historical causation that he understood thoroughly and that he could contribute a great deal to illuminate. He molded his narrative emphases accordingly.

Clarendon is always careful to separate the role of personal characteristics from that of personal motivation in evaluating causal elements in the *History*, and when he thinks it necessary, he disavows the role of either. For example, when Lambert is sent against Monck in late 1659, Clarendon gives a full character sketch of Monck's personal and political background and his military service. But he ends the sketch by emphasizing that at the time Monck had no intentions whatsoever of contributing to Charles II's restoration and that "the disposition that did grow in him afterwards did arise from those accidents which fell out, and even obliged him to undertake that which proved so much to his profit and glory" (*HR*, 6:156). Clarendon thus provides all the relevant information about Monck as a man, but he carefully qualifies the context in which it can properly be used for historical explanation. Later, he even more firmly establishes the dichotomy between Monck's attributes as an individual and the role he played in events:

And for . . . his understanding and ratiocination, alas! it was not equal to the enterprise. He could not bear so many and so different contrivances in his head together as were necessary to that work. And it was the King's great happiness that he never had it in his purpose to serve him till it fell to be in his power, and indeed till he had nothing else in his power to do. If he had resolved it sooner, he had been destroyed himself; the whole machine being so infinitely above his strength, that it could be only moved by a divine hand; and it is glory enough to his memory, that he was instrumental in bringing those mighty things to pass, which he had neither wisdom to foresee, nor courage to attempt, nor understanding to contrive. (*HR*, 6:164)

171

Although Monck's character is vastly insufficient to explain the Restoration, it represented historical causality on the level at which Clarendon was best equipped to deal. He thus depicts the man in detail, while maintaining the integrity of the event by deconstructing the character depiction through his narrative.

Finally, Clarendon's focus on causal characters is actually at many points in the *History* a literary device as much as it is a historical method. He makes some errors in historical interpretation because he misreads motivation (notably in his emphasis on the private ambitions of the Parliamentary leaders),[99] but these historical misinterpretations seldom significantly disrupt the narrative functions of his depictions of character. Although, as Boyce points out, the character sketch is "a literary form that did not naturally develop in the art of story-telling,"[100] one of Clarendon's major achievements was to make his sketches an integral part of his narrative. The character sketch as a form contains some story, for it usually portrays an individual's typical actions. However, because its primary concern is a man's essence, it is heavily explanatory and interpretive and is therefore predominantly composed of discourse. As a genre it thus suited Clarendon's preference for a high percentage of discourse in his work, and his sketches function well within the general narrative context he creates for the *History*. Faced with organizing a chaotic period, he often finds the character sketch a useful narrative tool with which to subsume and order unruly events. At the beginning of the *History* he surveys the problems that developed early in Charles I's reign by focusing on the Duke of Buckingham, because "the nature and character and fortune of the duke" were "the best mirror to discern the temper and spirit of that age" (*HR*, 1:55). Similarly, he uses Archbishop Williams' character as a narrative base from which to depict the withdrawal of all the Bishops from the House of Lords (*HR*, 1:464–73). In another section he manages to cover foreign military affairs succinctly by discussing maneuvers in Turenne's and Condé's campaigns in terms of their understanding of each other's personalities (*HR*, 6:82–84).

Treatments of character such as these directly advance the narrative; Clarendon can also use character sketches instead of narrative. Like many Restoration and eighteenth-century satirists, he recognized that properly deployed portraits could replace events in a narrative or compensate for a lack of physical action. Just as Dryden does in *Absalom and Achitophel*, Clarendon effectively juxtaposes groups of characters to remove the action in his text to the psychological level. For a conclusion to Book 6, at the end of the year 1642, he surveys the Privy Counselors who attended the King and those who stayed with the Parliament in a long series of character sketches. Individuals on both sides, poised against each other, illumine the motivations that had made the conflicts insoluble in order to set the stage for the next year of fighting. Through such strategies Clarendon joins personal concerns with political actions, which in turn translate later into military events. Finally, Clarendon also uses character sketches to pace his narrative. Before an important decision, he draws the characters of men representing different points of view to create suspense, even as they help to explain how various political and military policies evolved. The roll calls of the dead after battles heighten the tragedy of the engagements that are depicted, grounding public events in private losses to translate national history into directly human terms. Clarendon's character sketches provide several of his best narrative devices even as they enliven his text.

Clarendon's integration of character and event in his concept of history is reflected in the way he structured the context of his narrative so that the sketches are dispersed throughout at points relative to the character's participation in events. The *History* often includes several portraits of the same man, showing various facets of his character that were important in different situations. Some characters are depicted when they first appear in the *History*. In other cases, Clarendon will mention a man and give salient information about him, but will wait to draw a full character sketch until his role requires more extended explanation. He carefully deploys these sketches to serve the needs of his narrative. For example, the Marquis of Newcastle appears many times in the *History*, with details of his character relevant to the actions depicted, before Clarendon includes an abbreviated character sketch of him in the survey of the King's Privy Counselors in 1643 (*HR*, 2:533). But for both literary and historical reasons, Clarendon waits to offer an extended sketch until after Marston Moor, so that he can use Newcastle's personality and temperament to explain why the defeat occurred and why all Royalist efforts in Yorkshire were subsequently abandoned. Despite his disastrous mistakes at Marston Moor and his almost comically unmilitary temperament, Newcastle had long served Charles I faithfully and generously, and Clarendon rightly ends the character on a positive note, with Newcastle's "constant and noble behaviour" during the Royalist exile (*HR*, 3:384–85). By doing so he not only renders justice to Newcastle, but also begins shifting the emphasis of his narrative as a whole. The rout at Marston Moor sealed the fate of the Royalists in the first civil war, and after this defeat Clarendon's perspective in the *History* focuses predominantly on Royalist affairs abroad.

Thus his character of Newcastle concludes one larger set of events within the narrative and looks forward to the next.

As Clarendon traces his contemporaries through the *History*, he creates richly complex portrayals by supplementing his character sketches with short descriptive comments on the character's behavior in later situations, as well as by amplifying initial sketches with subsequent ones.[101] His depiction of Sir John Hotham, the hapless and reluctant Parliamentarian whose refusal to allow the King to enter Hull in 1642 was one of the several events Clarendon in the *History* terms "in truth, the immediate cause of the war" (*HR*, 3:526), shows how he shapes a character gradually throughout his text under the press of events. Hotham first appears in the *History* during debate in the Long Parliament as one of a group of Yorkshiremen opposed to Strafford (1:225), and short references to him occur sporadically in connection with other Parliamentary activities. When he is appointed governor of Hull to keep munitions there out of Royalist hands, Clarendon briefly summarizes his political principles to establish how lukewarm his adherence to the Parliamentary side actually was, noting that Parliament sent Hotham's son, whom they trusted entirely, "to assist . . . or rather to be a spy upon his father" (*HR*, 1:524). But he deliberately withholds any actual sketch of Hotham's character until Charles I approaches within a mile of Hull in his abortive attempt on the town and sends a messenger to inform the governor of his arrival. Clarendon then focuses on Hotham's personal attributes (his fearfulness and his inability to think fast) and his family and political background (his ample fortune, his fundamentally good inclinations toward the government, and his deep opposition to civil war) to explain Hotham's utter confusion when faced with the King's advance. As the sketch ends, Clarendon turns to show Hotham on the town walls, with the King and his entourage below. Literary character at this point translates directly into narrative action as Hotham babbles distractedly of his trust from the Parliament and simultaneously falls on his knees to swear his loyalty to the King (*HR*, 2:47–50). Clarendon's explanation of public events at Hull thus develops naturally from his portrayal of Hotham's personality, his background, and his private ideological conflicts.

References to Hotham and his actions recur, particularly in the charges and countercharges about Hull in the declarations that form much of Book 5 of the *History*. Then the man himself reappears as Lord Digby, whom Hotham considered "in the number of his most notorious enemies" (*HR*, 2:257), is captured in French disguise, and becomes a prisoner in Hull. Here Clarendon briefly sketches Hotham's character again, this time emphasizing his roughness, overweening pride, lack of generosity, and shrewd craftiness. These attributes highlight Digby's masterful achievement in duping him, as Clarendon shows Hotham's character ineptly in action once more in protracted conversations with his prisoner, who "so far prevailed and imposed upon his spirit that he resolved to practise that virtue which the other had imputed to him, and which he was absolutely without, and not to suffer him to fall into the hands of his enemies" (*HR*, 2:263). During these discussions Clarendon also begins to develop Hotham by contrasting him with his son, whose fanatic Parliamentarianism and "ill nature" his father despised (*HR*, 2:263). Digby not only manages to convince Hotham to protect him, but also embroils the governor in an abortive scheme to hand over Hull to the King. The plot fails because Hotham's character or his circumstances again prove inadequate: "Whether from his want of courage, or want of power to execute what he desired, remained still uncertain" (*HR*, 2:267). Clarendon by this time has rounded out Hotham's character fully enough so that later, when he wants to explain why Parliamentary forces did not entirely subdue Yorkshire despite their superior strength, he has only to refer to "Hotham's wariness," his "pride," and his "contempt" of Fairfax, and to contrast his quiescence with his son's military activity (*HR*, 2:464, 460).

Hotham makes his final appearance in the *History* to be imprisoned, tried, and executed in 1645 by the Parliament, along with his son. Before he is brought to the scaffold, "broken with despair" (*HR*, 3:529), Clarendon offers a final summary of his background, political principles, and actions during the conflicts, to emphasize the ironies his life embodies: "It was the more wonderful, that a person of a full and ample fortune, who was not disturbed by any fancies in religion, had unquestioned duty to the Crown, and reverence for the government both of Church and State, should so foolishly expose himself and his family, of great antiquity, to comply with the humours of those men whose persons he did not much esteem, and whose designs he perfectly detested" (*HR*, 3:526). Characteristically, Clarendon interprets Hotham's role through a combination of personal traits and historical circumstances. Personal animosity against Strafford first involved him with the Parliamentarians; his "vanity and ambition" led him to continue with them, but so did the King's concessions to Parliament's "unreasonable demands" (*HR*, 3:526–27). Again characteristically, despite the clarity with which he has developed Hotham's character and situation, Clarendon emphasizes that neither fully accounts for what happened to him by framing the final review of his life within a Providential context. He opens by calling the execution of the

Hothams "an act of divine justice"; as Hotham puts his head on the block, Clarendon ends the account by writing that in Hotham's life and his son's, "there were so many circumstances of an unusual nature, that the immediate hand of Almighty God could not but appear to all men who knew their natures, humours, and transactions" (*HR*, 3 : 526, 529).

Neither one of Clarendon's two discrete character sketches of Hotham adequately conveys the impression of the man that emerges from the *History* as a whole. Even the final summation depends heavily for its effect on the many details of Hotham's character embedded in earlier parts of the narrative. Clarendon's depictions of men in the *History* are always cumulative ones, resulting both from his various character sketches and from details of character in action developed throughout the narrative. His Cromwell, for example, is both the master dissimulator who dominates the narrative interpretations and the "brave bad man" (*HR*, 6:97) of the judiciously balanced character sketch after his death. It is because Clarendon's sketches are so dependent on the narrative context and so much a part of it themselves that detaching individual sketches—particularly the obituary ones, which are usually those excerpted—from the *History* misrepresents the scope of his achievement in rendering his contemporaries and also misrepresents their roles in the work as a whole.

Hotham is a relatively minor character in the *History*, albeit one whose most significant action had major consequences. Yet Clarendon depicts his personality and motivations so clearly that even in his small role Hotham emerges not simply as an inept political maneuverer or a foolish Parliamentary puppet—both of which he unquestionably was—but also as a misguided and confused human being, a man of average capabilities and reasonably good intentions who found himself in a situation beyond his control, and who endeavored with increasing desperation and without success "to disentangle himself, and to wind himself out of the labyrinth he was in" (*HR*, 3 : 527). Clarendon can finally call Hotham's death a "woful tragedy" (*HR*, 3 : 529) because he has with great care developed the human as well as the historical dimensions of Hotham's story.

Despite Clarendon's emphasis on personal causation, all of his characters exist in his text not simply as historical agents or instruments, but as *men*. Tolstoy baldly differentiated between historians' and artists' depictions of individuals: "As an historian would be wrong if he tried to present an historical person in his entirety, in all the complexity of his relations with all sides of life, so the artist would fail to perform his task were he to represent the person always in his historic significance." [102] But Clarendon puts this judgment to the test, for his interest in individuals is that of both the artist and the historian. Because at his best he joins both perspectives in drawing his characters, they do not become structurally or thematically teleological. He will not simplify them to fulfill only their historical roles or to function solely as moral or political examples. In him, the historian's knowledge of individuals, honesty about them, and fairness toward them combine with the artist's fascination with human beings and desire to depict them so that he renders rounded and credible men. His ability to do so accounts in part for the lasting appeal of his work. History is most easily accessible to the average reader at the human level; even Braudel admits that "to challenge the enormous role that has sometimes been assigned to certain outstanding men in the genesis of history is by no means to deny the stature of the individual as individual and the fascination that there is for one man in poring over the fate of another." [103] As Clarendon traces men's motives, analyzes their behavior, and illumines their complexities as individuals, his studies of his contemporaries offer a wealth of insight into human nature and human capabilities even as they provide a rich texture for his historical narrative.

THE CHARACTERS AND THE *HISTORY*

Because Clarendon rendered men in the *History* not only in terms of their public roles in the events of the times but also in terms of their own personalities as individuals, he managed one task that only a contemporary historian can undertake. He shows how the men of his age appeared to at least one acute observer who saw them living. Clarendon has preserved for posterity those "delicate features of the mind, the nice discriminations of character, and the minute peculiarities of conduct" that Samuel Johnson noted were so "soon obliterated" and that led Johnson to believe that historical characters were trustworthy only when drawn by those who had known them personally, such as Sallust and Clarendon. [104] However, Clarendon's achievement is not simply that he shows the personal significance along with the historical as he portrays his characters. Because of his narrative skill, he makes the two integrally connected, and he forges these connections so that the larger themes of his work are both clarified and strengthened. As early as Aristotle's *Poetics*, the tragic character's role as an agent was distinguished from his traits as a person. [105] Most seventeenth-century biographies and many histories structurally reflected such a distinction by separating their accounts of deeds and events from concluding character sketches. But in Clarendon's characters themselves, and in his integration of them into his text, he merged historical evidence about men's lives and psychological interpretation of their personalities to show how what men do derives directly from what they are, always within the irrational or circumstantial limitations that life itself continually imposes.

As Clarendon shows men's individual significances as human beings, and makes those personal significances historical, his interpretations assume the broad aesthetic and thematic validity associated with literature. They do so because the larger thematic concerns shaped by his imaginative referent led him to see men's historical significance as greater than— or at least different from—their particular roles in public affairs. Falkland, a relatively minor historical personage who assumed larger proportions for posterity because of the way his friend portrayed him, is the best of many examples of Clarendon's ability to develop his characters so that they illumine the times while pointing beyond the simultaneously personal and historical.

Although he had some colorful family involvements, Falkland's life before the war was mainly uneventful in public terms. Generous, warm, and impulsive in temperament, Falkland was preeminently an intellectual and an idealist, with the characteristic strengths and weaknesses of the breed: the driving curiosity, the ability and the need to develop subtle distinctions, the wholehearted commitment to moral behavior and the concomitant inability to commit himself to any monolithic ideological stance. Because he was constitutionally unable to make the compromises that for most men are the essence of daily life, when, as Cowley wrote, "this great *Prince* of *Knowledge* is by Fate / Thrust into th' noise and business of a State,"[106] the results were predictably unfortunate. Irene Coltman, who questions whether "the political world was somehow unreal to Falkland," writes that he seemed "to have thought of Parliament as a larger Great Tew."[107] Falkland's roles in the events of the early 1640s, first as a Parliamentary reformer and then as Charles I's Secretary of State, were not of exceptional political or historical importance. Horace Walpole could sum him up as "a virtuous, well-meaning man, with a moderate understanding, who got knocked on the head early in the civil war, because it [the war] boded ill."[108] Falkland's supreme achievement was the intellectual and spiritual community which he gathered around him at Great Tew. But even here his role could be unpropitiously interpreted. Thus Maurice Ashley reduced Falkland to "above all one of those personable young men

who (like the celebrated Edwardian hostesses) have a natural gift for at-
tracting brilliant company." [109]

Falkland would most naturally appear as an important figure in a
cultural or perhaps an intellectual history of the mid-seventeenth century
rather than in a predominantly political one. Although Clarendon listed
"the growth and improvement of arts and sciences" along with "great and
noble actions in peace and in war" as "the most proper subjects of history," [110] he seldom includes the arts and never the sciences in the *History
of the Rebellion*. In writing of Chillingworth's death in the *Life*, for example, he asserted that Chillingworth's "book will live," but he deleted
that observation from the final *History* (*HR*, 3:313, 335). Clarendon
makes his case for Falkland in the *History* not by focusing on the cultural
contributions of his intellect and ideals but by developing their potential
political ramifications. Characteristically, he was honest in describing
Falkland, showing both his political misjudgments and the ungracious-
ness sometimes produced by his rigid personal standards. He even included Falkland's concern with his clothes, which he attended to "with
more neatness and industry and expense than is usual to so great a mind"
(*HR*, 3:188). Nevertheless, because Clarendon was also able to so clearly
portray Falkland's essence—the absolute integrity of his intellect and his
uncompromising idealism—and to convey the importance of this kind of
integrity in shaping any individual, the character of Falkland assumes a
symbolic function in the *History* as a representative of the values of this
stance, despite his personal shortcomings. Moreover, when Clarendon
shows this kind of person choosing to in effect commit suicide since he is
no longer able to function in the world as he finds it, the public dimensions of a tragedy of private character emerge clearly. The kind of government Clarendon wanted, and the kind of nation he felt England should
be, required the intelligence, the loyalty, the courage, and above all the
integrity of individuals like Falkland. Thus in the *History* the loss of such
men assumes an importance disproportionate to their own particular historical roles. Because of Clarendon's ability to be faithful to his historical
evidence, while at the same time imbuing it with his vision of their larger
significances in human and ultimately moral terms, he merges public and
private elements so that through his characters he can both render and
measure the age as a whole.

The kinds of evaluations of individuals that Clarendon makes in the
History collectively convey a sense of the unusual configurations of the
age itself, a time of extraordinary demands on men when normal expectations and standards could not apply. Because of his diachronic under-

179

standing of character, he carefully evaluates individuals throughout the *History* in terms of their times. In such a period most men's characters prove inadequate for England's historical circumstances. Justice Reeve "in good times would have been a good judge"; the Earl of Cumberland was "a man of honour, and popular enough in peace, but not endued with those parts which were necessary for such a season" (*HR*, 2:241, 286). A rare few prove themselves superior. War brought out strengths in the Earl of Carnarvon that had lain dormant in peacetime (*HR*, 3:178). The second Duke of Hamilton possessed "a rare virtue in the men of that time," for he "was still the same man he pretended to be" (*HR*, 5:5). The Earl of Manchester was

of so excellent a temper and disposition that the barbarous times, and the rough parts he was forced to act in them, did not wipe out or much deface those marks: insomuch as he . . . performed always as good offices towards his old friends, and all other persons, as the iniquity of the time, and the nature of the employment he was in, would permit him to do; which kind of humanity could be imputed to very few. (*HR*, 2:545)

Through his relation of individuals' qualities to the age, Clarendon creates a rich sense of the moral and psychological climate of the nation, and of its evolution through the crises at midcentury.

Other patterns that collectively emerge from Clarendon's depictions of individuals in the *History* also render his conception of the age as a whole. Early English historians had found biography an easy organizing principle for individual reigns, but Clarendon employed the character sketch on so broad a scale that his work became at one level what Carlyle would later claim all history was—"the essence of innumerable Biographies."[111] Like modern prosopographers in social history, Clarendon molds his sketches of characters so that they can represent and in a sense explain the trends of an age. In his causal and obituary characters he traces the ways in which many different men reacted to the same events. Through this variety of perspectives, he recreates the national past through individual pasts. While each person's story remains his own, many also have ties to the experiences of others. For example, Clarendon portrays Hotham as a unique individual. But when he writes that Hotham "found himself more dangerously and desperately embarked than he ever intended to be" (*HR*, 3:529), Hotham's predicament becomes reminiscent of the dilemmas of Essex, of Pembroke, and of many other Parliamentarians in the *History*. As Clarendon allows the common perceptions and illusions of the men of his time to emerge through his depictions of character, the sketches as a group contribute to the emergence of larger thematic concerns, such as the relationships between private virtues and public good, individual integrity and national honor, effective ministers and a healthy state. Merging personal, political, historical, and moral concerns to depict individuals so that they illumine their times, he recreates the world of mid-seventeenth-century England through his literary methods of collective biography.

Finally, for all his interest in individuals and his belief in their importance, Clarendon's ultimate concern in the *History* was always the depiction of his age as a whole. He believed that it was "no less a part of history, and more useful to posterity, to leave a character of the times than of the persons, or the narrative of matters of fact, which cannot be so well understood as by knowing the genius that prevailed when they were transacted" (*HR*, 3:232). "Temper of the times" is a recurring expression in the *History*, suggesting the seriousness with which Clarendon viewed his age itself as a living entity with characteristics of its own. The character sketches are vital in revealing this temper, but he conveys it in many other ways as well, from the language used in certain declarations to the inclusion of events of "trivial moment" (*HR*, 2:244) that reveal the national mood.

Clarendon's perception of the nature of his own country and its people and his treatment of the national character in the *History* contribute greatly to the cumulative effect of his narrative. Throughout his career, Clarendon's strength as a statesman had been his understanding of England and the English people. Totally devoted to his country—fleeing into banishment, he was unconcerned about his destination, "all places out of England being indifferent" to him (*CL*, 2:453)—he had developed an encompassing sense of its regions, its traditions, its institutions, its customs, and its characteristic ways of life and thought. His ability to recognize where the deepest loyalties of the English people lay, what changes they would accept or reject, and what courses of action would best accord with the ways they instinctively thought had guided him in counseling Charles I and Charles II, and had finally enabled him to help bring about the Restoration. It is this sense of the essence of the English nation manifesting itself in time that informs the *History*.

Like his knowledge of individuals, Clarendon's conception of what the English people as a nation were during the period from the late 1620s until 1660 was diachronic, based on what they had been in the past, what they were in the present, and what they could be in the future. Similarly, he was as concerned to be fair to the nation during a tumultuous age as he was to the individuals whose characters he portrayed. He believed that "there are *vitia temporum*, as well as *vitia hominum*,"[112] but he felt that the age in which he lived, like too many of the men of it, had been unjustly maligned. In the opening sentence of the *History*, he emphasized his desire to show that the times were not characterized by "a general combination, and universal apostasy in the whole nation." In his exordium to Book 9, he again insisted that "lamentable effects" proceeded not from "a universal corruption of the hearts of the whole nation," but "only from the folly and the frowardness [*sic*], from the weakness and the wilfulness, the pride and the passion, of particular persons." He was determined that their "memories ought to be charged with their own evil actions, rather than they should be preserved as the infamous charge of the age in which they lived" (*HR*, 4:2). Clarendon's desire to protect his nation and his era from the recriminations of posterity was not only an attempt to place the blame where it was fairly due; it was also an expression of his deep affection for and loyalty to his fellow Englishmen, of whatever political persuasion. This magnanimity of outlook, coupled with his ability to use varied literary means to embody it, serves to make the *History* more than merely an accurate and well-written recounting of events and collection of sketches. In the prose he forged, in the narrative structure and point of view he evolved, and, above all, in the imaginative vision with which he infused his evidence, Clarendon reflects his capacious view of individual men, of an era, and of the nature of history itself.

Although the *History of the Rebellion* would be of far less literary value if it had included no character sketches, the sketches themselves do not provide the only, or even the major, literary merit of Clarendon's work. What he did with the literary conventions of the character represents microcosmically what he also accomplished with other literary elements in historical writing. At a time when writers like Izaak Walton were allowing moral concerns to submerge men's characters as individuals and others like Aubrey and Burnet were capturing individuality at the expense of essence, Clarendon showed how the character sketch could be made suitable for a history that would be both accurate and artistic. Between the old commemorative and memorial traditions of the character, which sacrificed life to art and evidence to interpretation, and the emerging realistic modes, which highlighted fact at the expense of art, Clarendon found a middle way that combined the strengths of both. Using all his insight and skill, in his character sketches he fused life and art, evidence and interpretation, in the same way that he forged his prose style and narrative structure by taking up available conventions, combining them to serve his own purposes, and, in the process, transforming them.

Clarendon's style molded the content of his *History* to meet the requirements of his subject as he conceived it, as well as the demands of his own personality, circumstances, and talents, and his view of history and literature. His attempt was an ambitious one, for he measured out a goodly portion of historical ground in order to find the most satisfactory form to encompass his own experiences and those of his age. His view of how events had evolved and how they should be told was at times more capacious than he had the art to control. At other times his literary abilities faltered when he was less sure in his grasp of the meaning of certain events. But if the literary quality of his masterpiece is occasionally uneven, the *History of the Rebellion* is nevertheless a work of art. Despite some flaws, Clarendon's work conveys a felt sense of human experience and historical reality that is never simply the result of scholarship but can only derive from the creative imagination.

Moreover, if Clarendon's merging of literary art and factual evidence was not a perfect one, it was of essential value in advancing the literary development of historical writing after a century in which both its contents and methods had irrevocably changed. The split that was developing between evidence and interpretation in the depiction of character during the seventeenth century can be viewed from one perspective as a manifestation of the larger divisions within historical discourse, as the antiquarians moved to reduce it to documentary evidence and the polemicists made it subservient to their own interested interpretations of events. These antiquarian and polemical elements, which threatened the literary quality of seventeenth-century histories and often the integrity of history itself by upsetting the balance between evidence and interpretation, continued to figure prominently in English historiography well into the eighteenth century.

In the position of Historiographer Royal, Thomas Rymer with his *Foedera* (1702–11) and then Thomas Madox with his *History of the Exchequer* (1711) provided documentary collections and continued to refine antiquarian methods. Richard Rawlinson's bibliographies traced the accumulated learning in historical areas. Polemical historians refought the civil wars from their studies. During the Restoration the Royalist (by then more accurately termed high Tory) John Nalson had published his *Impartial Collection of the Great Affairs of State* (1682, 1683) to counter the Parliamentary bias of the first three volumes of John Rushworth's *Historical*

Collections (1659, 1680). In the eighteenth century Laurence Echard followed Clarendon in his *History of England* (1707–18), only to be refuted by John Oldmixon's histories in 1724 and the 1730s. Next, Thomas Carte's work attacked what he saw to be the Whiggish interpretation of Rapin. Edmund Calamy and John Walker exhumed ecclesiastical and clerical issues from the previous century to debate them.[113] The tendency to separate historical truth and literary art also continued. In 1691, for example, John Harrington's Preface to *Athenae Oxonienses* asserted "it was thought more useful to publish . . . it, in an honest plain *English* dress, without flourishes or affectation of Stile, as best becomes a History of Truth and matter of Fact."[114] But in the midst of this historiographical mediocrity and confusion, the publication of Clarendon's *History* offered a giant alternative, the power of which was shown by its enthusiastic reception among scholars and the general reading public alike. Clarendon's literary skills and particularly his ability to evolve an imaginative overview of his subject set his work apart. Even as polemicists moved to attack his views, they were forced to acknowledge his art. After reading Clarendon, Burnet revised the manuscript of his own history, paying particular attention to the characters. No one until Hume would match Clarendon, but two generations of historians between them lived with the *History of the Rebellion* as an example overshadowing their own attempts.

Clarendon's work was also vital in combating another historiographical trend that emerged strongly in the late seventeenth and early eighteenth centuries. The focus on political instruction in history, which had developed from Machiavelli, Guicciardini, and Continental historians, and had entered English historiography in the works of Bacon, Camden, and others in the late sixteenth and early seventeenth centuries, had degenerated by the mid-seventeenth century mainly into polemical strains. These emphases, along with the increasing interest in individual personality characteristic of the later seventeenth century, combined to produce a focus on details of character in the histories written during the Restoration. Thus, even as literature was moving from subjective and private themes to public ones, history was taking the opposite tack, and the emphasis on the individual rapidly degenerated over the period to make the so-called "secret history" the most characteristic historiographical enterprise of the end of the century. At best such trends culminated in the work of Burnet, while at worst they led to the gossip and scandal of spurious histories produced by hack writers. In the eighteenth century, Pope and Swift particularly connected such histories with the Dunces, and Daniel Defoe, that quintessential reflector of the momentarily marketable, once wrote the secret history of a secret history.[115] That Burnet's model was not followed and that the secret histories ultimately contributed to enrich the emerging genre of the novel had a good deal to do with Clarendon's example of what historical narrative could be.

Out of the distilled richness of a lifetime of varied experience and careful observation, Clarendon in the *History of the Rebellion* recreated his England by presenting his own evidence and that of others with the literary skill and vision of an artist. Fusing personal and impersonal elements, he rendered his world so well because he was so much a part of it, so representative of it in so many ways, and yet at the same time was able to detach himself from it and view it with perhaps as much objectivity as any contemporary historian could hope to attain. Most of Clarendon's major writings were works he had planned or pondered for many years. In the late 1650s, he was anxious to see effective replies to Hobbes; several of his letters during the Royalist exile reveal the interest in papal power that would culminate in *Religion and Policy*.[116] Behind the final *History of the Rebellion* were two previous attempts at the same subject and almost three decades of thought. Clarendon wanted his works to be read, but he recognized that they would have to await the proper time; he wrote to his son that he was "willing to follow the advice of your friend Horace, 'Nonumque prematur in annum.'"[117] He also knew that he was writing for a particular kind of reader. In one of his polemical responses he repeatedly refers to readers who "will take the pains" to examine the events and issues involved;[118] because of his characteristic methods and emphases, all of his works demand such readers. But just as Clarendon placed his trust in literary methods at a time when most historians were turning away from them, he also trusted that the integrity of his story and his vision would in the end insure a place for himself and his work. He believed that his life and his ideals would be validated by his own portrayal of his times, and that his personal quest, as he subsumed it into historical writing, could guide others in the future. Because of his integrity and abilities as a man and a statesman, an artist and a historian, Clarendon was able to merge literature and history to create in the *History of the Rebellion* the kind of depictions and transformations of an era that mark great literary historiography.

Appendix: Hyde's Poems*

*Poems from William Davenant, *The Tragedy of Albovine, King of the Lombards* (London, 1629), n.p.; [John Donne], *Poems, By J. D. With Elegies on the Authors Death* (London, 1633), p. 377.

To his friend, M^r. W^m. D'avenant.

Why should the fond ambition of a friend,
With such industrious accents strive to lend
A Prologue to thy worth? Can ought of mine
Inrich thy Volume? Th'hast rear'd thy selfe a Shrine
Will out-live Piramids; Marble Pillars shall,
Ere thy great Muse, receive a funerall:
Thy wit hath purchas'd such a Patrons name
To deck thy front, as must derive to Fame
These Tragick raptures, and indent with Eyes
To spend hot teares, t'inrich the Sacrifice.

Ed: Hyde.

On the death of Dr Donne.

I cannot blame those men, that knew thee well,
Yet dare not helpe the world, to ring thy knell
In tuneful *Elegies*; there's not language knowne
Fit for thy mention, but 'twas first thy owne;
The *Epitaphs* thou writst, have so bereft

Our tongue of wit, there is not phansie left
Enough to weepe thee; what henceforth we see
Of Art or Nature, must result from thee.
There may perchance some busie gathering friend
Steale from thy owne workes, and that, varied, lend,
Which thou bestow'st on others, to thy Hearse,
And so thou shalt live still in thine owne verse;
Hee that shall venture farther, may commit
A pitied errour, shew his zeale, not wit.
Fate hath done mankinde wrong; vertue may aime
Reward of conscience, never can, of fame,
Since her great trumpet's broke, could onely give
Faith to the world, command it to beleeve;
    Hee then must write, that world [would] define thy parts:
    Here lyes the best Divinitie, All the Arts.

Edw. Hyde.

Notes

Introduction

1. Leopold von Ranke, *A History of England, Principally in the Seventeenth Century*, 6 vols. (Oxford: Clarendon Press, 1875), 6:29.

2. David Underdown, *Royalist Conspiracy in England: 1649–1660* (New Haven: Yale University Press, 1960), p. 354.

3. John Oldmixon, *Clarendon and Whitlock Compar'd. To which is occasionally added, A Comparison between the History of the Rebellion, and Other Histories of the Civil War* (London: J. Pemberton, 1727), p. 172; Samuel Rawson Gardiner, *History of the Great Civil War: 1642–1649*, 4 vols. (London: Longmans, Green, 1893), 3:121.

4. W. C. Brownell, *The Genius of Style* (1924; reprint ed., Port Washington, N.Y.: Kennikat Press, 1972), p. 113; H. R. Trevor-Roper, *Men and Events: Historical Essays* (New York: Octagon Books, 1976), p. 248; George Sherburn and Donald F. Bond, *A Literary History of England*, ed. Albert C. Baugh, 2nd. ed. (New York: Appleton-Century-Crofts, 1967), p. 787; A. L. Rowse, *The English Spirit: Essays in History and Literature* (New York: Macmillan, 1945), p. 158; Sir Charles Firth, *Essays Historical and Literary* (Oxford: Clarendon Press, 1938), p. 122.

5. Christopher Hill, "Clarendon and the Civil War," *History Today* 3 (1953): 703.

6. Frank Smith Fussner, *The Historical Revolution: English Historical Writing and Thought, 1580–1640* (London: Routledge and Kegan Paul, 1962), p. 300.

7. Although passing remarks on style often appear in articles on other aspects of Clarendon's work, more extended criticism has been sparse. Leo Braudy includes some literary analysis of Clarendon in *Narrative Form in History and Fiction* (Princeton: Princeton University Press, 1970), pp. 14–21. George Watson considers the style of Clarendon's opening sentence in "The Reader in Clarendon's *History of the Rebellion*," *Review of English Studies*, n.s., 25 (1974): 396–409.

George E. Miller in *Edward Hyde, Earl of Clarendon* (Boston: Twayne, 1983) includes a chapter on "The *History of the Rebellion* as Literature" (pp. 67–87), although the brevity of the format limits his coverage. E. M. W. Tillyard in *The English Epic and its Background* (1954; reprint ed., London: Chatto and Windus, 1966) evaluates epic elements in Clarendon's writings (pp. 448–51), and is followed by William E. Miller ("Clarendon's Mind and Art: A Literary Reappraisal" [Ph.D. diss., University of Rochester, 1974], pp. 127–28) and George Miller (pp. 74–76). One of the best discussions is Joan E. Hartman's "Clarendon: History, Biography, Style" (Ph.D. diss., Radcliffe College, 1960). Commentary on the character sketches alone is covered in the notes to Chapter 5 of this book.

8. On the possibilities of such a biography being written, see Chapter 3. The two earliest biographies of Clarendon are T. H. Lister's *Life and Administration of Edward, First Earl of Clarendon*, 3 vols. (London: Longman et al., 1837), and Sir Henry Craik's *The Life of Edward, Earl of Clarendon*, 2 vols. (London: Smith, Elder, 1911), of which Lister's is the more balanced and effective portrayal. R. W. Harris adds some new information in *Clarendon and the English Revolution* (London: Chatto and Windus, 1983), but the times rather than the man still predominate, and some of the documentation is faulty. B. H. G. Wormald's *Clarendon: Politics, History, and Religion, 1640–1660* (Cambridge: Cambridge University Press, 1951) gives very full political and intellectual biography for that period of Clarendon's life. Finally, Graham Roebuck's *Clarendon and Cultural Continuity: A Bibliographical Study* (New York: Garland, 1981) contains much biographical information about Clarendon and useful observations on his style in addition to bibliography.

Chapter 1: *Clarendon's Historical Writing in Context*

Epigraphs: Degoreaus Wheare, *The Method and Order of Reading Both Civil and Ecclesiastical Histories*, trans. Edmund Bohun (London: M. Flesher, 1685), p. 176. Wheare delivered the lectures on which this work is based in 1623, which is the year the work itself was first published in Latin—as *De Ratione et Methodo Legendi Historias*—in London (William H. Allison, "The First Endowed Professorship of History and Its First Incumbent," *American Historical Review* 27 [1922]: 737). Sir John Hayward, "The Epistle Dedicatorie," *The Lives of the III Normans, Kings of England* (London: R. B., 1613), n.p. Samuel Johnson, *Rambler 152*, in *The Rambler*, ed. W. J. Bate and Albrecht B. Strauss (New Haven: Yale University Press, 1969), 5:45. Marc Bloch, *The Historian's Craft*, trans. Peter Putnam (New York: Vintage Books, 1953), p. 8.

1. F. J. Levy, *Tudor Historical Thought* (San Marino, Calif.: Huntington Library, 1967), p. 233; Godfrey Davies, *The Early Stuarts, 1603–1660*, 2nd. ed. (Oxford: Clarendon Press, 1959), p. 392.

2. Fussner, *Historical Revolution*, p. 193.

3. Davies, *Early Stuarts*, p. 415.

4. Cicero, *De Oratore*, trans. E. W. Sutton and H. Rackham, 2 vols. (Cambridge: Harvard University Press, 1942), 1:242–43 (II.xv.62).

5. *The Institutio Oratoria of Quintilian*, trans. H. E. Butler, 4 vols. (New York: G. P. Putnam's Sons, 1922), 4:20–21 (X.i.31); "The Way to Write History," in *The Works of Lucian of Samosata*, trans. H. W. Fowler and F. G. Fowler, 4 vols. (Oxford: Clarendon Press, 1905), 2:130. See also Cicero, *De Oratore* 1:244–45 (II.xv.64).

6. Polydore Vergil, *An Abridgemēt of the notable worke of Polidore Vergile*, trans. Thomas Langley (London: Richarde Grafton, 1546), p. xxi[r].

7. *A Report and Discourse written by Roger Ascham, of the affaires and state of Germany and the Emperour Charles his Court, durying certaine years, while the sayd Roger was there* (1552), in *The Whole Works of Roger Ascham*, ed. Rev. Dr. Giles, 3 vols. (London: John Russell Smith, 1864–65), 3:6.

8. On the split between history and literature, see Herschel Baker, *The Race of Time: Three Lectures on Renaissance Historiography* (Toronto: University of Toronto Press, 1967), pp. 73–96; Fussner, *Historical Revolution*, pp. 46–48, 305; Levy, *Tudor Historical Thought*, pp. 37, 39, 45–46, 51; Joseph M. Levine, "Ancients, Moderns, and History: The Continuity of English Historical Writing in the Later Seventeenth Century," in *Studies in Change and Revolution: Aspects of English Intellectual History, 1640–1800*, ed. Paul J. Korshin (Menston, Yorkshire: Scolar Press, 1972), pp. 48–52; Hugh Trevor-Roper, *Queen Elizabeth's First Historian: William Camden and the Beginnings of English 'Civil History'* (London: Jonathan Cape, 1971), p. 23; George Huppert, "The Renaissance Background of Historicism," *History and Theory* 5 (1966): 48–54.

9. Edmund Bolton, "Hypercritica, or A Rule of Judgement, for writing or reading our History's" (1618?), in *Critical Essays of the Seventeenth Century*, ed. J. E. Spingarn, 3 vols. (Oxford: Clarendon Press, 1908), 1:83.

10. Jean Bodin, *Method for the Easy Comprehension of History*, trans. Beatrice Reynolds, Columbia University Records of Civilization—Sources and Studies, no. 37, ed. Austin P. Evans (New York: Columbia University Press, 1945), p. 55.

11. 1580 is the date cited by both Levy (*Tudor Historical Thought*, p. 128) and Fussner (*Historical Revolution*, p. xxii).

12. William Camden, *The History of the Most Renowned and Victorious Princess Elizabeth Late Queen of England: Selected Chapters*, ed. Wallace T. MacCaffrey (Chicago: University of Chicago Press, 1970), p. 3.

13. Ibid., p. 55.

14. Thomas Hobbes, *Hobbes's Thucydides*, ed. Richard Schlatter (New Brunswick: Rutgers University Press, 1975), p. 16.

15. John Hughes, "Preface," *A Complete History of England*, 3 vols. (London, 1719), 1:n.p.

16. Cicero, *De Oratore*, 2:236–37 (II.xii.54).

17. Camden, *History of Princess Elizabeth*, p. 8.

18. John Milton, "To Henry de Brass," no. 23 of *The Familiar Letters of John Milton*, ed. Donald Lemen Clark (New York: Columbia University Press, 1936), pp. 93–95; translation in Baker, *Race of Time*, p. 89.

19. Samuel Daniel, "Certaine Advertisements to the Reader," *The Collection of the History of England*, in *The Complete Works in Verse and Prose of Samuel Daniel*, ed. Alexander B. Grosart, 5 vols. (London: Hazel, Watson, and Viney, 1885–96), 4:83.

20. Thomas Carlyle, *Two Note Books of Thomas Carlyle*, ed. Charles Eliot Norton (1898; reprint ed., Mamaroneck, N.Y.: Paul P. Appel, 1972), pp. 22–23.

21. Cecil Seronsy, *Samuel Daniel* (New York: Twayne, 1967), pp. 61–62.

22. Quoted from Aubrey's manuscripts by Oliver Lawson Dick, "The Life and Times of John Aubrey," *Aubrey's Brief Lives* (London: Secker and Warburg, 1949), p. lv.

23. Morris W. Croll (*Style, Rhetoric, and Rhythm*, ed. J. Max Patrick et al. [Princeton: Princeton University Press, 1966]) and George Williamson (*The Senecan Amble: A Study in Prose Form from Bacon to Collier* [1951; reprint ed., Chicago: University of Chicago Press, 1966]) trace patterns that resulted from various reactions to the Ciceronian tradition during the century. R. F. Jones emphasizes the influence of contemporary science on prose style in *Ancients and Moderns: A Study of the Rise of the Scientific Movement in Seventeenth-Century England* (St. Louis: Washington University Studies, 1961), while W. Fraser Mitchell in *English Pulpit Oratory from Andrewes to Tillotson: A Study of Its Literary Aspects* (New York: Macmillan, 1932) considers the effects of Anglican and Puritan styles in preaching. More recent critics, such as Robert Adolph in *The Rise of Modern Prose Style* (Cambridge: M.I.T. Press, 1968) and Stanley Fish in *Self-Consuming Artifacts: The Experience of Seventeenth-Century Literature* (Berkeley: University of California Press, 1972), tend to work in terms of epistemological differences that shaped seventeenth-century styles. Three samples from Clarendon are included in Robert Cluett's computer analyses of style in *Prose Style and Critical Reading* (New York: Teachers College Press, 1976), although some of the charts and figures given for him seem to be contradictory (for example, see pp. 221 and 261, and also the numbers given for Clarendon and Coleridge on pp. 98 and 100 and their positions on Figure 5.2, p. 67). On seventeenth-century prose in general, see also Paul G. Arakelian, "The Myth of a Restoration Style Shift," *The Eighteenth Century: Theory and Interpretation* 20 (1979): 227–45.

24. Quintilian, *Institutio Oratoria*, 3:578–79 (IX.iv.129); Lucian, "Way to Write History," 2:133. See also Quintilian, 3:514–15 (IX.iv.18).

25. Hayward, "The Epistle Dedicatorie," n.p.

26. Fussner, *Historical Revolution*, p. 38.

27. Baker, *Race of Time*, p. 29; Davies, *Early Stuarts*, p. 408.

28. On their aims, see J. G. A. Pocock, *The Ancient Constitution and the*

Feudal Law: A Study of English Historical Thought in the Seventeenth Century (Cambridge: Cambridge University Press, 1957).

29. Levy, *Tudor Historical Thought*, p. 280; Matthew A. Fitzsimons, Alfred G. Pundt, and Charles E. Nowell, *The Development of Historiography* (Harrisburg, Pa.: Stackpole, 1954), pp. 137–38. In the early eighteenth century, John Hughes noted that Camden's work "had the natural Effect of a well-writ Piece of Modern History, for it gain'd him much Applause, and many Enemies" (*Complete History*, 1:n.p.)

30. Oldmixon, *Clarendon and Whitlock*, p. xviii. For general background on the historians of the civil war period, see Royce MacGillivray, *Restoration Historians and the English Civil War* (The Hague: Martin Nijhoff, 1974).

31. Joshua Sprigge, "To All True English-men," in *Anglia Rediviva; Englands Recovery: Being the History of the Motions, Actions, and Successes of the Army under the Immediate Conduct of His Excellency S⁰. Thomas Fairfax, K⁰.* (London: R. W., 1647), n.p.

32. Thomas May, *The History of the Parliament of England*, ed. Francis Maseres (1647; reprint ed., London: Robert Wilks, 1812), pp. xvi, xv.

33. Thomas, Lord Fairfax, *A Short Memorial of the Northern Actions; during the War there, from the year 1642 till the year 1644*, in *Stuart Tracts, 1603–1693*, ed. C. H. Firth (Westminster: Archibald Constable, 1903), p. 365.

34. Horace Walpole, *A Catalogue of the Royal and Noble Authors of England* (Edinburgh: J. Mundell, 1796), p. 321.

35. William Waller, *Vindication of the Character and Conduct of Sir William Waller, Knight* (London: J. Debrett, 1793), p. 197.

36. John Price, *The Mystery and Method of his Majesty's Happy Restoration, Laid Open to Publick View* (1680), reprinted in *Select Tracts Relating to the Civil Wars in England in the Reign of King Charles the First*, ed. Francis Maseres (London: R. Wilks, 1815), p. 745.

37. Jonathan Culler, *The Pursuit of Signs: Semiotics, Literature, Deconstruction* (Ithaca: Cornell University Press, 1981), pp. 169–70; Seymour Chatman, *Story and Discourse: Narrative Structure in Fiction and Film* (Ithaca: Cornell University Press, 1978), pp. 43–95.

38. Various uses of the term "story" by theorists are discussed by Culler, *Pursuit of Signs*, p. 170; Chatman, *Story and Discourse*, pp. 19–26; and Robert Scholes, *Semiotics and Interpretation* (New Haven: Yale University Press, 1982), pp. 88–93, 110–12, 148.

39. Scholes, *Semiotics and Interpretation*, p. 144.

40. John Donne, *Satyre IV*, in *The Satires, Epigrams and Verse Letters*, ed. W. Milgate (Oxford: Clarendon Press, 1967), p. 17, ll. 97–98.

41. Thomas Sprat, *History of the Royal Society*, ed. Jackson I. Cope and Harold Whitmore Jones (St. Louis: Washington University Studies, 1958), p. 36.

42. On Stowe, see Levy, *Tudor Historical Thought*, pp. 192–95, and C. L.

Kingsford, *English Historical Literature in the Fifteenth Century* (Oxford: Clarendon Press, 1913), p. 271. For Brady, see Fussner, *Historical Revolution*, p. 115, and Pocock, *Ancient Constitution*, pp. 224–26, 248, and "Robert Brady," *Cambridge Historical Journal* 10 (1951): 186–204.

43. Hugh G. Dick, "Thomas Blundeville's *The true order and Methode of wryting and reading Hystories (1574),*" *Huntington Library Quarterly* 3 (1940): 155.

44. Camden, *History of Princess Elizabeth*, p. 7; John Hughes, *Complete History*, 1:n.p.

45. Francis Bacon, *De Augmentis Scientiarum: Book II, Chapter VII*, in *The History of the Reign of King Henry the Seventh*, ed. F. J. Levy (Indianapolis: Bobbs-Merrill, 1972), p. 308; Bolton, "Hypercritica," 1:102. See also Wheare, *Method of Reading*, p. 17.

46. *Memoirs of Denzil, Lord Holles, Baron of Ifield in Sussex, From the Year 1641 to 1648* (1699), reprinted in Maseres, ed., *Select Tracts*, p. 310.   •

47. *A Narrative by John Ashburnham of his Attendance on King Charles the First From Oxford to the Scotch Army, and From Hampton-Court to the Isle of Wight*, 2 vols. (London: Payne et al., 1830), 2:63.

48. May, *History of the Parliament*, p. 208.

49. Hobbes, *Hobbes's Thucydides*, p. 7.

50. On these historiographers, see Felix Gilbert, "The Renaissance Interest in History," in *Art, Science, and History in the Renaissance*, ed. Charles S. Singleton (Baltimore: Johns Hopkins University Press, 1967), p. 378.

51. Hayden White, *Metahistory: The Historical Imagination in Nineteenth-Century Europe* (Baltimore: Johns Hopkins University Press, 1973), p. 31. In context, White ties the prefiguring "poetic act" to four basic tropes (Metaphor, Metonymy, Synecdoche, and Irony) in figurative language (pp. 31–38). These four tropological modes are integrally connected with three modes of historical explanation, each of which has four components: explanation by emplotment (Tragedy, Comedy, Romance, and Satire—pp. 7–11); explanation by formal argument (Formism, Organicism, Mechanism, Contextualism—pp. 11–21); and explanation by ideological implication (Conservatism, Liberalism, Anarchism, and Radicalism—pp. 22–29). White explains that "a historiographical style represents a particular *combination* of modes of emplotment, argument, and ideological implication" (p. 29). White's system in *Metahistory* is developed to be applied to nineteenth-century historiographers and philosophers of history, and it naturally presupposes both historical and literary self-consciousness and sophistication on the part of the historian that no writer in the seventeenth century could have possessed. Seventeenth-century historians were still at the early level of conceptualization that in White's system is briefly described as the "*transformation of chronicle into story*"—in his view, arranging events into rudimentary narratives with beginnings, middles, and ends (pp. 5–7). Because these writers are dealing only with what White calls "primitive elements" of the historical account (p. 5), his breakdown of additional components of the historical field and style is unnec-

essary for them. With some Procrustean alterations, White's system could perhaps be transposed to seventeenth-century historiography, but his complex of factors was evolved to explain very different kinds of historiographical problems in a very different intellectual climate.

52. On Thucydides, see Francis Macdonald Cornford, *Thucydides Mythistoricus* (1907; reprint ed., New York: Greenwood Press, 1969), and Kieran Egan, "Thucydides, Tragedian," in *The Writing of History: Literary Form and Historical Understanding*, ed. Robert H. Canary and Henry Kozicki (Madison: University of Wisconsin Press, 1978), pp. 87–88.

53. On More, see Levy, *Tudor Historical Thought*, pp. 68–72; for Bacon, see Fussner, *Historical Revolution*, pp. 253–74.

54. H. Stuart Hughes, *History as Art and as Science: Twin Vistas on the Past* (New York: Harper and Row, 1964), p. 81.

55. Ibid., pp. 80ff.; George Steiner, *In Bluebeard's Castle: Some Notes Towards the Redefinition of Culture* (New Haven: Yale University Press, 1971), pp. 3ff.

56. Carl L. Becker, "Everyman His Own Historian," *Everyman His Own Historian: Essays on History and Politics* (New York: Appleton-Century-Crofts, 1935), p. 245.

57. Virginia Woolf, "The New Biography," in *Collected Essays*, 4 vols. (New York: Harcourt, Brace and World, 1950), 4:233–34.

58. Lawrence Stone, "The Worst of Times?" review of *A Distant Mirror: The Calamitous Fourteenth Century*, by Barbara W. Tuchman, in *The New York Review of Books*, 28 September 1978, p. 3.

59. Frederick A. Pottle, *James Boswell: The Earlier Years, 1740–1769* (London: Heinemann, 1966), p. 43.

60. Jacques Barzun is acid on the subject: "What happens to a fine intelligence when subjected for years to a diet of archives? Quantification may be for such a mind the only recourse after ankylosis of the imagination has set in" (*Clio and the Doctors: Psycho-History, Quanto-History, and History* [Chicago: University of Chicago Press, 1974], pp. 117–18).

61. The definitive account of the composition of the *History of the Rebellion* is C. H. Firth's "Clarendon's 'History of the Rebellion,'" *English Historical Review* 19 (1904): 26–54, 246–62, 464–83.

62. *State Papers Collected by Edward, Earl of Clarendon*, ed. Richard Scrope and Thomas Monkhouse, 3 vols. (Oxford: Clarendon Printing-House, 1767–86), 2:288. Hereafter cited as *SP*.

63. *SP*, 2:288.

64. *Contemplations and Reflections Upon the Psalms of David*, in *A Collection of Several Tracts of the Right Honorable Edward, Earl of Clarendon* (London: T. Woodward and J. Peele, 1727), p. 485. Hereafter cited as *Psalms*.

65. MS. Clarendon 126, fol. 59. All Clarendon manuscripts are in the Bodleian Library, Oxford University. Clarendon referred again to Machiavelli in a similar context in a speech to the House of Lords on 19 May 1662, adding, "I am

sure, you are all good Historians, and need only to resort to the Records of your own Memories" (*Journals of the House of Lords, Beginning Anno Duodecimo Caroli Secundi, 1660,* [1660–66], 11:476).

66. *The History of the Rebellion and Civil Wars in England,* ed. W. Dunn Macray, 6 vols. (1888; reprint ed., Oxford: Oxford University Press, 1969), 4:184. Hereafter cited as *HR.*

67. *A Brief View and Survey of the Dangerous and pernicious Errors to Church and State, in Mr. Hobbes's Book, Entitled Leviathan* (Oxford, 1676), p. 116. Hereafter cited as *Lev.*

68. *HR,* 3:375; see also *HR,* 3:360; 6:107.

69. *The Difference and Disparity Between the Estates and Conditions of George Duke of Buckingham, and Robert Earl of Essex,* in Sir Henry Wotton, *Reliquiae Wottonianae,* 3rd ed. (London: T. Roycroft, 1672), p. 193. Hereafter cited as *RW.*

70. *Essays Moral and Entertaining, on the Various Faculties and Passions of the Human Mind,* ed. James Stanier Clarke, 2 vols. (London: Longman, 1815), 1:245. Hereafter cited as *Essays.*

71. *SP,* 2:289.

72. *Religion and Policy and the Countenance and Assistance Each Should Give to the Other,* 2 vols. (Oxford: Clarendon Press, 1811), 1:24. Hereafter cited as R & P.

73. *SP,* 2:336.

74. MS. Clarendon 47, fol. 389^v; MS. Clarendon 48, fol. 100^r.

75. *SP,* 2:289.

76. Ellis Farneworth, trans., "The Preface," *The History of the Civil Wars of France,* by Henrico Caterino Davila, 2 vols. (London, 1758), 1:v–vi.

77. In these writings, he was probably also trying to convince himself that Royalism, despite its shortcomings, was the only viable stance for a conscientious citizen, a motive that also underlies the *History.*

78. *Calendar of the Clarendon State Papers Preserved in the Bodleian Library,* ed. Octavius Ogle, W. H. Bliss, W. Dunn Macray, F. J. Routledge, 5 vols. (Oxford: Clarendon Press, 1869–1970), 4:266, 554. Hereafter cited as *Cal. Cl. SP.*

79. *Essays,* 1:244–45.

80. Firth, "Clarendon's 'History,'" p. 45.

81. *SP,* 2:350.

82. *SP,* 2:383.

83. *SP,* 2:385.

84. MS. Clarendon 29, fol. 101^r.

85. MS. Clarendon 28, fol. 179^r.

86. *SP,* 2:336.

87. *SP,* 2:357.

88. MS. Clarendon 28, fol. 179^r.

89. *SP,* 2:289.

90. MS. Clarendon 49, fol. 75^r; *Cal. Cl. SP,* 2:403.

91. Edward Gibbon, *Memoirs of My Life*, ed. Georges A. Bonnard (New York: Funk and Wagnalls, 1966), pp. 155–56.

92. Most of his changes occur at the beginning of the original history; by Book 4 of the manuscript (Book 5 in the final *History*), there are few alterations. The drafts of the *Life* (MS. Clarendon 123) and of later additions to the *History* (MS. Clarendon 112) are very clean copy.

93. *SP*, 2:333–35, 350. To see Clarendon's abilities in abridging, compare his accounts of the treaty of the Isle of Wight (*HR*, 4:391–93, 426–55) with the letters from the King that he was using (*SP*, 2:425–54).

94. MS Clarendon 36, fols. 80–83.

95. *SP*, 2:318.

96. British Library Add. MS. 18,982, fol. 159.

97. Firth, "Clarendon's 'History,'" pp. 464, 478.

98. Hartman, "Clarendon," p. 24.

99. "To the Kings Most Excellent Majesty: The Epistle Dedicatory," *Lev.*, n.p.

100. On the reception, see Levine, "Ancients, Moderns, and History," p. 72; H. R. Trevor-Roper, "Clarendon and the Practice of History," *Milton and Clarendon* (Los Angeles: William Andrews Clark Memorial Library, 1965), pp. 31–32; R. C. Richardson, *The Debate on the English Revolution* (New York: St. Martin's, 1977), pp. 25, 34.

Chapter 2: Clarendon's Literary Art

Epigraphs: Bolton, "Hypercritica," 1:107. Barzun, *Clio and the Doctors*, p. 114. Hayden White, "Rhetoric and History," *Theories of History* (Los Angeles: William Andrews Clark Memorial Library, 1978), p. 24. Herbert Butterfield, *Man on His Past: The Study of the History of Historical Scholarship* (Cambridge: Cambridge University Press, 1955), pp. xii–xiii.

1. Wormald, *Clarendon*, p. x.

2. Von Ranke, *History of England*, 6:11; Trevor-Roper, "Clarendon and the Practice of History," p. 27.

3. Firth, *Essays*, p. 121. See also Firth, "Clarendon's 'History,'" p. 470; Watson, "The Reader," p. 406; Rowse, *English Spirit*, p. 169; Harris, *Clarendon*, p. 393. Two brief positive views of the final *History* are offered by Rosalie L. Colie in *The Resources of Kind: Genre Theory in the Renaissance*, ed. Barbara K. Lewalski (Berkeley: University of California Press, 1973), p. 99, and C. V. Wedgwood, *Seventeenth-Century English Literature*, 2nd. ed. (Oxford: Oxford University Press, 1970), pp. 76–77. Although George Miller credits the final *History* with

unity (*Edward Hyde*, pp. 45, 86–87), he does so on different grounds than I do. He considers the *History* "a coherent work of art" because (1) it has "a beginning, middle, and an end"; (2) it shows "unifying concerns"; (3) it rests "upon a consistent set of values"; and (4) "most importantly, it exhibits the same fundamental literary elements that we expect to find in any work of literature [specifically, emplotment, character, and narrative voice]" (pp. 69, 86–87; see also p. 39). Miller continues the traditional emphasis on irreconcilable differences between the original history and the *Life*—"the *History* resulted from fusing together two separate works which had distinctly different intentions and methods"—and also the emphasis on the "patchwork nature" of the final *History* (pp. 68, 69, 86; see also p. 74).

4. *The Continuation of the Life of Edward Earl of Clarendon, Lord High Chancellor of England, and Chancellor of the University of Oxford; From the Restoration in 1660, to his Banishment in 1667*, in *The Life of Edward Earl of Clarendon, Lord High Chancellor of England, and Chancellor of the University of Oxford: In Which is Included A Continuation of His History of the Grand Rebellion*, 2 vols. (Oxford: Clarendon Press, 1817), 2:566. Hereafter cited as *CL*.

5. *The Life of Edward Earl of Clarendon; From His Birth to the Restoration of the Royal Family in the Year 1660*, in *The Life of Edward Earl of Clarendon*, 1:167. Hereafter cited as *Life*, with the page number, since all excerpts from the *Life* itself are in the first volume.

6. On Baxter, see Joan Webber, *The Eloquent "I": Style and Self in Seventeenth-Century Prose* (Madison: University of Wisconsin Press, 1968), pp. 122–23.

7. Quoted by David Nichol Smith, in *Characters from the Histories & Memoirs of the Seventeenth Century* (1918; reprint ed., Oxford: Clarendon Press, 1950), p. xxxvii, from the 1857 edition of the *Life*, Part 1, section 85. He points out its omission in the 1759 edition (n. 1).

8. For a good example, see Clarendon's accounts of Prynne, Bastwick, and Burton's triumphal entry into London (*HR*, 1:265—from the *Life*—and 1:269—from the original history).

9. Firth, "Clarendon's 'History,'" p. 259. Clarendon later included parts of this vindication in the *Continuation of the Life* (2:488–543).

10. Paul Delany in *British Autobiography in the Seventeenth Century* (London: Routledge and Kegan Paul, 1969) points out that "*res gestae* was, in that period, the orthodox and natural mode for *any* autobiographer to incline to; subjective works were exceptional" (p. 169).

11. *SP*, 2:246. Although in this instance Clarendon was encouraging others' contributions to the history, the remarks are nevertheless a fair indication of his general attitudes.

12. *Essays*, 2:84.

13. *SP*, 2:403.

14. *Lev.*, pp. 1–2.

15. *Essays*, 1:251.

16. *Essays*, 2:135.

17. *HR*, 3:90–91; *Bellum Civile. Hopton's Narrative of his Campaign in the West (1642–1644) and Other Papers*, ed. Charles E. H. Chadwyck Healey, Somerset Record Society Publication, vol. 18 (London: Harrison and Sons, 1902), pp. 52–55 (Sir Ralph Hopton) and 94–97 (Colonel Walter Slingsby). In other instances, however, Clarendon's narrative proved topographically inaccurate. On 13 August 1743, Walter Harte, the Vice Principal of St. Mary Hall, Oxford, wrote in a letter to Dr. C. Lyttleton: "With pleasure, attention, & Clarendon's history in my great coat pocket I surveyd the ground whereon the battle of Stratton was fought. . . . I thought L^d. C. the exactest of writers, till I reviewed the idea he had of this battle & the place twas fought on; but ex pede Herculem—." Harte explains: "You w^d. think by C. an attack was made on the East Side, but that way [is] impracticable, being exceedingly steep, skirted with wood, a rivulet & morass at bottom" (British Library MS. Stowe 753, fol. 38^r).

18. See, for example, Ascham, *Whole Works*, 3:6. Jacques Amyot's and Hobbes' prefaces to their translations of Plutarch and Thucydides, which notes in Clarendon's commonplace book indicate that he read, mention the stylistic importance of this kind of immediacy of representation (Hobbes, *Hobbes's Thucydides*, p. 18; "Amiot to the Readers," in Plutarch, *The Lives of the Noble Grecians and Romanes*, trans. James Amyot and Thomas North [1579 and 1603; reprint ed., London: Nonesuch Press, 1929], p. xx; MS. Clarendon 127, fols. 48^r, 50^r).

19. *Essays*, 2:84.

20. Hobbes, *Hobbes's Thucydides*, p. 8; MS. Clarendon 127, fol 50^r. "Ignorance in readinge" is Clarendon's marginal comment on the passage.

21. *Ben Jonson*, ed. C. H. Herford and Percy and Evelyn Simpson, 11 vols. (Oxford: Clarendon Press, 1925–52), 1:138.

22. Evelyn twice credited Clarendon with supporting and encouraging plans for the Royal Society, and Sprat in his *History* rendered the Society's "publick thanks" to Clarendon for his legal assistance as Chancellor in establishing it (Evelyn to Samuel Pepys, 12 August 1689, *Diary of John Evelyn*, ed. William Bray, revised by Henry B. Wheatley, 4 vols. [New York: Scribner's, 1906], 3:446, hereafter cited as Wheatley; John Evelyn, "To the Right Honourable Edward, Earl of Clarendon," *Instructions Concerning Erecting of a Library . . . by Gabriel Naudeus* [London, 1661], A$_2$^{v}–A$_3$^{r}; Sprat, *History*, p. 143, and also pp. 136–37, 142, 144). Although Clarendon was named a Fellow, the designation seems to have been an honorary one; there is no indication that he participated in any of the Society's intellectual enterprises. On Clarendon and the Royal Society, see also Hartman, "Clarendon," pp. 218–20; P. H. Hardacre, "Clarendon and the University of Oxford, 1660–1667," *British Journal of Educational Studies* 9 (1961): 131.

23. For general use of these metaphors, see Bernard N. Schilling, *Dryden and the Conservative Myth* (New Haven: Yale University Press, 1961), pp. 74–76, 242–50. The ubiquity of Clarendon's metaphors can be seen by their appearance in an address to Charles II in 1656 from the Levellers (*HR*, 6:67–74).

24. Sir Edward Walker, "The Happy Progress and Success of the Arms of K. Charles I. of ever blessed Memory, from the 30th of *March*, to the 23ᵈ of November, 1644," in *Historical Discourses*, ed. H. Clopton (London, 1705), p. 22; *HR*, 3:356.

25. Walker, "Happy Progress," p. 22; *HR*, 3:356.

26. Hopton, *Bellum Civile*, p. 56; *HR*, 3:96.

27. Hopton, *Bellum Civile*, p. 96; *HR*, 3:91.

28. Hopton, *Bellum Civile*, p. 95; *HR*, 3:91.

29. *R & P*, 2:581; MS. Clarendon 54, fol. 278ʳ. See also *Cal. Cl. SP*, 3:xi–xii, 397–98.

30. *SP*, 3:165.

31. *SP*, 3:171.

32. *SP*, 2:288.

33. Gilbert Burnet, *Burnet's History of My Own Time: Part I—The Reign of Charles the Second*, ed. Osmund Airy, 2 vols. (Oxford: Clarendon Press, 1898), 1:169.

34. D. C. Muecke, *The Compass of Irony* (London: Methuen, 1969), p. 80; Norman Knox, *The Word Irony and Its Context, 1500–1755* (Durham: Duke University Press, 1961), pp. 9–10. For additional discussions of Clarendon's irony, see William Miller, "Clarendon's Mind and Art," pp. 123–24, 153–55, and George Miller, *Edward Hyde*, pp. 85–86.

35. Hartman associates each of Clarendon's three major syntactical modes with specific subject matter in the *History*: the loose with factual narrative, the periodic with commentary, and antithetic point with brief observations at the end of his sentences for emphatic or ironic effect, particularly in the character sketches ("Clarendon," pp. 172–89, 229–30). However, Clarendon's practice of mixing syntactical modes in the *History* seriously undermines the schematic neatness of these specific associations of context and form.

36. *SP*, 2:357; *CL*, 2:567.

37. Ralph H. Major, "Angina Pectoris: The Earl of Clarendon," in *Classic Descriptions of Disease*, 2nd ed. (Springfield, Ill.: Charles C. Thomas, 1939), pp. 452–55.

38. *SP*, 2:478.

39. *SP*, 3:125, 66, 151. One other reason for Clarendon's characteristic copiousness is suggested by two apologies for long letters. From March 1644/5 on, he suffered from increasingly severe attacks of gout. To Hopton in 1648, he wrote: "The truth is, if I had bene able to stand or goe, you had not now had so long [a] letter, but beinge not at ease enough to study, I can do nothinge but write" (MS. Clarendon 31, fol. 63ᵛ). He told Dr. Cosin in 1656 that the length of his letter is due "to my Goute, wᶜʰ keepes me in my chaire, so that I can doe nothing but write or reade" (MS. Clarendon 51, fol. 115ᵛ). Harris, who suggests that Clarendon's gout may have been psychosomatic, connects the attacks with periods of crisis and stress (*Clarendon*, pp. 140, 202, 313, 392).

40. An additional difficulty for the modern reader of Clarendon's long sentences is created by seventeenth-century grammatical practices, for only in the eighteenth century were the conventions governing modern sentence structure developed. Ian A. Gordon points out that in seventeenth-century prose, "much of what appears to be subordination is really coordination by a link no longer current: 'as,' 'that,' 'where' and 'which' introduce clauses which later grammarians insisted on calling adjectival, and so subordinate" (*The Movement of English Prose* [London: Longmans, 1966], p. 115). Also, as Hartman notes, Clarendon's "punctuation was rhetorical, based on delivery rather than on syntax, and denotes pauses rather than grammatical stops." Hartman emphasizes that not even Macray's edition has faithfully reproduced the punctuation in Clarendon's manuscripts ("Clarendon," pp. 173–74). Since the characteristics of Clarendon's style which concern me here are equally clear in both versions, I have referred to Macray rather than to the manuscripts for the reader's convenience.

41. Lister, *Life and Administration*, 2:579.

42. G. M. Trevelyan, *England Under the Stuarts* (New York: Putnam's, 1949), p. 45. See also C. H. Firth, "The Development of the Study of Seventeenth-Century History," in *Transactions of the Royal Historical Society*, 3rd. ser. (London: Offices of the Society, 1913), 7:46–47.

43. *Essays*, 1:250.

44. The terminology denoting the duration of an action and the time required to read a depiction of it varies among critics; see Chatman, *Story and Discourse*, pp. 62–63. Probably the best-known discussion of the relationships between the two kinds of time is Gérard Genette's, in *Narrative Discourse: An Essay in Method*, trans. Jane E. Lewin (Ithaca: Cornell University Press, 1980).

45. Although Camden uses annalistic form, his occasional violations of strict chronology, as in his treatment of the rebellion in Ireland in 1580, could possibly have been models for Clarendon. On Camden's structure, see Fussner, *Historical Revolution*, pp. 249–50.

46. Robert Scholes and Robert Kellogg, *The Nature of Narrative* (London: Oxford University Press, 1966), pp. 72, 243–44. George Miller, however, connects Clarendon's use of first-person narrative with elements of defensive apologia in the *History*: "At still other points in the narrative when Clarendon feels the need to defend either the king or himself, he lapses into the first person" (*Edward Hyde*, p. 82).

47. Firth points out that "in very many cases a vague periphrasis is substituted for a definite statement, so that the turns and changes of royalist politics become involved in unnecessary obscurity" ("Clarendon's 'History,'" p. 470).

48. Roland Barthes, "Introduction to the Structural Analysis of Narrative," *Image—Music—Text*, trans. Stephen Heath (New York: Hill and Wang, 1977), p. 112.

49. Roland Barthes, "Historical Discourse," in *Introduction to Structuralism*, ed. Michael Lane (New York: Basic Books, 1970), p. 149.

50. For these letters, on which this account of the conversion crisis is based, see *Cal. Cl. SP*, 2:403–39, and the corresponding Clarendon manuscripts in the Bodleian Library.

51. *SP*, 3:259.

52. *Cal. Cl. SP*, 2:420–21, 423–24, 427.

53. *Essays*, 2:139. See also Clarendon's "A Dialogue between the Same Persons and a Bishop, concerning Education," in *A Collection of Several Tracts of . . . Clarendon*, p. 326. Hereafter cited as *Ed.*

54. Thomas Carlyle wrote that the "Uxbridge-treaty is graphically delineated" (*Two Note Books*, p. 11).

55. Genette, *Narrative Discourse*, p. 189.

56. Ibid., pp. 192, 191.

57. Firth, *Essays*, pp. 118–19, and *Dictionary of National Biography*, ed. Leslie Stephen and Sidney Lee, 22 vols. (1885–1900; reprint ed., Oxford: Oxford University Press, 1967–68) 10:386—hereafter cited as *DNB*; Christopher Hill, *Puritanism and Revolution* (London: Secker and Warburg, 1958), pp. 213–14.

58. For the conspiracy theory, see Wormald, *Clarendon*, pp. 156–60, 235, and Thomas H. Robinson, "Lord Clarendon's Conspiracy Theory," *Albion* 13 (1981): 96–116.

59. Hill, "Clarendon and the Civil War," pp. 698–701; G. E. Aylmer, *The Struggle for the Constitution: England in the Seventeenth Century* (1963; reprint ed., London: Blandford Press, 1971), pp. 118–19.

60. Denys Hay, *Annalists and Historians: Western Historiography from the Eighth to the Eighteenth Centuries* (London: Methuen, 1977), p. 119; Fussner, *Historical Revolution*, p. 250.

61. *SP*, 2:386.

62. *SP*, 3:206.

63. *Psalms*, p. 427.

64. *SP*, 2:359.

65. E. I. Carlyle emphasizes that Clarendon's view of the council is his own personal creation: "Clarendon believed that his conception of the privy council was in accordance with the traditional practice of the state. It was in fact ideal, and never had had an historical existence" ("Clarendon and the Privy Council, 1660–1667," *English Historical Review* 27 [1912]: 253). See also Clayton Roberts, *The Growth of Responsible Government in Stuart England* (Cambridge: Cambridge University Press, 1966), pp. 138–39, and Harris, *Clarendon*, pp. 327–28, 363.

66. There are 2,819 pages in Macray's edition, but certain sections of the *Life* and the original history deleted in the final *History* are included.

67. In the *Continuation of the Life*, he notes: "I should not have enlarged thus much upon the ceremony of the coronation, it may be not mentioned it, (a perfect narration having been then made and published of it, with all the grandeur and magnificence of the city of London,) but that there were two accidents in it" (1:170).

68. Irene Coltman, *Private Men and Public Causes: Philosophy and I English Civil War* (London: Faber and Faber, 1962), pp. 110–15; Wor endon, p. 238–39; W. G. Roebuck, "Charles II: The Missing Portrait, ~~~~~~~~ ton Library Quarterly* 38 (1974–75): 216, 219; Royce MacGillivray, "Clarendon Among the Pre–Clarendonians," *Humanities Association of Canada Bulletin* 20, no. 3 (1969): 14–15; George Miller, *Edward Hyde*, pp. 70–73; Harris, *Clarendon*, pp. 394–95. For Clarendon's own view of the miraculous aspects, see *Psalms*, pp. 584, 726–27, 744–45.

69. For instance, *Psalms*, pp. 468, 534, 605–6, 662.

70. George Miller's explanation of Clarendon's ending presents it as growing "out of the particular emplotment": "If the restoration of Charles II was evidence of God's providence, the deaths of the two power brokers of France and Spain, who had done everything they could to obstruct any assistance toward that restoration, was evidence of God's retribution" (*Edward Hyde*, p. 73).

71. Hayden White, "The Value of Narrativity in the Representation of Reality," in *On Narrative*, ed. W. J. T. Mitchell (Chicago: University of Chicago Press, 1981), p. 22.

Chapter 3: *The Man Behind the Historian*

Epigraphs: *A Letter of Meric Casaubon to Peter du Moulin Concerning Natural Experimental Philosophie (1669)* and *Of Credulity and Incredulity (1668; 1670)* (Delmar, N.Y.: Scholars' Facsimiles and Reprints, 1976), p. 312. Carl Becker, "Detachment and the Writing of History," *Detachment and the Writing of History: Essays and Letters of Carl L. Becker*, ed. Phil L. Snyder (Ithaca: Cornell University Press, 1958), p. 12. Johan Huizinga, "The Idea of History," in *The Varieties of History: From Voltaire to the Present*, ed. Fritz Stern (1956; reprint ed., New York: Vintage, 1973), p. 301. Carlyle, *Two Note Books*, p. 20.

1. Bodin, *Method*, p. 42.

2. *Essays*, 1:249.

3. See his discussion in "The Death of the Author," in *Image—Music—Text*, pp. 142–48.

4. J. H. Hexter, *Doing History* (Bloomington: Indiana University Press, 1971), p. 17.

5. H. Stuart Hughes, *History as Art and as Science*, p. 94.

6. Quoted in Fitzsimons et al., *Development of Historiography*, p. 218.

7. On Clarendon's rank, see Firth, *Essays*, p. 104, and *DNB*, 10:384; Rowse, *English Spirit*, p. 171; Coltman, *Private Men and Public Causes*, p. 16; Aylmer, *Struggle for the Constitution*, p. 24.

8. Craik, *Life*, 1:2, n. 2.

9. *Essays*, 1:270. In the essay he argues that in the country, "the best and the most exact survey is taken of the nature of man . . . ; what brings most and best advantages to the public, and what most contradicts or destroys it, is most effectually discovered; the errors in policy itself . . . are first taken notice of, and proper remedies foreseen in those climates" (269).

10. On the Tew group, see *Life*, p. 31; Kurt Weber, *Lucius Cary: Second Viscount Falkland*, Columbia University Studies in English and Comparative Literature, no. 147 (New York: Columbia University Press, 1940), p. 82; Hugh Trevor-Roper, "Clarendon," *Times Literary Supplement*, 10 January 1975, p. 31. Trevor-Roper, Wormald, *Clarendon* (pp. 243–61), Coltman, *Private Men and Public Causes* (pp. 152–79), and Thomas H. Robinson ("Lord Clarendon's Moral Thought," *Huntington Library Quarterly* 43 [1979]: 41–49) are particularly good on the ideas of the Tew circle.

11. *HR*, 3:180, n. 1 locates Tew sixteen miles from Oxford; Weber says the distance was eighteen or nineteen miles (*Lucius Cary*, pp. 74, 77). Weber points out that Falkland's establishment at Burford as well as Tew "should be thought of as the scenes of these *convivia*, at least during the earlier years"; Falkland sold Burford Priory in 1637. Weber adds, however, that "the traditional association of the circle with Tew rather than with the Priory is not unjust, for the former appears to have been the Viscount's favorite seat" (p. 79).

12. Weber, *Lucius Cary*, p. 82.

13. MS. Clarendon 87, fol. 206ʳ. Commentators have correctly emphasized the merging of political and religious issues in Hyde's thought (for example, see Wormald's section "Religion" in *Clarendon*, pp. 240–325, and William Miller's "Clarendon's Mind and Art," pp. 140, 148, 208). However, such overstatements as Craik's—"Sincerely as he was attached to the ceremonies of the Church, Hyde was statesman first, and churchman only second" (Craik, *Life*, 2:64)—have sometimes failed to do justice to the personal faith that was central in his life. During the Royalist exile, for example, he constantly urged on others the total reliance and trust in God that he himself always showed (*SP*, 3:22 is typical). Toward the end of his life, he wrote that "to my unspeakable discomfort, during the whole Time of this my Second Banishment, I have been without a Chaplain, and consequently without any Exercise of that Religion which I have always embraced with my Soul" (*Psalms*, p. 374). See also *Psalms*, p. 573.

14. Wormald discusses the differences between Hyde and the Tew group, particularly emphasizing their varying attitudes toward the relationship between religion and politics (*Clarendon*, pp. 292–316).

15. MS. Clarendon 126, fol. 150ᵛ.

16. Wormald's *Clarendon* is the definitive treatment of Hyde's politics until 1660; a parallel study of his chancellorship is still needed.

17. *SP*, 3:171.

18. Bodleian Library MS. Carte 35, fol. 762.

19. H. Stuart Hughes, *History as Art and as Science*, p. 102; his entire discussion (pp. 99–103) is excellent.

20. David Ogg, *England in the Reign of Charles II*, 2 vols. (Oxford: Clarendon Press, 1934), 1:150; Firth, *Essays*, p. 103.

21. A second character sketch of himself as one of Charles I's advisers focuses primarily on his political and religious beliefs (*Life*, pp. 82–84).

22. Delany, *British Autobiography*, pp. 49, 108, 155; Wayne Shumaker, *English Autobiography: Its Emergence, Materials, and Form* (Berkeley: University of California Press, 1954), pp. 33–35; Donald A. Stauffer, *English Biography Before 1700* (Cambridge: Harvard University Press, 1930), p. 167.

23. Roy Pascal, *Design and Truth in Autobiography* (London: Routledge and Kegan Paul, 1960), pp. 6, 120.

24. Lister, *Life and Administration*, 2:70–71; Hartman, "Clarendon," pp. 103–4; Sir James Fitzjames Stephen, *Horae Sabbaticae*, 1st ser. (London: Macmillan, 1892), 1:342.

25. MS. Clarendon 47, fol. 357^r.

26. *Essays*, 2:3.

27. Carlyle, *Historical Sketches of Notable Persons and Events in the Reigns of James I and Charles I*, ed. Alexander Carlyle (London: Chapman and Hall, 1898), pp. 340–41.

28. *SP*, 2:236, 366, and 3:214; MS. Clarendon 39, fol. 199^r; *SP*, 3:673.

29. *SP*, 3:97; see also *HR*, 2:535, 536.

30. MS. Clarendon 51, fol. 175^r. See also *Life*, pp. 83, 114; Lister, *Life and Administration*, 3:226.

31. *SP*, 3:120, 177, also 196, 617; MS. Clarendon 53, fol. 9^r.

32. *SP*, 2:237.

33. MS. Clarendon 39, fol. 102^r.

34. *SP*, 3:367.

35. MS. Clarendon 50, fol. 111^r.

36. *SP*, 2:315, 327.

37. *SP*, 3:104, 219.

38. *SP*, 3:194, 45, 371; *Cal. Cl. SP*, 2:271.

39. *SP*, 3:243, 240; MS. Clarendon 53, fol. 4^r. Hyde also created problems for others with cipher. In 1656 Ormonde wrote to him that "it is well your choler & some probabillity of the cause let me in to your meaning for I can finde no cypher that would doe it." Hyde replied sheepishly that "I am glad you have recovered [?] at last the cypher, but ashamed that my choler gave you any light into the businesse" (MS. Clarendon 52, fols. 219^r, 231).

40. *Cal. Cl. SP*, 4:184.

41. *Cal. Cl. SP*, 3:198.

42. MS. Clarendon 48, fol. 311^r.

43. B. L. Add. MS. 35,029, fol. 2; *SP*, 3:Suppl. xvi.

44. MS. Clarendon 55, fol. 284ʳ; Burnet, *Burnet's History*, 1:169.

45. Samuel Pepys, *The Diary of Samuel Pepys*, ed. Robert Latham and William Matthews, 9 vols. (London: G. Bell and Sons, 1970–76), 3:303; 5:205; 7:321.

46. See *Cal. Cl. SP*, 5:293–94, 299, 304–5 and *passim*; B. L. Add. MS. 22,919, fol. 151.

47. *SP*, 2:328; 3:201.

48. MS. Clarendon 53, fols. 35ʳ, 36ᵛ.

49. MS. Clarendon 53, fols. 55ᵛ, 36ᵛ; MS. Clarendon 59, fol. 340. Ironically, Bristol also uses Hyde's phrase about being "weary of his Life" (MS. Clarendon 53, fol. 55ʳ).

50. MS. Clarendon 53, fol. 9ʳ.

51. Pepys, *Diary*, 8:427; 7:377.

52. Ibid., 5:203.

53. Ibid., 8:507. Coventry himself fell from power less than two years after Clarendon.

54. *SP*, 2:525.

55. See, for example, MS. Clarendon 81, fol. 191ᵛ, and various references in the fifth volume of the *Cal. Cl. SP* (pp. 256, 548, etc.); see also *DNB*, 10:377–78; Lister, *Life and Administration*, 2:540–41, and 3:535–40; Burnet, *Burnet's History*, 1:457; MS. Clarendon 84, fol. 39; Aylmer, *Struggle for the Constitution*, p. 180; Miller, *Edward Hyde*, p. 20; Harris, *Clarendon*, pp. 374, 388, 390, 407. Harris notes the difficulties in determining Hyde's financial status during the Royalist exile (p. 224).

56. MS. Clarendon 31, fol. 3ʳ.

57. MS. Clarendon 40, fol. 184ʳ.

58. Lister, *Life and Administration*, 3:480–81. See also *Cal. Cl. SP*, 5:540, 557.

59. *Cal. Cl. SP*, 4:539; MS. Clarendon 65, fol. 27; *Cal. Cl. SP*, 3:379; MS. Clarendon 56, fol. 59ʳ.

60. *DNB*, 10:385.

61. *CL*, 2:548; *DNB*, 10:385.

62. A possible exception here would be certain letters to his friend Lady Morton, in which he is amusing and even playful. See, for example, MS. Clarendon 39, fol. 112ʳ; MS. Clarendon 40, fol. 184ʳ.

63. *The Diary of John Evelyn*, ed. E. S. de Beer, 6 vols. (Oxford: Clarendon Press, 1965), 4:339.

64. *DNB*, 10:384; B. L. MS. Stowe 770, fol. 170; Harris, *Clarendon*, pp. 4, 411; *Cal. Cl. SP*, 5:463, 470. The entry on Anne in the *DNB* points out that the identities of her four sons "have been much confused" (10:367).

65. *Psalms*, 440. In fairness, it should also be noted that he wrote in the *Life* that "not the least" of his encouragements to pursue his profession vigorously was his "excellent" (second) wife, and his children, "which he then and ever

looked upon, as his greatest blessing and consolation" (p. 56). In his *Contempla-tions* on the Psalms, he also wrote that "amongst the infinite Blessings which God hath vouchsafed to confer upon me, from my Cradle to this Time, I look upon it as the greatest, that he hath given me such Children"—but the statement occurs in the dedication specifically addressed "To My Children" (p. 375).

66. *Essays*, 1:118.

67. Godfrey Davies, "The Date of Clarendon's First Marriage," *English His-torical Review* 32 (1917): 406.

68. His grandfather had established his fortune by marrying a wealthy widow (Craik, *Life*, 1:2).

69. B. L. Add. MS. 34,727, fols. 74–80, 83–85. For his concern for her, see *Cal. Cl. SP*, 3:108–9, 112–14, 118, and *SP*, 3:355. However, in a letter to John Earle on 16 March 1646/7, Clarendon commented: "I am willing to think myself as uxorious a man as lives (I ought to be so)" (*SP*, 2:348–49). A series of letters written in 1657 and 1658 to Secretary Nicholas' son John offers a rare glimpse of his wife's attitudes (British Library Egerton MS. 2536, fols. 144, 209, 211, 213, 218, 227, 255, 275, 279, 292), as do two letters to Hyde in MS. Clarendon 129, fols. 32, 34.

70. *Essays*, 2:39.

71. MS. Clarendon 54, fol. 205ʳ; see also MS. Clarendon 53, fol. 113.

72. For examples of these attacks, see "The Downfall of the Chancellor," *Poems on Affairs of State*, ed. George deF. Lord (New Haven: Yale University Press, 1963), 1:158; "Upon Hides ministry," B. L. Add. MS. 34,362, fol. 51ᵛ; "The Chancellour turn'd Tarpaulin," *Poems on Affairs of State, The Second Part* (London, 1697), pp. 134–35; [George Wither], "Post-Script," *Vox & Lacrimae Anglorum: Or, The True English-mens Complaints, To their Representatives in Parliament* (1668), pp. 12–16; "A Hue and Crie After the Earl of Clarendon" (1667). Plays on his surname were a popular tactic.

73. It is possible that personal letters that have not yet surfaced could alter the picture, but the consistency of the evidence now available makes significant revi-sion unlikely.

74. *Essays*, 1:245.

75. Burnet, *Burnet's History*, 1:160.

76. *The Prose Works of Jonathan Swift*, ed. Herbert Davis, 14 vols. (Oxford: Blackwell, 1939–68), 5:11–12.

77. *Psalms*, p. 745.

78. *SP*, 2:205; see also *HR*, 2:192.

79. *SP*, 2:329. See also *Psalms*, p. 397; *Lev.*, p. 91; Clarendon, *A Full Answer to an Infamous and Trayterous Pamphlet, Entituled, A Declaration of the Commons of England in Parliament assembled, expressing their Reasons and Grounds of passing the late Resolutions touching no further Addresse or Application to be made to the King* (R. Royston, 1648), p. 152. Hereafter cited as *A Full Answer*.

80. *A Dialogue of the Want of Respect due to Age*, in *A Collection of Several Tracts of . . . Clarendon*, p. 309. Hereafter cited as *Age*.

81. *Psalms*, p. 758; see also pp. 569–70, 716–17. In Clarendon's later commentaries on the Psalms written during his banishment, the theme of the absolute submissiveness owed by the subject to his monarch is propounded in such excessive terms that Clarendon seems to be trying to convince himself as well as the reader. But in addition, just as in his life, this theme alternates with an emphasis on the importance of being true to one's own conscience.

82. *SP*, 3:170.

83. *SP*, 3:8, 18. See also *HR*, 2:250, 527, and 5:316; *CL*, 2:286; *Life*, p. 83; *SP*, 2:232, and 3:24–25; *A Full Answer*, p. 137; and Coltman's second chapter, "Clarendon and Conscience," *Private Men and Public Causes*, pp. 69–99.

84. *SP*, 2:353.

85. *SP*, 2:417.

86. *SP*, 2:459.

87. On the Lord Keeper, see *HR*, 2:106–19; on legal forms in exile, see P. H. Hardacre, "The Royalists in Exile During the Puritan Revolution, 1642–1660," *Huntington Library Quarterly* 16 (1952–53): 359.

88. See the letters from Hyde in Peter Barwick, *The Life of the Reverend Dr. John Barwick, D.D.*, trans. H. Bedford (London, 1724); see also *SP*, 3:613.

89. *SP*, 2:459, 411.

90. *SP*, 3:568.

91. Burnet, *Burnet's History*, 1:309.

92. James Macpherson, *The History of Great Britain, from the Restoration, to the Accession of the House of Hanover*, 2 vols. (London: Strahan and Cadell, 1775), 1:53.

93. *Psalms*, p. 647. See also pp. 424, 555, 716; *CL*, 1:9; *SP*, 2:525, and 3:294; *HR*, 3:229; MS. Clarendon 51, fol. 176ʳ (also 177).

94. *SP*, 2:459.

95. *SP*, 2:318.

96. MS. Clarendon 40, fol. 188ʳ; MS. Clarendon 41, fol. 180ʳ; see also *Essays*, 2:42.

97. *SP*, 3:101.

98. *SP*, 3:65.

99. *SP*, 3:18, 117.

100. *Essays*, 2:161; *Psalms*, p. 500. In 1646/7 Hyde wrote to Earle that Charles I's surrendering himself to the Scots "it may be, had more of Philosophy or Metaphysicks in it, than practical reason" (*SP*, 2:338).

101. *Lev.*, pp. 168, 85, 79.

102. Trevor-Roper, "Clarendon," pp. 32–33. On Clarendon's general tendencies toward expediency, see also Lister, *Life and Administration*, 2:519–22.

103. De Beer, ed., *The Diary of John Evelyn*, 3:493.

104. Ogg, *England*, 1:150, 193; Percy Lewis Kaye, *English Colonial Admin-*

istration Under Lord Clarendon, 1660–1667, Johns Hopkins University Studies in Historical and Political Science, series 27, nos. 5–6 (Baltimore: Johns Hopkins University Press, 1905), pp. 18, 83, and *passim*.

105. J. R. Jones, *Country and Court: England 1658–1714* (Cambridge: Harvard University Press, 1978), p. 156.

106. Samuel Rawson Gardiner, *History of England from the Accession of James I to the Outbreak of the Civil War*, 10 vols. (London: Longmans, Green, 1883–84), 10:169–70; see also *DNB*, 10:372, 380; Davies, *Early Stuarts*, p. 124; Osmund Airy, *The English Restoration and Louis XIV: From the Peace of Westphalia to the Peace of Nimwegen* (New York: Scribner's, 1889), p. 161.

107. D. T. Witcombe, *Charles II and the Cavalier House of Commons* (New York: Barnes and Noble, 1966), pp. 2–3.

108. *HR*, 1:5, 260, 353, 570, 594; 2:72; 3:526. See also 1:103, and 2:341. Similarly, Clarendon never produces a coherent explanation of his fall from political power in the *Continuation of the Life*.

109. *Essays*, 1:230; *CL*, 2:81.

110. *SP*, 2:334.

Chapter 4: Clarendon's Literary Background

Epigraphs: Bodin, *Method*, p. 44. *SP*, 3:187. Wheatley, ed., *Diary of John Evelyn*, 3:446. Basil Willey, *The Seventeenth Century Background* (1934; reprint ed., Garden City, N.Y.: Doubleday, 1953), p. 50.

1. Maurice Ashley, *England in the Seventeenth Century* (Baltimore: Penguin Books, 1962), p. 108.

2. Ed., p. 328.

3. Anthony à Wood, *Athenae Oxonienses*, ed. Philip Bliss, 3rd ed., 5 vols. (London: 1813–20), 3:column 1022.

4. Clarendon's youthful experiences must have given impetus to his continuing concern with educational discipline and reform. When he became Chancellor of Oxford in 1660, he particularly "recommended the restoration of its ancient discipline" (*DNB*, 4:385). During his final exile, Clarendon wrote "Reflections upon some Reformations of great Benefit to both Universities, principally with Reference to Oxford" (*A Catalogue of a Collection of Manuscripts of the Great Earl of Clarendon* [1764], p. 4, #25; hereafter cited as *MSS. Catalogue*). In contrast to his eighteenth-century counterpart Edward Gibbon, Clarendon maintained a high regard for the university for the rest of his life, undoubtedly because, unlike Gibbon, he blamed himself as much as Oxford for his problems there.

5. James Bowen, *A History of Western Education: The Modern West, Europe and the New World*, 3 vols. (New York: St. Martin's, 1981), 3:66; Wilfred R. Prest, *The*

Inns of Court under Elizabeth I and the Early Stuarts, 1590–1640 (Totowa, N.J.: Rowman and Littlefield, 1972), p. 159.

6. Herford and Simpson, eds., *Ben Jonson*, 3:421; Alfred Harbage, *Sir William Davenant: Poet, Venturer, 1606–1668* (Philadelphia: University of Pennsylvania Press, 1935), p. 37.

7. A. Wigfall Green, *The Inns of Court and Early English Drama* (1931; reprint ed., New York: Benjamin Blom, 1965), p. 3. Prest points out, however, that the role of the Inns as creative centers declined in the late sixteenth and early seventeenth centuries. After about 1610, those at the Inns tended to be "consumers and patrons" rather than "producers" of literature (*Inns of Court*, p. 157; also pp. 155–56, 158, 168). See also Pocock, *Ancient Constitution*, p. 241.

8. Prest, *Inns of Court*, pp. 160, 138; see also p. 155.

9. Green, *Inns of Court*, p. 2.

10. Harbage, *Sir William Davenant*, p. 35.

11. Arthur H. Nethercot, *Sir William D'Avenant: Poet Laureate and Playwright-Manager* (Chicago: University of Chicago Press, 1938), p. 52.

12. Ibid., p. 82. Information about Davenant's early plays is from Harbage, *Sir William Davenant*, p. 34, and Nethercot, pp. 52–54, 79–81. Harbage claims that *Albovine* was Davenant's second play, which the actors could not be persuaded to produce because his first play had been unsuccessful. Nethercot, while conceding that Davenant's first two plays were written at about the same time, believes *Albovine* was first (p. 52).

13. Nethercot, *Sir William D'Avenant*, pp. 70–71; Harbage, *Sir William Davenant*, p. 38.

14. Roger Lorte, "To my Friend, M^r. D'avenant," in William Davenant, *The Tragedy of Albovine, King of the Lombards* (London, 1629), n.p., ll. 10–12.

15. *DNB*, 12:142 (Lorte); *DNB*, 8:858 (Habington); Nethercot, *Sir William D'Avenant*, p. 69 (Clerke); *DNB*, 2:709 (Blount).

16. "To his friend, M^r. W^m. D'avenant," in *The Tragedy of Albovine*, n.p., ll. 3–4. Both of Hyde's poems are printed in the appendix of this book.

17. Nethercot, *Sir William D'Avenant*, p. 83.

18. *DNB*, 5:553; Lorte, "To my Friend," l. 6.

19. Sir Geoffrey Keynes, *A Bibliography of Dr. John Donne* (Oxford: Clarendon Press, 1973), p. 52. All of the elegies are in John Donne, *The Epithalamions, Anniversaries, and Epicedes*, ed. W. Milgate (Oxford: Clarendon Press, 1978), pp. 81–107.

20. John Sampson, "A Contemporary Light upon John Donne," *Essays and Studies by Members of the English Association* 7 (Oxford: Clarendon Press, 1921), pp. 98–103.

21. Keynes, *Bibliography*, p. 187, and "A Footnote to Donne," *The Book Collector* 22 (1973): 166–67.

22. For the Donne portrait, see Wheatley, ed., *Diary of John Evelyn*, 3:444. Three volumes of Donne's sermons (1640) seem to have been in Clarendon's li-

brary, according to *Bibliotheca Clarendoniana: A Catalogue of the Valuable and Curious Library of the Right Honourable Edward Earl of Clarendon*, p. 15; hereafter cited as *Bib. Cl.* This catalogue was prepared for a sale that began on 26 August 1756. All references to the catalogue are phrased tentatively because it is difficult to know which books in it were actually Clarendon's own. The second Earl considerably augmented the library he had inherited from his father; see P. H. Hardacre, "Portrait of a Bibliophile I: Edward Hyde, Earl of Clarendon, 1609–1674," *The Book Collector* 7 (1958): 367. In 1646 Clarendon wrote down extracts in his second commonplace book from Donne's first work, his *Pseudomartyr* (MS. Clarendon 126, fols. 182–87).

23. MS. Clarendon 19, fol. 270. See also R. C. Bald, *John Donne: A Life* (Oxford: Oxford University Press, 1970), p. 549, and Margaret A. Beese, "John Donne the Younger: Addenda and Corrections to his Biography," *Modern Language Review* 33 (1938): 356–59. Beese notes that Donne's son was also associated with Waller (p. 356). Thus it is possible that his connection with Hyde could have come through Waller rather than his father.

24. *DNB*, 11:133; Keynes, *Bibliography*, p. 53; Weber, *Lucius Cary*, p. 140.

25. For example, in Milgate, ed., *The Epithalamions*, see King, ll. 51–55 (p. 82); Walton, ll. 79–81 (p. 88); Carew, ll. 9–10 (p. 88), ll. 95–98 (p. 90); Falkland, ll. 11–12 (p. 91); Mayne, ll. 1–2, 13–18 (pp. 93–94); Busby, ll. 77–82 (p. 99); and Porter, ll. 25–26 (p. 100).

26. Green, *Inns of Court*, p. 7.

27. Harbage, *Sir William Davenant*, p. 37; Green, *Inns of Court*, p. 125.

28. Green, *Inns of Court*, pp. 123–24. On Prynne, see also Bulstrode Whitelocke, *Memorials of the English Affairs from the Beginning of the Reign of Charles the First to the Happy Restoration of King Charles the Second*, 4 vols. (Oxford: Oxford University Press, 1853), 1:51–52; *DNB*, 16:432–37; Lister, *Life and Administration*, 1:19.

29. Whitelocke, *Memorials*, 1:53–54.

30. Harbage, *Sir William Davenant*, p. 36; Green, *Inns of Court*, p. 123, n. 72. But see also Prest, *Inns of Court*, p. 158, n. 55.

31. Green, *Inns of Court*, p. 126. Whitelocke, Hyde's friend Selden, a Mr. Gerling, Sir Edward Herbert (later to be Attorney General and a bitter enemy of Hyde's), and an unidentified member from Gray's Inn completed the group (Whitelocke, *Memorials*, 1:54; J. Bruce Williamson, *The History of the Temple, London* [London: John Murray, 1924], p. 398, n. 1).

32. Prest, *Inns of Court*, p. 154; for evaluations of *The Triumph of Peace*, see Ben Lucow, *James Shirley* (Boston: Twayne, 1981), pp. 40–41, and Green, *Inns of Court*, p. 132.

33. Green, *Inns of Court*, p. 123.

34. Whitelocke says the cost was above £21,000 (*Memorials*, 1:61); Green estimates it at over £24,000 (*Inns of Court*, pp. 125–26).

35. *The Earl of Strafforde's Letters and Dispatches*, ed. William Knowler, 2 vols. (London: William Bowyer, 1739), 1:177.

36. Whitelocke, *Memorials*, 1:54–55.

37. Williamson, *History of the Temple*, p. 405.

38. Green, *Inns of Court*, p. 132, n. 101; Knowler, ed., *Strafforde's Letters*, 1:207; *DNB*, 13:143. On the next day, Pembroke apologized and gave May £50, after Charles I had rebuked Pembroke and called May "his poet." In "Tom May's Death," Andrew Marvell has Ben Jonson in the underworld whip May with his laurel wand "ore the pate / Like *Pembroke* at the Masque" before berating him (*The Poems and Letters of Andrew Marvell*, ed. H. M. Margoliouth, 3rd ed., 2 vols. [Oxford: Clarendon Press, 1971], 1:95, ll. 37–38).

39. Whitelocke, *Memorials*, 1:60, 54; see also Green, *Inns of Court*, pp. 126–27.

40. Knowler, ed., *Strafforde's Letters*, 1:207.

41. Whitelocke, *Memorials*, 1:62.

42. Quoted by Lucow, *James Shirley*, p. 41.

43. Whitelocke, *Memorials*, 1:61–62.

44. Identification of the literary men associated with Falkland's group is based on Weber, *Lucius Cary*, pp. 61–63, 75, 82, 110, 125–27, 131–33; Kenneth B. Murdock, *The Sun at Noon: Three Biographical Sketches* (New York: Macmillan, 1939), pp. 79–87, 91, 109; and Trevor-Roper, "Clarendon," p. 31.

45. Falkland aided the aging Laureate financially and wrote several poems to him; he also suggested the title for the volume of memorial verses after Jonson's death (Herford and Simpson, eds., *Ben Jonson*, 11:428).

46. Weber, *Lucius Cary*, p. 63.

47. J. C. Hayward, "The *Mores* of Great Tew: Literary, Philosophical and Political Idealism in Falkland's Circle" (Ph.D. diss., Cambridge University, 1981), p. 44.

48. Weber, *Lucius Cary*, pp. 160–61; Murdock, *Sun at Noon*, pp. 76–77.

49. *The Works of Sir John Suckling*, ed. Thomas Clayton (Oxford: Clarendon Press, 1971), pp. 71–72, ll. 9, 10, 12; p. 75, ll. 95–98; see also pp. 266, 273.

50. Divines known to have been at Tew whom Hyde omits are Thomas Barlow, John Duncon, George Eglionby, Charles Gataker, Dr. Walter Raleigh, Thomas Triplet, and probably Hugh Cressy (Weber, *Lucius Cary*, p. 82). For Hobbes, see Murdock, *Sun at Noon*, p. 112, and also Weber, *Lucius Cary*, pp. 130–31.

51. Clayton, ed., *Suckling*, p. 75, ll. 99–102. Suckling is guilty of some exaggeration. Earle more accurately summed up Falkland's poetic abilities when he said that he "would not allow him to be a good poet, though a great wit; he writt not a smoth verse, but a great deal of sense" (Murdock, *Sun at Noon*, p. 81).

52. Murdock, *Sun at Noon*, p. 102.

53. Weber, *Lucius Cary*, pp. 124, 126.

54. Wood, *Athenae Oxonienses*, 3:column 716.

55. Weber, *Lucius Cary*, p. 103 (Morley); *DNB*, 13:162–63 (Mayne); Murdock, *Sun at Noon*, p. 82 (Killigrew).

56. Marchette Chute, *Ben Jonson of Westminster* (New York: Dutton, 1953), p. 32.

57. *Table Talk: Being the Discourses of John Selden Esq.* (1689), in *English Reprints*, ed. Edward Arber (London: Alexander Murray, 1868), pp. 85–86.

58. *DNB*, 13:164.

59. *DNB*, 5:796.

60. *DNB*, 5:553, and Harbage, *Sir William Davenant*, p. 102 (Davenant); *DNB*, 4:1305 (Cowley); *DNB*, 5:968 (Digby).

61. *A Letter from a True and Lawfull Member of Parliament and One faithfully engaged with it, from the beginning of the War to the end* (1656), p. 65. Hereafter cited as *1656 Letter*.

62. MS. Clarendon 25, fol. 209^v.

63. Sir Philip Warwick, *Memoirs of the Reign of King Charles I* (London, 1702), p. 258.

64. Nethercot, *Sir William D'Avenant*, p. 183.

65. On Davenant during the wars, see Harbage, *Sir William Davenant*, pp. 99–101, and Nethercot, *Sir William D'Avenant*, pp. 187, 199, 203, 207, 217, and 221.

66. Clayton, ed., *Suckling*, p. 74, l. 76.

67. For the contributors, see *Jonsonus Virbius*, in Herford and Simpson, eds., *Ben Jonson*, 11:428ff.

68. Evelyn's letter to Clarendon, 18 March 1666/7, quoted in *The Diary of John Evelyn*, ed. William Bray (New York: Dutton, 1911), 2:39, n. 2. All other quotations from and references to Evelyn's comments on the portraits in this paragraph are taken from his letter to Pepys, 12 August 1689, in Wheatley, ed., *Diary of John Evelyn*, 3:443–44. On the collection, see MS. Clarendon 92, fols. 253–54 (list of the pictures mended and repaired for the second Earl of Clarendon at Cornbury); Lady Theresa Lewis, *Lives of the Friends and Contemporaries of Lord Chancellor Clarendon*, 3 vols. (London: John Murray, 1852), 1:*15–*58, and 3:239–435; Robin Gibson, *Catalogue of Portraits in the Collection of the Earl of Clarendon* (Wallop, Hampshire: BAS Printers, 1977). Gibson questions the accuracy of Evelyn's memory of the collection (pp. xii–xiii).

69. Evelyn indicated that Beaumont and Fletcher "were both in one piece"; the 1750 inventory of paintings lists only "Fletcher the Poet" (Wheatley, ed., *Diary of John Evelyn*, 3:444; Lewis, *Lives*, 3:252, 256, 304–5). Among the strictly literary figures in the collection, only Beaumont and Fletcher appear among the books Clarendon could have owned in the list in the *Bib. Cl.* It shows both Beaumont and Fletcher's *Comedies and Tragedies* (1647) and Beaumont's *Poems* (1659) (pp. 16, 53). The catalogue includes very little literature; only about half a dozen of the works of English poetry that it lists could have been Clarendon's.

70. *Lev.*, p. 255.
71. Lewis, *Lives*, 1:*28. She cites no source, but the two would have been very natural inclusions.
72. MS. Clarendon 67, fol. 147ʳ.
73. Weber, *Lucius Cary*, pp. 69–72.
74. Williamson, *History of the Temple*, pp. 418–19. Books are mentioned in connection with similar orders quoted on other residents, but not manuscripts. On 12 May 1660 Robert Reynolds, who received Hyde's chambers, books, and manuscripts, wrote to Hyde to say that although he had been forced to sell the chambers, he would return Hyde's possessions and give him the proceeds of the sale when Hyde returned (*Cal. Cl. SP*, 5:31).
75. British Library Sloane MS. 3986, fol. 1.
76. *Cal. Cl. SP*, 4:180.
77. *Cal. Cl. SP*, 2:268.
78. *Cal. Cl. SP*, 3:202.
79. *Cal. Cl. SP*, 2:112, 95, and 4:520–21, 544; Wheatley, ed., *Diary of John Evelyn*, 4:314, 317; *Cal. Cl. SP*, 4:4, 71, 96, 172, 114, and 2:238–39.
80. *SP*, 3:732. It was appropriate that Evelyn's translation of Naudé's work on libraries was dedicated to Clarendon. Evelyn also addressed some proposals for improving printing in England to him (*DNB*, 4:385).
81. *SP*, 3:App. xi; *DNB*, 4:385–86; Burnet, *Burnet's History*, 1:457.
82. Hardacre, "Portrait," p. 367.
83. Hardacre, "The Royalists in Exile," p. 361. See also *Cal. Cl. SP*, 4:321, 473; 5:68.
84. "Viro, Favore Regio, et Meritis Suis Honoratissimo, Amplissimoque Domino, Edvardo Hide, . . . Carmen Gratulatorium" (1660). Hardacre notes that Clarendon was a "warm friend of the Bodleian" and "urged an extensive programme of publication" for the University Press ("Clarendon and the University of Oxford," p. 128).
85. *The Dramatic Works of Sir William Davenant*, ed. James Maidment and W. H. Logan, 5 vols. (London: H. Sotheran and Co., 1872–74), 3:257.
86. "Prologue for the Temple: at the Acting of *Five hours Adventure*, to my Lord Chancelor," in Sir William Davenant, *The Shorter Poems, and Songs from the Plays and Masques*, ed. A. M. Gibbs (Oxford: Clarendon Press, 1972), p. 203.
87. "To My Lord Chancellor," *Poems, 1649–1680*, ed. Edward Niles Hooker, H. T. Swedenberg, Jr., and Vinton A. Dearing (Berkeley and Los Angeles: University of California Press, 1956), p. 38, l. 5. Subsequent references are by line number within the text.
88. MS. Clarendon 87, fol. 244; B. L. Add. MS. 17,018, fol. 227.
89. Craik, *Life*, 1:302; *SP*, 2:289.
90. MS. Clarendon 87, fol. 247ʳ.
91. *SP*, 2:400.
92. *SP*, 3:166, 211.

93. *SP*, 3:215.

94. MS. Clarendon 28, fol. 297ᵛ.

95. *SP*, 2:345.

96. *A Voyage to England, Containing many Things relating to the State of Learn-ing, Religion, and other Curiosities of that Kingdom. By Mons. Sorbiere. As also Ob-servations on the same Voyage, by Dr. Thomas Sprat* . . . (London, 1709), pp. 52, 154–56. Evelyn in a dedication to Clarendon described him as "verifying by your univesal [*sic*] knowledge, the Rank you hold over the *Learned Republique*, as well as over the *Political*; which is, in summ, to be the greatest and most accomplish'd *Minister*, that this Nation has ever celebrated" ("To the Right Honourable Ed-ward, Earl of Clarendon," *Instructions Concerning Erecting of a Library*, p. A₂ᵛ).

97. *Ed.*, p. 344.

98. *Ed.*, p. 345.

99. *Ed.*, p. 345.

100. *Ed.*, p. 327.

101. *RW*, p. 200. See also *HR*, 1:92, 97, 265, 406; *CL*, 1:175; *Essays*, 1:233–34, and 2:27.

102. Hardacre, "Portrait," p. 367.

103. "June 26. 1636." appears on fol. 48ᵛ, at the end of the second set of ex-tracts (Plutarch). Even without this date, the handwriting in the book, which is much more legible than Hyde's later scrawl, would suggest a dating at least before the mid-1640s.

104. A few entries in it date from his final exile.

105. *SP*, 2:363. For a memorandum by Clarendon of some contemporary political tracts, see MS. Clarendon 92, fol. 344ᵇ.

106. MS. Clarendon 127, fols. 28–30. His old friend Tom May had trans-lated the *Argenis*.

107. MS. Clarendon 126, fols. 156–65, 177–79, 180–82, 182–87.

108. *HR*, 3:64, 184, and 6:91 (Cicero); he also quotes Cicero in the *Life* (pp. 83, 141). *HR*, 2:543, 3:112, and 5:281 (Seneca).

109. *MSS. Catalogue*, p. 9, #77.

110. *SP*, 2:335.

111. On parallels with Seneca in Clarendon's essay on anger, see Coltman, *Private Men and Public Causes*, pp. 165–66.

112. *MSS. Catalogue*, p. 12, #93 (Spelman); p. 9, #75 (Cicero).

113. *SP*, 2:375.

114. For example, *R & P*, 1:109, and *Essays*, 1:111. On Clarendon and Cicero, see also Roebuck, *Clarendon*, p. 140, and Robinson, "Lord Clarendon's Moral Thought," p. 49.

115. *Essays*, 1:244–51.

116. Charles I greatly encouraged the translation by William Aylesbury and Sir Charles Cotterill (1647) and read the entire manuscript before the work was published (*DNB*, 1:750). See also *Cal. Cl. SP*, 4:81.

117. *Essays*, 2:118; see also 120. Hardacre in "Portrait" discusses many of the minor Continental historians whose works Hyde requested in his correspondence (pp. 362–64).

118. *Cal. Cl. SP*, 3:xvi, 153, and 4:172; *SP*, 2:386; *Life*, p. 9. While in Madrid, Hyde found that the Spanish were "careful in writing their own histories, which I am studying diligently, and out of them inform myself more of the state of England than I could do by my own Chronicles" (*SP*, 2:520).

119. *SP*, 2:333–34.

120. Admitting that Book 5 (at that time the fourth book of the history) "consists upon the matter of little else but declarations," Hyde wrote that he "had a great mind to have avoided" including so many declarations "even *in terminis*" (*SP*, 2:334). Firth wrote that the predominance of these declarations in the book created "a sort of Serbonian bog in which many readers of the *History of the Rebellion* flounder and sink." Firth also points out that Hyde was not simply imitating Davila by inserting the declarations, but was also justifying himself and his policies: "He was proud of his declarations and regarded them as having produced an important practical effect" ("Clarendon's 'History,'" pp. 39, 40). On Clarendon and Davila, see also William Miller, "Clarendon's Mind and Art," p. 134, n. 45.

121. *Essays*, 1:244–45.

122. *Essays*, 2:83.

123. MS. Clarendon 126, fols. 20–49 (Speed); fols. 166–75 (Camden); *MSS. Catalogue*, p. 11, #91 (Calvisius). Clarendon must have liked Mariana, whose works he undoubtedly encountered while on the Spanish embassy, for he excerpts from him twice (*MSS. Catalogue*, p. 7, #48; p. 9, #76).

124. MS. Clarendon 126, fols. 140–49. He excerpted from Grotius in 1647. On 29 August 1653 he requested Grotius' *History of the Low Countries* (*SP*, 3:187).

125. MSS. Clarendon 127, fols. 33–48 (Plutarch); fols. 50–54 (Thucydides); fols. 66–71 (Commines).

126. MS. Clarendon 126, fols. 74–81 (Plutarch); fols. 86–97 (Livy); fols. 64–73 (Josephus).

127. *SP*, 2:375.

128. *MSS. Catalogue*, p. 1, #11.

129. *MSS. Catalogue*, p. 1, #10.

130. *MSS. Catalogue*, p. 10, #79. Clarendon quotes from Velleius Paterculus three times in Book 15 (*HR*, 6:1, 82, 91) and once in Book 16 (*HR*, 6:154–55), in sections taken from Part 7 of the *Life*, which he completed 1 August 1670 (MS. Clarendon 123, fol. 614). However, he had already used one of these quotations in Book 9, in the section concerning affairs in the west that was written in 1646 (*HR*, 4:23). He similarly reused a quotation from Tacitus, both times comparing the violent party in Parliament to Tacitus' Jews (*HR*, 1:250; 2:410).

131. MSS. Catalogue, p. 1, #11; *HR*, 4:511.

132. MS. Clarendon 126, fol. 64ʳ; *HR*, 2:292.
133. All quotations from the letter to Earle are from *SP*, 2:386.
134. *SP*, 2:375.
135. Peter Burke, "A Survey of the Popular Ancient Historians, 1450–1700," *History and Theory* 5 (1966): 151. Information about the popularity of individual historians and their reputations is taken from Burke as follows: Tacitus, pp. 149, 151; Plutarch, pp. 142, 151; Livy, pp. 146–47, 151; Polybius, p. 151. Information on Tacitus is also from Croll, *Style*, pp. 96, 190–95; information on Livy also from Edwin B. Benjamin, "The Spectacles of Tacitus," unpublished ms. in the possession of Professor William Frost, p. 159; and information on Polybius also from Arnaldo Momigliano, "Polybius' Reappearance in Western Europe," *Essays in Ancient and Modern Historiography* (Middletown, Ct.: Wesleyan University Press, 1977), pp. 76–77, 90–91, 93–95.
136. MS. Clarendon 126, fol. 144ʳ; see also *Essays*, 1:244.
137. MS. Clarendon 127, fols. 50–54; *HR*, 1:86, 87, 96.
138. *Lev.*, p. 85.
139. *1656 Letter*, p. 35.
140. *SP*, 2:335.
141. Levy, *Tudor Historical Thought*, pp. 196–97, 199.
142. Croll, *Style*, p. 96.
143. *Psalms*, p. 382. On Clarendon's general sensitivity to language and style, see Hartman, "Clarendon," pp. 189–200, 212–16.
144. MS. Clarendon 30, fol. 61.
145. MS. Clarendon 49, fol. 92ʳ; *SP*, 3:135, 190; MS. Clarendon 53, fol. 17.
146. *SP*, 2:335.
147. *Essays*, 1:40.
148. MS. Clarendon 52, fol. 231; *Life*, pp. 115–16. See also Roebuck, *Clarendon*, pp. 71–96.
149. *Cal. Cl. SP*, 2:256; 4:203, 266.
150. W. G. Crane, *Wit and Rhetoric in the Renaissance* (New York: Columbia University Press, 1937), pp. 134, 224; Croll, *Style*, pp. 54, 90.
151. Hyde's writings on and extracts from the Bible are in MS. Clarendon 138*, and *MSS. Catalogue*, pp. 1, #1; 4, #30 and #31; 9, #74 and #75; 10, #81. He often quotes from the Apocrypha in his meditations on the Psalms and in letters (for example, *Cal. Cl. SP*, 1:368; 2:319; MS. Clarendon 48, fol. 98ʳ).
152. See, for example, *Mr. Edward Hydes Speech at A Conference betweene both Houses, on Tuesday the 6th of July, 1641* (London, 1641), and Craik, *Life*, 1:109.
153. MS. Clarendon 112, fols. 573, 597, 614. The transcripts from which the *History* was printed (MSS. Clarendon 114–20) have verses before each book that do not appear in Clarendon's original manuscript.
154. Edward Gibbon, *The Decline and Fall of the Roman Empire*, ed. J. B. Bury, 7 vols. (1911; reprint ed., New York: AMS Press, 1974), 5:139.
155. Firth, *Essays*, pp. 107–8.

156. Gardiner, *History of England*, 10:170; Perez Zagorin, *The Court and the Country: The Beginning of the English Revolution* (London: Routledge and Kegan Paul, 1969), pp. 307–8; Aylmer, *Struggle for the Constitution*, pp. 113–14.

157. Sprat, *History*, pp. 41–42, 111–12. On Clarendon and political language in the *History*, see Hartman, "Clarendon," pp. 200–216, 227–35; William Miller, "Clarendon's Mind and Art," pp. 100–111. Roebuck in *Clarendon* often focuses on Hyde's concern with polemical language: pp. 4–5, 17, 23, 25, 33–34, 38–39, 44, 56, 64.

158. *1656 Letter*, p. 39.

159. *Essays*, 1:255, 254. He also attacks the schoolmen in *Lev.*, pp. 301–302.

160. *Lev.*, p. 2.

161. Lister, *Life and Administration*, 3:233.

162. Huntington Brown, *Prose Styles: Five Primary Types* (Minneapolis: University of Minnesota Press, 1966), pp. 91, 92, 94. Brown analyzes legal style in his chapter on "The Indenture Style," pp. 90–124.

163. Clarendon, *An Appendix to the History of the Grand Rebellion* (London: H. P., 1724), pp. 1–245.

164. See, for example, *SP*, 2:287; 3:53, 190, 611.

165. *Preface to Shakespeare*, in *Johnson on Shakespeare*, ed. Arthur Sherbo, 2 vols. (New Haven: Yale University Press, 1968), 2:74. On Clarendon's love of argument, see also Harris, *Clarendon*, p. 400, for limits Clarendon placed on religious controversy.

166. On Clarendon and Hooker, see Hartman, "Clarendon," pp. 61–69, 71–77, 82–83; Roebuck, *Clarendon*, pp. 36, 69; H. R. Trevor-Roper, "The Good & Great Works of Richard Hooker," review of *Of the Laws of Ecclesiastical Polity, Preface and Books I–V*, by Richard Hooker, *The New York Review of Books*, 24 November 1977, pp. 53–54. On the Tew Circle's general connections with Hooker, see Trevor-Roper, "Clarendon," p. 32; Harris, *Clarendon*, pp. 398–99. Hooker may also have influenced Clarendon's tendency to use parenthetical expressions frequently in his prose.

167. Hugh Trevor-Roper, "Three Historians: I—The Earl of Clarendon," *The Listener* 74 (1965): 487.

168. Gibson, *Catalogue of Portraits*, p. x; see also Lewis, *Lives*, 1:*16, *30.

Chapter 5: Clarendon's Achievement in Perspective

Epigraphs: Walpole, *A Catalogue*, p. 136. Quoted from "MS. essay on 'Romance' and 'History', in the Abinger collection," by Gary Kelly, in *The English Jacobin Novel, 1780–1805* (Oxford: Clarendon Press, 1976), pp. 200–201. Trevelyan in Stern, ed., *Varieties of History*, p. 234. Bloch, *Historian's Craft*, p. 26.

1. *Mr. Le Clerc's Account of the Earl of Clarendon's History of the Civil Wars,* trans. J. Ozell (London, 1710), p. 8.

2. *The Clarendon-Family Vindicated, from the Gross Falshoods and Misrepresentations of John Oldmixon, Esq., . . . and George Duckett, Esq. . . .* (1732), p. 13.

3. Edward Ward, *The History of the Grand Rebellion; . . . . Together With the Impartial Characters of the most Famous and Infamous Persons, for and against the Monarchy,* 3 vols. (London, 1713).

4. Sir John Bramston, *The Autobiography of Sir John Bramston* (London: Camden Society, 1845), p. 255. Although the comparison of Buckingham and Essex has traditionally been considered the earliest of Hyde's historical writings (*DNB*, 4:371), recently Roebuck has suggested "tentatively enough, that it was written (or at least revised) after Hyde was declared a delinquent excepted from possible pardon (1642), and perhaps later than *The King's Cabinet opened* (1645)." Roebuck considers it "likely to have been a product of his Jersey period when he composed forgeries in a variety of styles" (*Clarendon,* p. 95). But Bramston, who was Hyde's chamberfellow in the Middle Temple and maintained a "strict friendship ever after" with him, indicates that Hyde's marriage, which connected him with the Villiers family, led him to write the comparison (pp. 103, 255). Godfrey Davies has shown that this marriage occurred around the end of 1631, in December or January 1631/2 ("The Date of Clarendon's First Marriage," pp. 405–6). From the dates in Bramston's account, he seems to have entered the Middle Temple in 1630 or 1631, and therefore would have been around Hyde during the period when, if an early date is accepted, Hyde wrote the piece (pp. 99, 102, 103). Bramston began his autobiography in 1683 (p. xii), and thus was covering events that had occurred half a century earlier; nevertheless, without more evidence to discredit his account, revision seems the more likely of Roebuck's hypotheses. In addition, Clarendon wrote in the *History* that he "had lamented [Buckingham's death] at that time, and endeavoured to vindicate him from some libels and reproaches which vented after his death" (1:55). If the comment is actually an oblique reference to the comparison of Buckingham and Essex, it could be read as relating the vindication to a period at least somewhat close to the assassination itself, which occurred on 23 August 1628. On the dating, see also Hartman, "Clarendon," pp. 111, 105–6.

5. *R & P,* 1:328.

6. Stauffer, *English Biography,* p. 235.

7. For the individual historians, see Stauffer, *English Biography,* pp. 271–72, and Fussner, *Historical Revolution,* pp. 176–77. As late as Boswell, the bipartite structure was considered the standard format for biographies (*Boswell's Life of Johnson,* ed. George Birkbeck Hill, revised by L. F. Powell, 6 vols. [Oxford: Clarendon Press, 1934–64], 4:424–25).

8. George Philip Krapp, *The Rise of English Literary Prose* (1915; reprint ed., New York: Frederick Ungar, 1963), pp. 396, 399; Fussner, *Historical Revolution,*

p. 250; Levy, *Tudor Historical Thought*, pp. 197–98. These obituaries derived mainly from Tacitus and the classical historians, although their placement had some connection with the chronicle tradition.

9. MS. Clarendon 126, fols. 166–75.

10. MS. Clarendon 127, fols. 66–71; *Essays*, 1:245–49.

11. By the eighteenth century, this view of Davila appears often. See, for example, Hugh Blair, *Lectures on Rhetoric and Belles Lettres* (Philadelphia: T. Ellwood Zell, 1833), pp. 406–7; *Letters from Mrs. Elizabeth Carter to Mrs. Montagu*, ed. Montagu Pennington, 3 vols. (1817; reprint ed., New York: AMS Press, 1973), 1:276–77.

12. *MSS. Catalogue*, p. 1, #10.

13. G. B. Townend, "Suetonius and His Influence," *Latin Biography*, ed. T. A. Dorey (London: Routledge and Kegan Paul, 1967), pp. 82–84, 97, 116; Delany, *British Autobiography*, p. 154.

14. MS. Clarendon 127, fols. 33–48; MS. Clarendon 126, fols. 74–81; *HR*, 1:1.

15. *SP*, 2:375, 386.

16. *MSS. Catalogue*, p. 1, #11.

17. *SP*, 2:386; *HR*, 3:183, 185, 188.

18. MS. Clarendon 126, fol. 80^v.

19. MS. Clarendon 126, fols. 180–82. In addition, Bishop Hall's *Works* (3 vols., 1647) appear in the sale catalogue of his library (*Bib. Cl.*, p. 16), and he must have known Hall as a polemical writer.

20. Wendell Clausen, "The Beginnings of English Character-Writing in the Early Seventeenth Century," *Philological Quarterly* 25 (1946): 41.

21. Benjamin Boyce, *The Theophrastan Character* (Cambridge: Harvard University Press, 1947), p. 287.

22. Coltman, *Private Men and Public Causes*, p. 157; George Miller, *Edward Hyde*, p. 92; Boyce, *Theophrastan Character*, p. 247. Earle's sketches would have offered Clarendon a broad overview of character writing, for, as Boyce points out, Earle was "both one of the best and one of the most imitative of Character-writers," whose characters "repeatedly echo the words and ideas of Theophrastus, Hall, and Stephens" (*Theophrastan Character*, pp. 238, 188).

23. Some caveats are in order. Hyde could have known Earle at Oxford, for Hyde was at Magdalen from 1622 to 1625, while Earle was at Merton or Christ Church in 1619, received his M.A. in 1624, and was a Fellow at Merton (*DNB*, 6:321). However, Clarendon usually notes this kind of connection in the character sketches of the Tew group in the *Life*. Earle's *Microcosmographie*, published in 1628, was very popular, and Hyde might well have read it. Falkland did not receive the inheritance that included Great Tew until 1629. For about the next two years he was involved in family problems, his marriage, and a trip to the Continent in an abortive attempt to serve with the Dutch army. He then returned to Great Tew; Harris dates his settling there in 1632 (*Clarendon*, p. 11). In the *Life*

Clarendon focuses on the period when Falkland returned to the country after set-tling his father's will in London as the time when the Tew circle especially flour-ished; the elder Falkland died in 1633. But see also note 4 of this chapter.

24. Boyce, *Theophrastan Character*, p. 287.

25. Ibid., pp. 58–59, 67–69.

26. F. P. Wilson, *Seventeenth Century Prose* (Berkeley: University of Califor-nia Press, 1960), p. 13; A. M. Kinghorn, *The Chorus of History* (London: Bland-ford Press, 1971), p. 27; Boyce, *Theophrastan Character*, pp. 46–50, 129; Boyce, *The Polemic Character* (1955; reprint ed., New York: Octagon Books, 1969), pp. 23–31.

27. On possible French influence, Nichol Smith writes: "The literary career of Clarendon poses the question in a simple form. Most of his characters, and the best as a whole, were written at Montpelier towards the close of his life. Did he find in French literature an incentive to indulge and perfect his natural bent? Yet there can be no conclusive answer to those who find a sufficient explanation in the leisure of these unhappy years, and in the solace that comes to chiefs out of war and statesmen out of place in ruminating on their experiences and impressions" (*Characters*, p. xxviii; see also pp. xxvi–xxvii). Hartman argues persuasively against influence from the French portraits on Clarendon ("Clarendon," pp. 170–71). He did request the memoirs of Cardinal de Retz, which had character sketches, and those of Richelieu. It would seem doubtful that Clarendon was a reader of French heroic romances.

28. Warren Anderson, *Theophrastus: The Character Sketches* (Kent: Kent State University Press, 1970), pp. xii–xviii; see also Boyce, *Theophrastan Character*, pp. 11–14.

29. Boyce, *Theophrastan Character*, p. 160.

30. Quoted by Henry Gally, in "A Critical Essay on Character-Writings," *The Moral Characters of Theophrastus* (London: John Hooke, 1725), p. 7.

31. Blair, *Lectures*, p. 405.

32. Boyce, *Theophrastan Character*, pp. 78–79, 186.

33. Gilbert Burnet, "The Life and Death of Sir Matthew Hale," in *The Works, Moral and Religious, of Sir Matthew Hale*, 2 vols. (London: R. Wilks, 1805), 1:50.

34. Quoted from manuscript by James L. Clifford in "Roger North and the Art of Biography," in *Restoration and Eighteenth-Century Literature: Essays in Honor of Alan Dugald McKillop*, ed. Carroll Camden (Chicago: University of Chicago Press, 1963), p. 283.

35. Stauffer, *English Biography*, pp. 271–72.

36. For Speed, see Levy, *Tudor Historical Thought*, pp. 197–98.

37. Crane, *Wit and Rhetoric*, pp. 138, 157–58; *Essays*, 1:246.

38. *Essays*, 1:247.

39. See, for example, Ascham, *Whole Works*, 3:6; Amyot, "Amiot to the Readers," p. xx; Hobbes, *Hobbes's Thucydides*, p. 18.

40. *SP*, 2:386.

41. *Essays*, 1:248.

42. Townend, "Suetonius," p. 82.

43. For his sources, see William Miller, "Clarendon's Mind and Art," p. 151.

44. MS. Clarendon 51, fols. 267, 115ʳ. For the character of Julian, see *R & P*, 1:23–25.

45. *SP*, 2:373.

46. *SP*, 3:Suppl. lvii.

47. *Psalms*, p. 698.

48. *Psalms*, p. 644.

49. *Essays*, 1:188.

50. *SP*, 3:396.

51. *SP*, 3:465; see also *SP*, 3:87, 536, 582.

52. *SP*, 3:115, 135, 119, 144.

53. Boyce, *Theophrastan Character*, p. 315; *Polemical Character*, pp. 3, 93.

54. *SP*, 3:594; see also *SP*, 3:677.

55. MS. Clarendon 56, fol. 17.

56. Clarendon, *Appendix*, p. lx; Burnet, *Burnet's History*, 1:162.

57. *SP*, 3:200–201; see also *SP*, 3:101, 172–73, 186, 194, 214, 217, 540; *Cal. Cl. SP*, 2:262–63; *Psalms*, p. 540.

58. *SP*, 3:118.

59. *SP*, 3:228; see also *SP*, 3:123, 245.

60. *RW*, p. 195.

61. *SP*, 3:609.

62. *1656 Letter*, p. 8.

63. *Cal. Cl. SP*, 5:29; see also 2, 7, 8, 11–12, 19, 22, 28, 30, and *passim*.

64. Pepys, *Diary*, 4:115; see also 8:418.

65. *SP*, 2:350; see also *SP*, 3:410.

66. Martin J. Havran, *Caroline Courtier: The Life of Lord Cottington* (Columbia: University of South Carolina Press, 1973), p. 176; MS. Clarendon 83, fol. 253.

67. On Baxter, see Webber, *Eloquent "I,"* p. 124.

68. MS. Clarendon 48, fol. 97ʳ.

69. *SP*, 2:376.

70. MS. Clarendon 52, fol. 173ʳ.

71. *SP*, 2:358.

72. *SP*, 2:284–85.

73. *SP*, 2:322.

74. *Psalms*, p. 698.

75. *Essays*, 1:245.

76. The basic structure of Warwick's sketch of Cromwell is an extreme example of this tendency:

I have no mind to give an ill character of Cromwell, for in his conversation towards me he
was ever friendly. . . .
The first time that ever I took notice of him, ...
And yet I liv'd to see this gentleman. . . .
Of him therefore I will say no more, but that verily I believe. . . . (*Memoirs*, pp. 273, 275)

77. Camden, *History of Princess Elizabeth*, p. 104.
78. Warwick, *Memoirs*, pp. 273, 275.
79. *HR*, 3:178; see also *SP*, 2:328.
80. *Psalms*, p. 460.
81. *Essays*, 2:135.
82. *Essays*, 2:134.
83. MS. Clarendon 28, fol. 179ʳ; see also *HR*, 1:3, and 4:2.
84. *HR*, 1:2–3; *SP*, 2:357; MS. Clarendon 28, fol. 179ʳ.
85. *SP*, 2:386.
86. Lucian, "Way to Write History," 2:134–35; Amyot, "Amiot to the Readers," pp. xii; MS. Clarendon 126, fol. 69ᵛ.
87. Lister, *Life and Administration*, 3:43.
88. *SP*, 3:109.
89. *SP*, 2:374–75, 478.
90. Craik, *Life*, 1:315–16; MacGillivray, "Clarendon Among the Pre-Clarendonians," pp. 16–17.
91. *The History of England from the Invasion of Julius Caesar to the Abdication of James the Second, 1688*, 6 vols. (Philadelphia: Claxton et al., n.d.), 5:380, 379.
92. MS. Clarendon 40, fol. 106ʳ.
93. Cicero, *De Oratore*, 1:244 (II.xv.63).
94. MS. Clarendon 31, fol. 63ᵛ.
95. *A Full Answer*, p. 137. On Clarendon's memorial characters, and also on the differences between characters in the original history and the *Life*, see George Miller, *Edward Hyde*, pp. 95–100.
96. Again and again, a tantalizing "if" in the *History* shows how the roles individuals assumed during the period could have national consequences:

If that stratagem . . . of winning men by places had been practised as soon as the resolution was taken at York to call a Parliament, . . . and if Mr. Pim, Mr. Hambden, and Mr. Hollis, had been then preferred with Mr. St. John, before they were desperately embarked in their desperate designs, and had innocence enough about them to trust the King and be trusted by him, having yet contracted no personal animosities against him, it is very possible that they might either have been made instruments to have done good service, or at least been restrained from endeavouring to subvert the royal building. (*HR*, 1:431)

If the staff had remained still in the hands of the earl of Essex, by which he was charged with the defence and security of the King's person, he would never have been prevailed with to have taken upon him the command of that army which was afterwards raised against the King's, and with which so many battles were fought. And there can be as little doubt, . . . that it had been utterly impossible for the two Houses of Parliament to have raised an army then if the earl of Essex had not consented to be general of that army. (*HR*, 2:16)

It concerned him [Prince Charles] the more to be solicitous to put the west into such a posture that it might be able to repair any loss the King had received; which it might easily have done if the jealousies and animosities between particular persons could be reconciled, and a union made amongst all men who pretended [to wish,] and really did wish, prosperity to the King's affairs, which yet were disturbed, and even rendered desperate, by the intolerable pride and incorrigible faction of and between such persons. (*HR*, 4:55–56)

97. May, *History of the Parliament*, p. 201.

98. Paul Lacombe's term, discussed by Paul Ricoeur, *The Contribution of French Historiography to the Theory of History* (Oxford: Clarendon Press, 1980), pp. 10–11; Fernand Braudel, *On History*, trans. Sarah Matthews (Chicago: University of Chicago Press, 1980), p. 10.

99. Wormald, *Clarendon*, pp. 155–56; George Miller, *Edward Hyde*, pp. 77–78.

100. Boyce, *Theophrastan Character*, p. 88.

101. Both Hartman ("Clarendon," p. 86) and William Miller ("Clarendon's Mind and Art," pp. 78–83) have emphasized the cumulative biographical nature of Clarendon's characters and the need for their context.

102. Leo Tolstoy, "Some Words about *War and Peace*," in *War and Peace*, ed. George Gibian (New York: Norton, 1966), p. 1368.

103. Braudel, *On History*, p. 20.

104. Johnson, "Addison," in *Lives of the English Poets*, ed. George Birkbeck Hill, 3 vols. (Oxford: Clarendon Press, 1905), 2:116; Boswell, *Boswell's Life of Johnson*, 2:79, and 3:404.

105. Aristotle, *Poetics*, trans. Ingram Bywater, in *Rhetoric and Poetics* (New York: Modern Library, 1954), pp. 231–32; see also O. B. Hardison, Jr., "A Commentary on Aristotle's *Poetics*," *Aristotle's Poetics* (1968; reprint ed., Tallahassee: University Presses of Florida, 1981), pp. 82–83, 123–26, 199.

106. Abraham Cowley, "To the Lord Falkland. For his safe Return from the Northern Expedition against the Scots," in *Poems*, ed. A. R. Waller (Cambridge: Cambridge University Press, 1905), p. 19.

107. Coltman, *Private Men and Public Causes*, pp. 163, 59.

108. Walpole, *A Catalogue*, p. 317.

109. Ashley, *England in the Seventeenth Century*, p. 109.

110. *Essays*, 1:250.

111. Thomas Carlyle, "On History," in *Carlyle: Selected Works, Reminiscences, and Letters*, ed. Julian Symons (Cambridge: Harvard University Press, 1970), p. 49.

112. *Essays*, 2:41.

113. For Rymer and Madox, see David C. Douglas, *English Scholars, 1660–1730* (London: Eyre and Spottiswoode, 1951), pp. 17, 222, 229–30; Clark, *Later Stuarts*, p. 366; for Rawlinson, see Hay, *Annalists and Historians*, pp. 156–57; for Nalson and Rushworth, see MacGillivray, *Restoration Historians*, pp. 96–119; for Echard, Oldmixon, Carte, Calamy, and Walker, see Richardson, *Debate*, pp. 35–37, 40–41.

114. Quoted by Adolph, *Rise of Modern Prose*, p. 262.

115. Pat Rogers, *Grub Street: Studies in a Subculture* (London: Methuen, 1972), p. 324; see also pp. 205, 281, 354–55, and Firth, "Development," p. 27.

116. Barwick, *Life of John Barwick*, pp. 430–31; *Cal. Cl. SP*, 1:462; 2:227; 3:12.

117. *SP*, 3:Suppl. xliv.

118. *A Full Answer*, pp. 48, 75, 97; see also p. 113.

Index

Note: Titles of historical and literary works are entered under the names of their authors. For consistency, Edward Hyde, first Earl of Clarendon, is referred to as "Clarendon" throughout this index, even when the title may be anachronistic.

Index

Cavendish, William. *See* Newcastle

Character sketches: abstraction in, 151–52, 162; balance in Clarendon's, 24, 157, 160, 161, 164–68, 176–77; in Clarendon's *Life*, 31, 35; Clarendon's, of himself, 84–85, 205n.21; content of Clarendon's, xv, 137, 148, 153–54, 161–63, 174–77, 182–83, 223n.95; in French memoirs and romances, 150, 221n.27; in histories and biographies, 10, 61–62, 147–48, 150, 151–53, 158, 162–63, 168, 169, 177–78, 182, 219n.8; homiletic, 147, 149, 150; humour, 147, 149, 150; literary influences on Clarendon's, 136, 146–53, 220nn.22–23; moral bias in, 148, 150–51, 182; narrative contexts of (*see* Narrative); narrative functions of Clarendon's (*see* Narrative); personal influences on Clarendon's, 58, 65–66, 103, 153–61, 164–67, 170; polemical, 150, 155–56; prose style of (*see* Prose style); prose style of Clarendon's (*see* Prose style); purposes of Clarendon's, 163–64, 167–73, 176–77, 180; satirical, 147, 150; thematic functions of Clarendon's, 58, 68, 146, 153, 166, 177–81; Theophrastan, 147, 149–51, 152. *See also* Genre

Charles I: during civil wars, 8, 11, 33, 35, 36, 41, 44, 50, 51, 56, 57, 58, 59, 60, 79, 86, 106, 122, 123, 140, 142, 145, 167, 169, 170, 173, 174, 175, 178, 208n.100; early reign of, 48, 60, 117, 118, 146, 168, 170, 172, 212n.38, 223n.96; execution of, 19, 34, 39, 43, 134; Clarendon's service to, 18, 20–21, 23, 24, 64, 80, 81, 84, 86, 89, 97, 98, 99, 105, 138, 140, 155, 157, 158, 181; portrayal in Clarendon's *History*, 21, 22, 34, 69, 165–66; mentioned, 12, 110, 163

Charles II: Clarendon's problems with, 34, 81, 82, 83, 97, 101, 102, 105, 123, 134, 157, 159; in exile, 25, 33, 44, 53–54, 55, 56–57, 59, 60, 62, 63, 71, 88, 89, 98, 99, 100, 102, 106, 122, 127, 134, 155, 156, 199n.23; as Prince of Wales, 18, 23, 26, 81, 98, 128, 223n.96; reign of, 86, 90, 91, 99, 101, 102, 123; Restoration of,

Charles II (*continued*)
39, 40, 43, 57, 67, 69–72, 106, 107, 171; mentioned, 94, 181

Chaucer, Geoffrey, 125

Cherbury, Edward Herbert, Lord of, 147; *Henry VIII*, 15

Chillingworth, William, 79, 120, 149, 179; *Religion of Protestants*, 79

Chronology: in Clarendon's *History*, 35–37, 51, 158, 181; in historical writing, xv, 10–11, 12, 17, 51, 67, 148, 201n.45

Cicero: *Brutus*, 131; Clarendon's reading of, 131; *De Oratore*, 131; *De Natura Deorum*, 131; on historical style and writing, 2, 3, 4, 167; *Orator*, 131; mentioned, 129, 136. *See also* Prose style, Ciceronian

Cinna, 148

Clanricarde, Ulick de Burgh, Marquis of, 23

Clarendon, Edward Hyde, first Earl of
—life (chronological summary): parents and background, 77, 93, 132, 133, 207n.68; at Oxford, 112, 220n.23; at Inns of Court (*see* Inns of Court); with Jonson circle (*see* Jonson, Ben); marriages and children, 86–87, 92–94, 100, 123–24, 206n.65, 207n.69, 219n.4; legal career, 43, 56, 77, 78, 79, 94, 98, 105, 106, 113, 116–17, 123–24, 155; with Great Tew group (*see* Great Tew); early Parliamentarianism, 19, 66, 80, 83, 84, 158, 159; counselor to Charles I, 18, 20–21, 22, 24, 33, 56, 64, 69, 80, 81, 84, 86, 89, 97, 98, 99, 105, 106, 119, 122–23, 138, 140, 155, 157, 158, 159, 181; experiences in west of England, 18, 33, 53, 56, 81, 82–83, 156; on Jersey, 18–19, 22, 24, 26, 30, 33, 53, 83, 88–89, 92, 101, 127, 128, 130, 131, 133, 134, 154, 160, 219n.4; counselor in exile to Charles II, 25, 26, 33, 44, 53–54, 56, 60, 68, 71, 80, 81, 83, 88–89, 93, 97, 98, 99–100, 105–6, 122, 126, 155, 156, 157, 159, 181, 205n.39; Spanish embassy, 33, 53, 62, 68, 71, 83, 92, 93, 126, 127, 139, 154, 157, 216n.123; role in Restoration, 25, 33, 69–71, 80, 82, 106, 107, 156, 158, 181; as Lord

229

Index

Clarendon, first Earl of (*continued*)
Chancellor, 25, 56, 71, 72, 80, 81, 82,
84, 89, 90, 91, 93, 94, 98, 99–101, 102,
104, 105, 106, 123, 126, 127, 128–29,
156, 158, 159, 181; impeachment, 25,
122, 125, 158; final exile, xiii, 25–27, 30,
32, 33, 70, 82, 83, 84, 85, 88, 91, 92,
102, 108–9, 126, 127–28, 130, 131,
133, 134, 139, 154, 159, 181, 204n.13,
221n.27
—attitudes and opinions: on argument, 56,
142, 162; on drama and theater, 129–30;
on education, 112, 125, 130, 209n.4; on
family, 86–87, 89, 92–94, 206n.65,
207n.69; on finances, 77, 84, 91, 92, 107,
206n.55; on friendship, 66, 92, 93, 94,
124, 158–59, 163, 165; on government,
64–67, 71, 80, 82, 97, 103, 106–7, 159,
179; on historians, 19, 22, 37–38, 76,
116, 126, 130–36, 147, 148, 152–53,
163–64, 165, 216nn.117, 123; on history
and historical writing, 19–22, 31–32,
37–42, 47–51, 56, 61–63, 72, 76, 95,
108–9, 113, 130–36, 137–39, 142–43,
152–53, 160, 161, 163–64, 165–67, 179,
181, 185, 195n.65, 216n.118; on language and style, 24–25, 37–50, 61–63,
123, 127, 128, 130, 131, 135, 137–43,
146, 148, 149, 151, 152–53, 185; on law,
33, 64, 78, 80, 81, 84, 95, 100, 106, 129;
on literature, xiv, 62–63, 112–13, 116,
119–31, 133–39, 142–43, 146, 147–49,
150, 151, 153, 213n.69, 214n.84; on
politics, 19, 21–22, 33–34, 64–68, 71,
73, 77, 78, 79, 80–82, 84, 97–108, 114,
121–23, 125, 129, 140–41, 143, 155,
159, 169, 179, 181, 202n.65, 204n.9; on
religion and theology, 19, 22, 33, 59,
64–65, 70, 78, 79, 80, 81, 82, 84, 85, 97,
98, 99, 100, 101, 104, 105, 110, 129,
130–31, 133, 141, 149, 154–55, 160,
204n.13; self-view, 77, 83–87, 91, 94,
95, 154; on work, 82, 84, 88–91, 94,
104, 105, 107, 108, 156–57
—characteristics: book collector, 111,
125–26, 128, 130, 132, 210n.22,
214nn.74, 84, 216n.124; constitu-

Clarendon, first Earl of (*continued*)
tionalism, 22, 26, 33, 64, 80, 81, 84, 98,
100, 116; devotion to duty, 84, 88–90,
97–99, 101–2; habits of writing, 24–25,
48, 108, 127, 137–38, 142, 159, 185,
200n.39; idealism, 66–68, 95, 97,
101–2, 104–8, 110; magnanimity, 67,
84–85, 88, 158, 161, 182; moderation,
82, 84–85, 95, 116, 156; morality, 20,
77, 82, 84, 90–91, 100–101, 104, 105,
123, 129, 131, 135–36, 148, 150, 151,
154, 164, 179; move from literature to
law, 78, 94, 113, 116–17, 120, 123–24,
126, 128–29, 130–31, 133; negative
traits, 42, 56, 85, 89–91, 92, 95, 104,
205n.39; optimism, 18, 19, 85, 88, 96,
103, 110; physical, 25, 94, 99, 200n.39;
portrait collector, 115, 125, 143, 154,
213nn.68–69, 214n.71; position as outsider, 77–83, 110; pragmatism, 67–68,
79–80, 97, 101–6, 110, 129–30, 143,
156, 158, 159, 208n.100; private life elusive, xiv, 83–85, 86–87, 91–94, 96;
rank, 59, 61, 64, 77; records of reading,
126, 130–36, 148, 199n.18,
216nn.117–18, 123–24; sense of tradition, 33, 64, 71, 80, 82, 97, 99–100, 104;
subordination of private concerns to
public, xiv, 30–32, 84–87, 89, 91–94,
96, 97, 110, 156; tolerance, 85, 88, 94,
156–57; as viewed by others, 89–92, 94
—works:
Brief View and Survey of . . . Leviathan:
attacks in, 102–3, 141; composition
of, 128, 185; quoted, 19, 26, 38, 136;
themes of, 64, 84; mentioned, 125
Clarendon manuscripts, 87–89, 91, 94,
138, 195n.65
Commonplace books: dates of, 130,
215n.103; quoted, 19, 80; records of
reading in, 130–36, 147, 148, 149,
199n.18
*Contemplations and Reflections upon the
Psalms of David*: composition of, 127;
quoted, 19, 96, 100, 102, 137, 154,
161, 206n.65; style of, 84, 139, 217n.
151; themes of, 64–65, 70, 208n.81

Index

Continuation of the Life: Clarendon's depictions of himself in, 82, 84, 92, 94, 98, 209n.108; purposes of, 72, 108; style in, 139

Dialogue . . . concerning Education, 65, 112, 128, 129–30, 131, 138

Dialogue of the Want of Respect due to Age, 39, 65, 128, 131, 138, 142

Difference and Disparity Between . . . George Duke of Buckingham, and Robert Earl of Essex, 56, 84, 146, 149, 157, 219n.4

Essays: composition of, 128; purpose, 108; quoted, 77, 87, 93, 102, 132; style, 131, 138, 142, 215n.111

Full Answer, 142

History of the Rebellion: audience for, 42–43, 109; autobiography in (*see* Autobiography); causation in, 57, 61, 65, 108, 163, 168–72, 176–77, 223n.96; character sketches in (*see* Character sketch); classical and contemporary models for, 130–36, 142, 147–49, 153, 162, 216n.120; composition of, xii–xiii, 18, 26–27, 30, 34–35, 72, 96, 128, 130, 148, 185, 197n.92; dramatic elements in, 39–40, 69, 152–53; imaginative referent in (*see* Imaginative referent); literary merit of, xii–xv, 18, 24–25, 27, 30, 34, 35, 37, 46–47, 49–50, 53, 56, 58, 59, 61–66, 68–73, 104, 108–10, 129, 132, 133–34, 137–39, 142–43, 146, 151, 153, 161–62, 167–68, 176–77, 182–85, 216n.120; narrative structure of (*see* Narrative); point of view in, xii, xiii, xv, 26, 32, 34–37, 42–45, 51–53, 56–60, 63–64, 68–69, 72–73, 77–78, 82–83, 92, 95, 96, 104, 107–10, 129, 138, 164–68, 169–71, 173, 176–82, 185, 201nn.46–47; polemical elements in, xiii, 18, 26, 42–43, 83, 95, 97, 164, 167–68; prose style of (*see* Prose style); Providential elements in (*see* Providential history); publication of, xi, 20–21, 24, 27, 164, 184; purposes of, xiii, 20, 40, 87, 107–10, 135–36, 150, 160, 163–64,

History of the Rebellion (continued) 182; quotations in, 133–34, 138, 139, 148, 216n.130; reception of, xi–xiv, 53, 143, 146, 184–85; sources for, 18, 25–27, 30–31, 49, 51, 56, 88, 137–38; thematic structure of, xiv, xv, 63–73, 77, 104, 110, 146, 176–82; unity of, 30–37, 72, 197n.3; mentioned, 84, 88, 112, 125, 126, 140, 157, 159. *See also* Biography; Chronology; Dialectic, abbreviated; Discourse; Focalization; Genre; Geography; Rhetoric; Story; Syntax

King's Cabinet opened, 219n.4

Letter from a True and Lawfull Member of Parliament, 122, 157

Life: audience for, 31, 42; as autobiography (*see* Autobiography); composition of, 18, 25–26, 31–32, 128, 197n.92, 216n.130; point of view in, 26, 31, 34–37, 52, 164; prose style of (*see* Prose style); purposes, 26, 30–32, 33–34, 55, 72, 87; sources for, 18, 25–26, 31, 32, 34, 88; mentioned, 84, 88, 92, 93, 96, 97, 113, 119, 122, 132, 135, 138, 159, 179, 197n.3

On an active and on a contemplative Life, 93

"On the death of Dr Donne," 115–16, 187–88

Original history: audience for, 31, 42, 51, 109, 164; autobiography in (*see* Autobiography); composition of, 18–19, 22–25, 127, 128, 130, 197n.92; moral and political instruction in, 19–20, 22, 30, 55, 138; point of view in, 21–22, 33–37, 51–52, 108, 164; polemical elements in, 18, 20–22, 33–34; prose style of (*see* Prose style); purposes of, 19–22, 33–34, 55, 72, 108; sources for, 18, 22–24, 32, 34, 88; mentioned, 26, 108, 122, 138, 197n.3

Religion and Policy: composition of, 128, 131, 185; stylistic problems in, 109, 153–54; themes in, 56, 65, 146

"To his friend, M^r. W^m. D'avenant," 114–15, 116, 187

231

Index

Hyde, Nicholas (Clarendon's uncle), 113, 114

Imaginative referent: in Clarendon's *History*, xv, 64–69, 71–73, 154, 178; in historical writing, xv, 13–17, 66
Impeachment, of Clarendon. *See* Clarendon, life
Independents, 11, 42, 67, 101
Inns of Court: Clarendon at, 78, 112–19, 125–26, 127, 219n.4; connections with drama and literature, 112–14, 117–19, 210n.7
Irony, 43–45, 50, 63, 70–71, 151, 194n.51, 200n.35
Ives, Simon, 118

James, Duke of York, 23, 86, 100, 117, 137
Jersey. *See* Clarendon, life
Johnson, Samuel, 142, 177; *Rambler 152*, 1
Johnston, Robert, 132
Jones, Inigo, 118
Jones, J. R., 105
Jonson, Ben: circle of, 113, 119, 121, 123, 212nn.38, 45; *Every Man Out of his Humor*, 112; Hyde's association with circle of, 78, 113, 116, 119, 123, 124, 125, 149; opinions of, 39, 112; mentioned, 122
Josephus, 103, 126, 133, 134–35, 165
Julian the Apostate, 153–54

Kellogg, Robert, 51
Kennet, White, xi
Keynes, Sir Geoffrey, 115
Killigrew, Henry (divine), 119, 121
Killigrew, Sir Henry (Cornish Royalist), 165
King, Henry, 115
Knolles, Richard, 147

Lambert, John, 171
Langdale, Sir Marmaduke, 44, 155
Lansdown, Battle of, 38–39
Laud, William, 39, 117, 154, 155, 159, 160
Lauderdale, John Maitland, Earl of, 60, 162
Lawes, William, 118
Le Clerc, John, xiii, 146

Lenton, Francis, 113
Levellers, 103, 199n.23
Lewis, Lady Theresa, 125, 214n.71
Lilburne, John, 102, 110, 130
Lilly, John, *History of His Life and Times*, 86
Lister, T. H., 49
Literary historiography. *See* Historiography, literary
Litotes, 42
Livy, 10, 14, 132, 133, 134, 135, 136
Lorte, Roger, 114
Louis XIV, 126
Lucan, 113
Lucian of Samosata, 2, 6, 76, 165
Ludlow, Edmund, *Memoirs*, 7

Macaulay, Thomas Babington, xiii, xv
Machiavelli, Niccolò, 17, 19, 20, 83, 101, 184, 195n.65
Madox, Thomas, *History of the Exchequer*, 183
Manchester, Edward Montagu, Earl of, 180
Mariana, Juan de, 133, 216n.123
Marsden Moor, Battle of, 60, 86, 173
Marten, Henry, 158
Marvell, Andrew, 212n.38
Mary, Princess of Orange, 54
Massey, Edward, 155
Maurice, Prince, 59
May, Bab, 81
May, Thomas: as historian, 7–8, 12, 122, 133, 169; *History of the Long Parliament*, 8; literary connections of, 113, 118, 123, 124, 212n.38, 215n.106
Mayne, Jasper, 115, 121, 124
Mazarin, Cardinal Giulio, 69, 70, 71, 162, 203n.70
Memoir: French, characters in, 150, 221n.27; relationship of history to, in seventeenth century, 11, 15, 18, 86; style of, 7, 37
Metaphor, 36, 40, 138, 139, 151, 194n.51, 199n.23
Mézeray, François Eudes de, 132
Middle Temple, 78, 112, 113, 117, 125, 219n.4

Index

Sorbière, Samuel, *Relation d'un Voyage en Angleterre*, 128

Sorel, Georges, 15

Southampton, Thomas Wriothesley, Earl of, 99, 156, 162

Spanish embassy. *See* Clarendon, life

Speed, John, 2, 133, 136, 147, 152

Spelman, Sir Henry, 22, 131

Spenser, Edmund, 125

Sprat, Thomas, 10, 40, 129, 140, 199n.22

Sprigge, Joshua, *Anglia Rediviva*, 7

Stanley, Venetia, 123

Stapleton, Sir Philip, 40

Steiner, George, 15

Stillingfleet, Edward, 65

Story: in Clarendon's *History*, 32, 51, 53–61, 63, 109, 172; in historical writing, 9–10, 12, 13, 172

Stowe, John, 10, 132, 135; *Chronicle*, 126

Strada, Famianus, 131, 153

Strafford, Thomas Wentworth, Earl of: Clarendon's character sketch of, 154; execution of, 39, 44, 140, 171; Hotham's animosity toward, 174, 175; as royal adviser, 81, 105, 159, 160; mentioned, 94, 118

Suckling, Sir John, 119, 120, 122, 123, 212n.51; "The Wits," 120

Suetonius, 61, 133, 148

Swift, Jonathan, xiii, 96, 184

Syntax: in Clarendon's *History*, 41–42, 45–50, 108, 109, 131, 142, 200n.35, 201n.40; during seventeenth century, 8, 45–47, 50; in historical writing, 5–6

Tacitus: *Agricola*, 133, 134, 135, 148; *Annals*, 133, 135; character sketches of, 10, 61, 148, 151, 153, 168, 219n.8; Clarendon's reading of, 132, 133, 134, 135, 136; *Histories*, 133, 134, 135; imaginative referent of, 14; mentioned, 216n.130

Tew. *See* Great Tew

Theophrastus, 147, 150–51, 220n.22. *See also* Character sketch, Theophrastan

Thucydides: Clarendon's reading of, 133, 136; Hobbes's translation of, 12, 39, 121,

Thucydides (*continued*) 199n.18; imaginative referent in, 14, 17; mentioned, 83

Thurloe, John, 71

Titus, Colonel Silas, 91; *Killing No Murder* (with Edward Sexby), 44

Tolstoy, Leo, 176

Townend, G. B., 153

Tragedy, 36, 110, 176, 178, 194n.51

Trajan, Emperor, 134, 153

Trevelyan, G. M., 49; *Clio, A Muse*, 145

Trevor-Roper, H. R., 30, 104, 143

Tuke, Sir Samuel, *Adventures of Five Hours*, 127

Turenne, Henri de la Tour D'Auvergne, Vicomte de, 172

Underdown, David, xii

Ussher, James (Archbishop), 121

Uxbridge, 23, 24, 57

Van Dyck, Sir Anthony, 145

Vane, Sir Henry, 44

Vaughan, John, 113, 119

Vega, Bernardo de la, *History of Peru*, 126

Velleius Paterculus, 133, 134, 136, 148, 216n.130

Vergil, Polydore, 3, 61, 147

Virgil, *Georgics*, 113

Verney, Sir Edmund, 36

Villiers, George. *See* Buckingham

Vossius, G. J., 126

Walker, Sir Edward, 41, 137

Walker, John, 184

Waller, Edmund: Clarendon's opinion of, 119–20, 121, 122, 125; and Great Tew group, 78, 120, 124; poetry of, 120, 121, 124; in politics, 122; mentioned, 211n.23

Waller, Sir William, 41, 59, 169; *Vindication*, 8

Walpole, Horace, 8, 178; *A Catalogue of the Royal and Noble Authors of England*, 145

Walton, Izaak, 182

Ward, Ned, 146

Warwick, Sir Philip: character sketches of, 162, 163, 166, 222n.76; mentioned, 122